CRACKED VASES

CRACKED VASES

Online Alter Ego Betrayals

Teri Brooks

To order additional copies of this book, contact:
Xlibris Corporation
1-888-795-4274
www.Xlibris.com
Orders@Xlibris.com
44560

DEDICATION

To my men:
To Ryan, the one I always seemed to find my way back to.
To Tony, my Italian funny guy, who always makes—my heart smile.
To Daniel, there for me in some of my darkest hours.
To Will, my rock. To my husband, who lives in my heart still.

Prologue

For all those lost or lonely women and men out there who find themselves caught between an unhappy relationship and the fantasy world of online chatting, which can turn into an addiction as well as challenge ones self worth. You are not alone. I stand with you and I hold out my hand for you to reach out for, in hopes that you will know that there are many of us who share in this pain. As addicts of all kinds of addictions have asked those that they love, "Please don't give up on me." Don't give up on yourself.

COMMON CHAT EMOTICONS
AND ABBREVIATIONS

:o) :) smiles
:o(:(sad face
<g> grin
<smile> the one writing the message is smiling
<wink> the one writing the message is winking
? I have a question
ASL age, sex, location
AWHFY are we having fun yet?
B4N bye for now
BF boy friend
BFD big frickin deal
BIF before I forget
BRB be right back
BTHOM beats the hell out of me
BTW by the way
CU see you
CUL see you later
CUL8R see you later
CWYL chat with you later
DK don't know
FOAD fuck off and die
F2F face to face

GF girl friend
GTG got to go
H&K hugs and kisses
H4U hot for you
IC I see
IMAO in my arrogant opinion
IWALU I will always love you

JC just chilling
KK Teri's version of okay
KMA kiss my ass
L8R Later
LMAO laughing my ass off
LOL laughing out loud
LY love you
NBD no big deal
PITA pain in the ass
POS piece of shit
QT cutie
R U There? are you there?
NM never mind
NP no problem
OBTW oh by the way
OMG oh my God

ROFL rolling on the floor laughing
ROFLMAO rolling on the floor laughing my ass off
ROTFL rolling on the floor laughing
SOB stresses out big time
SOL shit out of luck
TTYL talk to you later
UOK are you okay?
WTF what the fuck?
WTG way to go

CHAPTER ONE

December '06

It's not like I was ever the most pretty or even the smartest girl on the block, but when it came to chatting online, I seemed to had transformed into a goddess that men desired. Horny married men, but who cared? I was married as well.

There are a million stories and reasons why people do the things that they do online. For me, my story begins with the color *fuchsia*. I find myself never watching the news only because it's so depressing and takes me to a "not so happy" place. I get my current events from those *brave* ones who do watch the news and share it with me. As an interior designer, I tend to notice color, and as I was passing through the living room one day, the color fuchsia caught my eye. My story begins with a fuchsia screen.

A cute, petite brunette anchorwoman is speaking, sporting a serious face as if she were reporting news on some sort of tragedy. "The Web site is called the Cheaters Club, and it is a site for married people who go online to find other married people and have affairs with. Consisting of over eight thousand members worldwide," the anchor woman announces as she slightly squints one eye. You can hear the judgment in her voice.

Cut to a man whose face is blotched out. He is sitting in a coffee shop with the anchorwoman, who had posed to be a married as well and who found him earlier this week online. As the camera is rolling, she comes clean with him and tells him who she is then proceeds to asks him, "Does your wife know that you meet married women in coffee shops?"

He shifts uncomfortably in his chair, and his voice has panic in it.

"No, and I'm sorry. I will never do this again, I'm sorry."

Noticing this, she doesn't stop there, playing on his panic, "Is this worth your marriage? Or do you even think about how it would affect someone else's marriage?"

"I love my wife, I'm sorry," he says. "I will never do this again," he repeats himself almost as if he's in shock.

I'm fixated on the purplish screen as it flashes in front of me again. I'm almost in a trance as it screams "LOOK AT ME!" and I do. I can't help but pity the sorry cheater guy, and I want to knock out the sassy anchorwoman for being so smug and happy to catch him. The whole thing is pathetic to me as I think to myself, *Nothing much must be happening in Utah today if they are featuring this shit on the news.* I walk away and don' t look back at the television, but the words on fuchsia site flash in my mind: When Monogamy becomes Monotony.

It is December now, and eight months and about five hundred chat buddies later, I sit on this plane flying home from seeing my main "boy toy" and decide that I must stop this behavior or die, realizing that continuing this would be the bane of my existence. Binge drinking has consumed me, and I was never really much of a drinker. People who drank a lot didn't have control. As soon as the thought of not chatting online or meeting men hits my little brain, I panic and think to myself, *Okay, I will give it up for my New Year's Resolution. Well, maybe.* So here I am, and I feel as if I have missed out on "living" the past eight months of my life by literally being online for the majority of my waking hours.

I have to admit as well if I could get online now, on this airplane, and chat, I would probably be doing that instead of writing this. Yet I feel compelled to write and to share my story, however painful it is to remember not only for myself, but for all my sisters out there who sit in front of their computer screens seeking for whatever it is they are missing in their lives. The contents and events written are true and happened, yet the names of the men and W eb sites have been changed to protect the identity of these individuals, whom don't know I' m writing this.

Blame it on the seven-year itch or maybe lack of sex and attention in my marriage, but I started to feel the desire to cheat growing within me. I fought it for a very long time. I even went as far as to take a class at the college on the history and philosophy of religion. No, I'm not a Mormon, which most people assume when you tell them you live in Utah. I' m what I like to consider as spiritual. I say my prayers every night and believe in a higher power I consider to be God, the traditional Christian monotheist God posessing all the characteristics and traits to which God is. This is the God who I pray to every night, but for some reason, God must have been busier than usual because I don' t think he heard my prayers of desperation to be rid of the feelings of adultery.

"Dear Father in Heaven," would be the way it started, and the prayer was always the same one.

"Save me from these feelings that burn this black hole into my soul, these feelings of desire, and from the need of wanting more. Save me from myself, before I step into a life that will end my life as I know it." Every night it was the same prayer, and every morning I would wake up with the feeling of *sin to come.* As the semester was coming to an end, I chose to write my final paper on the concepts of evil. Now remember that I don't even watch the news, so researching logical and moral evils put me in a state of distress in Teri-Ville, where things are always happy and sunny and pretty. Evil's face snuck into my dreams at night, turning my happy, fuzzy yellow thoughts into something resembling a Salvador Dali painting and leaving me cold. My first instinct was to try arguing that there is no such a thing as evil and that it does not exist within itself alone. I had read somewhere that evil was just the absence of good as dark is just the absence of light. But really, I didn't believe that for one minute. I struggled through writing my final paper, and weeks of darkness surrounded me as I landed in a state of depression while I researched evil in all of its horror. On the last day of class, I handed in my final paper to my instructor and went home and logged online.

I saw the color fuchsia in my mind and closed my eyes and tried to remember the name of that Web site that I saw featured on the news several weeks earlier, the one where "bad people go to cheat on their spouses." I could not remember the name of it, and my hands were trembling as my heart was pounding at the thought of entering a chat room for the first time. Not just a chat room but an *evil* chat room.

"Don't do this, Teri," I said out loud to myself. Speaking out loud to myself is something that I do under distress.

"Remember what Mom told you about marriage?" Years ago, when I was married to my first husband, my mother gave me some marital advice, as many mothers do for their daughters.

My mother was born in China, so much of the advice she gives me has a Chinese influence to it. "Honey, marriage is like a precious Ming vase, unique, fragile, and you must not neglect it or handle it poorly. If you become careless and drop this vase, it will surely crack. You may be able to glue the pieces back together, but the crack will always be there, and it will never be whole again." This was my mother's way of telling me to stay faithful to my husband. Remembering these words from my mother, I almost logged off the computer, but then I said out loud, "Oh so what, Mother, since when have I ever listened to you? Why start now?"

Then the justification hit me. I felt satisfied and dizzy, somewhat like I do when I have that first cigarette in the morning. As the justification of why I should log into this evil site started to become clearer, I thought to myself, *This is not evil, it is my balance.* I convinced myself at that moment it would be more of an "evil" if I were to leave my husband because he was not in good health and he was older—he would *die* if I were to leave him. Logging onto this site was the lesser of the two evils in my mind. Then it came to me—the name of the Web site. I whispered it quietly to myself, saying the name out loud for the first time as I typed it into the address bar and hit Search. There it was. Little did I know as I entered the pretty fuchsia site that this was my first of many visits to hell.

CHAPTER TWO

April '06—How it began

What was I going to call myself? Having never been in any sort of a chat room before, I was wondering if I should use my first name. No, probably not, I decided. Not a good idea. Even strippers don't use their first names, and most of them aren't the brightest Barbies. What then—something sexy, maybe? Like Sweet Sin? Or maybe Sexy Kitty Kat ? Too porn star-ish. Maybe I should appear to be smart and go with Renaissance Girl? No, then they would expect for me to be able to spell. I opted to just be myself and came up with "Designgirl11." Design girl because that is what I am, an interior designer, and the eleven is because that is my favorite number. It has been ever since I was a little girl and my older sister Kirsten would listen to the song "One." I remember that it seemed so sad, so I thought if there are two "ones," then it won't stand alone anymore, hence the eleven. That is the reasoning of an eight-year-old that should have maybe been on Ritalin.

Designgirl was born that rainy April morning. She would be my *alter ego*, and my secret *other* life would begin with that first chat. I created my profile, answering all of the questions as honestly as I possibly could. My caption read, "It's getting hot in here, can you take the heat?" Now if that didn't catch some bad boy's attention then what would? I filled in the boxes of the questions asked.

Age:	41
Height:	5'4". Really I am only five feet, three inches, but there wasn't a box for 5'3", so I decided to round it up rather than down. Guys like taller chicks.
Weight:	135 lbs. This is the only part that I wanted to kind of *twist* the truth. I mean, it's okay that one does this on her driver's license, right? Any woman whose booty is larger than a soccer ball understands that a little *twist* on what she weighs is not the same as a lie.
Hair:	Dark Brown
Eyes:	Brown
Body Type:	Curvy

Ethnic Background: Caucasian. If there were a "mutt" box to check, I would have. Smoking Habits: Regularly. Again there was not a "chain-smoke like hell" box.

There were sections on "What Really Turns Me On" and "Preferences and Encounters I Am Open To" as well as "What I Am Looking For." As I glanced through the list of things to check, I felt desolate and confounded by what I read in front of me. Threesome, being submissive/slave, fetishes, video taping, spanking, being watched, whips, role playing, transvestism were some of the things listed. *What the hell is transvestism?* I decided to leave the boxes unchecked. Designgirl was now born so I logged online.

It was almost instantly that that I received my first instant message from someone called HOTROD.

HOTROD: Hi sexy
Designgirl: Oh, hi there, this is my first time here, I wasn't sure if this was working!
HOTROD: So you are a virgin then huh? I will be gentle
Designgirl: Oh, no I'm not a virgin, I have three children. Do you have kids?
HOTROD: LOL, I meant that you are new and this is your first chat which makes you a virgin
Designgirl: Oh, ok then. So what is "LOL"?
HOTROD: Damn girl, you really are a virgin! It means—laughing out loud

There was something flashing at the top of the right-hand part of the chat box. It read "3 waiting"; an instant later, it read "4 waiting." Four waiting for what? I clicked the flashing icon, and there was a new screen with someone who I really don't remember, so I will just call him Dickboy1.

Dickboy1: Hi baby, are you wet?
Designgirl: What did you just say? You are kidding right?
Dickboy1: I'm hard, do you want to play?

I was done chatting with this ass wipe so I clicked the flashing icon once again. Dickboy 2 appeared.

Dickboy2: Hey
Designgirl: Hi
Dickboy2: Whatcha up to?
Designgirl: Just checking out this site, what about you?
Dickboy2: Chillin and relaxin

I was curious to know more about who Dickboy2 was, so I clicked on his profile. He was twenty-five years old, which explained his laid-back grammar, and he was from Canada.

Designgirl: So how are things in Canada today?
Dickboy2:   Same ol, where are you from?
Designgirl: Utah, it should say that in my profile
Dickboy2:   Kewl, oh ic you are 41, older women are hot

However much fun this was, Dickboy2 was boring me, so I clicked the flashing icon another time.

Dickboy3:   Hello, how are you today?
Designgirl: Hi, I'm doing well thank you and yourself?
Dickboy3:   Same here TY, it's nice to see someone local online

I pulled up Dickboy3's profile and saw that he was also from Provo. He was thirty-eight years old, and his photo was posted in his profile. He was very handsome, with wavy dark hair and kind brown eyes and had that sexy dimpled chin thing going. He had that sexy foreign look about him—maybe Italian or perhaps Spanish? The kind of look that makes you fantasize of sticking dollar bills down his britches. I liked what I saw.

Designgirl: You live in Provo? I'm originally from California myself
Dickboy3:   I'm from Florida but I moved here several years ago

We chatted for a long time, and I ignored the other eager men waiting for a chance to say hello. Dickboy3 was easy to talk to, and I found myself wanting to know more about him.

Designgirl: I'm Teri, btw
Dickboy3:   I'm Paul, nice to meet you Teri

Paul and I continued to chat, and I glanced at the time. Over an hour had passed. Paul had a rule to never meet local women because it was too risky. However discrete he had intended to be, I must have intrigued him because by the end of our conversation, I became the exception to his rule.

Paul: So Teri, would you like to meet sometime? You really have me
              captured in a spell here
Designgirl: Oh, I bet you say that to all the girls don't you?

Paul:	Only you
Designgirl:	Right . . . . well, really, I didn' t expect to land a date on my first chat! Are your photos current? I mean, they weren't taken like ten years ago and if I meet you I will find that you are now an ugly fatty with no hair will I?
Paul:	ha ha . . . you have a quick wit about you, I like that. No, my photos are current and I'm not an ugly fatty without hair. I'm more a stinky though . . . .

I was hooked. The *stinky* statement sealed the meeting for me. Paul was handsome if indeed his photos were current, and he was both intelligent and funny. We set up a time and place to meet the following night. I was so enthralled in our conversation that I had not noticed that there were now ten men waiting to chat with me. It was 1:00 p.m., and I fought the temptation to click the flashing icon to see who else was there. The temptation won out, and I my finger found its way to the key, clicking the flashing button again.

Dickboy4:	Can you chat?
Designgirl:	Hi, sure
Dickboy4:	I'm Randolph what is your name?
Designgirl:	Olga
Dickboy4:	Hi Olga!! (He inserts a smiley face) Do you have any photos?
Designgirl:	No, I'm new and really, I don't think I want to post my photo here yet
Dickboy4:	I just sent you my key, take a look

I wasn't certain what a key was, but up came an icon with a key symbol, so I clicked on it.

Dickboy4:	Did you get it doll?

Before I could view it, it had a "rating warning," and not quite knowing what this meant, I accepted it anyways.

Dickboy4:	So what do you think?

Have you ever noticed someone who sucked on a lemon and made that sour lemon face? Well, that was what happened to me when I saw what was before me. I looked as if I just sucked on the sourest lemon of them all. There it was—it was about four inches long and wrinkly and blue.

Dickboy4:	So?

I felt nauseous, and I didn't know how to respond. I clicked on his profile and started to read it. That explained the penis picture—he was sixty-two.

Designgirl: Nice
Dickboy4: Thank ya darling, so what would ya like to do with that?

I wanted to tell him that I would like to get him on an oxygen tank and pump some major circulation in that direction, yet I said nothing. I clicked the flashing icon in hopes to seek out someone to save me from blue Dickboy4. It was that nasty Dickboy1 again.

Dickboy1: I'm ready to blow a huge load here baby, ready for me?

This dude was sick and wrong. I clicked on his profile and discovered that Dickboy1 was only thirty years old, from Ohio, 190 pounds, and six feet tall. He claimed to be athletically built, and not to my surprise, every box possibly available of what he desired was checked Curiosity got the best of me, so I responded.

Designgirl: So what is it that you do for a living horny guy?
Dickboy1: I'm an Attorney sweet thing, and my cock is throbbing here so help me out! LOL

This very moment confirmed that I really did not like attorneys, and all the jokes that I ever heard about attorneys flashed through mind, making me want to share one or two of them with him.

Designgirl: Santa Claus, the tooth fairy, an honest lawyer and an old drunk are walking down the street together when they simultaneously spot a hundred dollar bill. Who gets it?
Dickboy1: (no response)
Designgirl: The drunk, of course, the other three are mythological creatures!
Dickboy1: (still no response)

I was never good at telling jokes, and it seemed as if I was always the only one who ever laughed at them. My timing was always off, or I would get the punch line wrong. Really, it was my older sister Kirstin who was the joke teller in the family. It occurred to me that when I wanted to get rid of a "Dickboy" who I didn't want to chat with, I would just tell him a joke. I felt smart that I figured that one out, until . . .

Dickboy1: That's really funny baby, so are you wet yet?

Designgirl: Sorry Mr. Counselor, I'm pleading the fifth on that one.

Dickboy1:   I need to blow a load so L8R

He did not just diss me! Some horny-ass, arrogant attorney just gave ME the boot? I made a mental note to learn more insulting jokes about attorneys. I clicked the flashing button once more.

Dickboy5:   Hello, are you there?

Designgirl: Hi, I'm here yes, how are you?

Dickboy5:   You must be popular I have been waiting to chat with you for awhile now!

Designgirl: No not at all, I'm new to this site and have only chatted with a few so far, do you like it here?

Dickboy5:   It's ok. I just got back on it, I was on it for about a year and then left for six months or so and decided to see if anyone interesting is here now.

Designgirl: Oh well I will do my best to try to be interesting to you then! (I found the icons with the smiley faces and choose to send him a "wink" face)

Dickboy5:   So do you have MSN?

I did have MSN, but I was not sure if I should say I did. It had my first and last name on it, and I didn't know this guy, so I opted not to tell him that I did.

Designgirl: Nope I don't have MSN

Dickboy5:   What about Yahoo?

Designgirl: Not that either

Dickboy5:   You should create one; this site is expensive to chat on!

Designgirl: I noticed that when I looked at the prices for credits.

One had to purchase credits for "chat time" if you wanted to chat. Most women did not buy credits, so the men were the ones who would normally pay for time to chat. The prices were exorbitant, and one could easily spend up to a hundred dollars a day if they were serious chatters. This was an addiction for many, and instead of using drugs or alcohol, they would spend their money on credits to chat with people they have never met. Later down the road, I would find myself purchasing credits after discovering that there are a lot of cheap men out there requesting collect chats.

Designgirl: I will create a Yahoo email and let you know, how's that?

Dickboy5:   Deal. I will look forward to that. So what do you look like?

Designgirl:	I'm 5'3" and brunette and my eyes are brown. My mothers Chinese and my fathers a white boy so people often mistake me for being Hispanic or Italian. What do you look like?
Dickboy5:	I bet you are beautiful then, I will send you my key, hold on.
Dickboy5:	There, did you get it?

I pull up his photos, and "HOLY SHIT!" came out of my mouth.

Designgirl:	Is this really you???????
Dickboy5:	Naw, it's the guy who's doing my wife, JK, yes it's me!
Designgirl:	Wow, you are HOT! Ok, I lied, this is my MSN addy . . . .
Dickboy5:	See how you women are? Lol! Ok I will meet you on MSN in a sec

I didn't want to close the screen. He was perfect. He had sandy blond hair and what appeared to be either green or blue eyes, but it was not his eyes I was looking at. He had about five photos posted. The first one was a close-up of his face; he could have been a Calvin Klein model. The others were ones of him posing and flexing his muscles. He must have been one of those gym guys by the way he posed, showing off the ripples in his abs. I noticed he had some "rated photos," and I thought to myself, *Today I go to heaven for a few minutes.* Forgetting all about the last time I clicked this button only minutes ago, my finger was fast to hit that button and open the page. There it was, perfect, erect, and nicely pinkish. It was HUGE! The first thing that came to my mind was, *Ouchy, this would HURT!*

Who was gym boy, and how far away did he live from me? Before I could click off the photo of his perfect pinkish "thing" and find the answers to these questions, I received a pop-up on MSN from him to be invited as an instant—messenger friend. I immediately accepted it and logged off the Cheaters Club site for now.

Gym boy's name was Scott. Or that's what it said on his MSN messenger screen. Scotty-licious was more like it. He had a picture of his perfect torso in a Speedo on his display picture. Normally, a dude in a Speedo would be a major turnoff for me, kind of like when a guy wears flip-flops and jeans and it's not summer, or overalls. Yet I was finding myself staring right at that Speedo, thinking, *I'm buying stock in Speedo after I say good-bye here.*

MSN Chat:

Scott:	Hi, are you there?
Teri:	Yes you found me! Hi Scott, I' m Teri, nice display picture!
Scott:	Glad you like it Teri, nice, ummm . . . duck

I knew that I needed to change out the duck that was displayed as my picture. I made a mental note to do this soon. I needed to get some current photos of myself and was thinking of how I was going to do that.

Teri: You makin fun of my duckie?

Scott: No way, your duck is cute. Do you have any photos that you want to share with me?

Teri: Only ones of me and my children and I don't feel comfortable sending you any of those, no offense but really I'm amazed I gave you my MSN! It must have been your . . . kind smile which convinced me to do so.

Scott: Sure it was lol! Maybe you can take some then and throw in a few naughty ones?

Teri: You wish! I will get some G-rated ones for you soon.

Scott and I chatted for a long time, and I found out that he was from Florida, hence the sexy tan. He was a structural engineer, so we had some things in common to talk about. He was thirty-four, and he had been married for twelve years and had two sons. His story was sad. His wife paid no attention to him, and they would go months without having sex. As he typed away, sharing his pain with me, I felt a connection to him. He turned from being this sex symbol fantasy guy into a real person. I wondered how many married people were unhappy and put on a front for their friends and family. I assumed it was more than most would think. Scott seemed perfect to me. He was sexy and smart, and there was tenderness about him. He was this big, strong, macho guy who seemed to open up to me, sharing a small piece of his life. I was amazed to how easy it was to chat with him, and a mutual trust began between us on this first chat.

I would continue to chat with Scott for months, and since then I have chatted with hundreds of men, yet there was something different and special about my chats with Scott that I have not felt with anyone since him.

Teri: OMG! It's three o'clock I have to go get my son

Scott: I should go too; will you be back online tonight?

Teri: Yes I should be . . . look for me k?

Scott: Ok sexy, until tonight then

Teri: Kisses

Kisses? Did I just type that? This would be the standard way I would say good-bye from this time on. I logged off my computer knowing that I had just crossed a forbidden line. I felt something amiss as I realized the fallacy of my behavior. Knowing that I committed something so uncharacteristic of who I was gave me a chill, and a small rush went through my body. I felt instantly alive—as if something or someone had breathed a breath of fire into my lungs stirring up feelings of arousal long forgotten.

The phone rang, and it was my husband. "What are you doing baby?" he asked as he does every day when he calls me to check in.

"I was working on the Anderson job, done for now, though. What are you doing?" I lied so easily, surprising myself.

"Just killing alligators like always. Just like that movie, *Groundhog Day*, my days are just like the day before. I always know what is going to happen next. So what did you design for the Andersons? Did you finish the kitchen plan?"

"Nope, but I did get a good start on it. I will probably be working on it tonight all night after the kids go to bed." My alibi to why I would be up late on the computer was established.

"Okay, just checking to see how my baby is doing. I' ll be late getting home tonight, hangin out with the boys for a while."

"All right, talk to you later then, bye honey." I hung up the phone, grabbed my purse, and headed out the door to get my son with the same normality I did every day, as if the events of the past six hours didn't really happen.

CHAPTER THREE

May '06

I met my husband almost eight years ago. I was a bartender in a club he used to own, and he would come in several times a week. I was recently divorced, with three young children, and working double shifts to try to stay afloat. My future husband would come in and order a diet Coke and talk to me for hours. He had owned several clubs and lost them recently and was driving commercial trucks. He went from having millions to living in a trailer.

He was much older than I was, nineteen years my senior. He was funny and made me laugh. On the days he would come in to visit, I always knew that it would be a good day.

"Diet Coke? Or something stronger today, cowboy?" I asked him one November afternoon.

"Diet Coke is good. I opened up a new club. Why don't you leave this shit hole and come work for me?" he asked in his "always to the point" way of speaking.

"You can't afford to hire me! I'm expensive, you know."

"Ha! Honey, I believe it! Give me a call if you change your mind."

It would be months before I would go to work for him, and when I did, I would still not know for a very long time the reason for his visits to see me. He would later tell me, "The first time I saw you, I said to myself, 'There is my next future ex-wife.'"

We became engaged two months after I started working for him, and I became wife number four to him two years later. Our courtship was rocky, but I found security with this man who I did love, and I could see myself spending the rest of his life with him. I say the rest of *his* life because realistically I knew the possibility of me surviving him was high.

We worked hard together establishing the club, and eventually, after a year, it did take off. I decided to leave bartending and seek out something that was a more a "happy" profession, without the undertone of ugliness that hides itself behind the club scene. Decorating was something that always came so easily to me. I could always see shapes and color and had a talent for putting a room together. I went to school to become an interior designer and worked hard to get through my courses in half the time because I was anxious to start my new profession. This, and because when I become driven to do something, I plunge myself into it. Diving in, head first.

My children and husband were very supportive of me despite the long hours of schooling and design projects that took me away from them. The day I graduated was one of the happiest days of my life. It would take a few years for my design business to flourish, but I became one of the busiest designers in town. I stayed busy and happy in my work, yet I felt my marriage drifting from me. He would work long hours at the club, and I would throw myself into more work than I could handle. It was about eight months ago when I crashed and burned. Going back to that time in early May . . .

I met Scott online that night and we chatted for hours. I felt as if I were a schoolgirl again, flirting with the captain of the football team. I was nervous, and that night, before I logged online, I did something that I had never done I poured myself a vodka cranberry. This was the first time I ever drank at home. Even when I'd host parties at my house I would have a diet Coke or water. I would go out occasionally and party, but drinking to me was not fun unless I could dance and be in the environment of a club. After my first cape cod, I logged online and found him instantly; he was waiting for me.

The more we chatted, the more drinks I poured. Vodka never tasted so sweet. I felt as if I were on this "secret" first date, and even though I could not hear or see him, he was just as real as if he were standing right in front of me. We agreed to meet online the next day as we said goodbye after chatting until midnight. I was drunk and was starting to spell badly; not that spelling was ever a strong point of mine to begin with. He seemed not to have noticed, and if he had, he was a gentleman and would never correct me on it.

My binge drinking started on this night, and I would not put two and two together as to why I started to drink until several months later. I would drink my cape cods in a coffee mug so that my children and husband did not see what it was that I was drinking.

I woke up the next morning a bit hung over, and the first thing I did was drink a huge glass of water and log onto my computer. Scott was not online, so I decided to visit the Cheaters Club site. I logged in and had several messages from guys requesting my photo, or "key" as it was called. I started to chat with several guys, and Paul popped up.

Cheaters club site:

Paul: Hey you, are we still on for tonight?
Designgirl: Yes, but you are aware that this is my first meeting right?
Paul: Yes, you mentioned that

Designgirl:	Ok then, I am a bit nervous and really, I don't know if I will be able to kiss you or anything
Paul:	Lol! Who said anything about kissing you? Maybe I will see you and think YOU are an ugly fatty! But I will still stay for a drink even if you are, until my diarrhea kicks in and I will have to go
Designgirl:	That's funny! Hey, I'm not an ugly fatty though so I don' t think you should expect a case of instant diarrhea
Paul:	It would be nice to know what you look like. I don't usually meet blindly; don't you have a photo you can send me?
Designgirl:	Really I don't. You will just have to trust that I look like I say I do. Plus, it's not what I may look like that you like about me, it's because I'm a gud spellar
Paul:	Right again, I have a weakness for women who can spel gud
Designgirl:	Good, I'm glad to hear that, I will remember to put my teeth in before we meet then. So, see you later tonight? Do you know where the club is? I will leave your name at the door
Paul:	I have been there a few times so I know where it is. I will see you at seven then Beautiful
Designgirl:	Ok and I will bring the Pepto-Bismol so you won't have an excuse to bail, kisses

I logged off the site and noticed that Scott was still not online. I decided to take a shower and to eat something to settle my stomach.

The door bell rang at about one o'clock that afternoon; it was Dustin, the guy who cleaned the pool.

"Hi, Teri, sorry to bother you, but I forgot my key to the pool cover. Can you open it up for me?"

"No problem, Dustin. Come in and I will find the key for you."

Dustin was in his early thirties and a quiet guy. He would come and clean the pool weekly, and I had noticed that he would check me out in my bikini when I would lay out by my pool and he would steal glances when I would fetch a drink. A thought occurred to me as I handed him the key to the pool cover.

"Dustin, can I ask you to do me a weird favor?"

"Sure, what's that?"

"Okay, this is going to sound really strange, but can you take some photos of me so I can send them to my sister? She has been bugging me for some, and I promised to get a few to her this week."

"Sure, no problem, I can do that." He said with a huge grin on his face.

"Great, I need to get changed, and I will be back up. It won't take me long, okay? Help yourself to a soda in the outside fridge, and here's the key if you want to start cleaning the pool."

"Okay, but photography is not one of my talents, just to let you know. I'm sure the camera loves you, though."

The camera is not my friend. It's true that it makes one look ten pounds heavier, but in my case double that number. My sisters are both photogenic, as well as my mother, and in viewing photos of myself, I would wonder what I must have done to piss off the "camera goddess." The only photo of me which I considered "cute" was one taken when I was eighteen months old and I was in a little red one-piece bathing suit, little white sneakers, and wearing a white hat. I was on the grass at what appeared to be a park, bending over to pick up something not visible in the photo. One day, when I was looking through my baby album, I asked my father about this photo since he was the one who photographed it.

"Dad, where was that photo taken?"

"In Okinawa, when we lived in Japan. It was at a place called White Beach."

"You and Mom must have fed me well 'cause I was a chunk. What was I picking up?"

He laughed and said, "Bird shit."

"EW! NO WAY! You let me do that?" I asked, almost afraid to hear what he would answer.

"I thought it was cute, but I didn't know that you would pick it up and eat it." I was horrified at what I just heard.

"Dad, that really should be considered some sort of child abuse, you know." I never asked what I was doing in another baby photo after that day.

I went downstairs to my bedroom and looked through my closet to find something that would make me look "thinnish." I chose a short brown baby doll dress with spaghetti straps. I fixed my hair and put on my favorite shade of lipstick. I was looking hot-ish, so I hoped the camera goddess was in a good mood today and would smile upon me.

"Wow, you look great, Teri. Your sister should like these photos," he said, looking straight at my ample cleavage.

"Thanks, I just threw this on. I have nothing in my closet, and I hate that." I gave a huge sigh and a "what's a girl to do?" look, but I could tell he didn't believe it for a second.

He took several pictures of me, and I could tell that he would be thinking that my pool would be the best pool he cleaned that day.

"Thanks, Dustin. I really appreciate this a lot."

"Welcome, Teri. It was fun, and maybe I will think of taking up photography now. Let me know if you need me to reshoot any!"

"You got it. You will be the first I call."

She must have been in a pleasant mood that day, the camera goddess, because the photos were not half bad. I spent an hour cropping and cutting out all of my "fat" parts. It was ready to post on my profile. I logged in and posted the photos that Dustin took of me. *I HAVE A KEY!*

I took another look at Paul's key, and my stomach was in knots. What if he did think I was an ugly fatty? Or worse, what if he lied, and he looked nothing like his photos? I glanced at the time and decided to change into some jeans and go early. I thought that I needed a few drinks before he met me there.

I arrived at the club at six o'clock. He would be here in an hour. I took a seat on a bar stool at the main bar in front of a video machine. The bartender was an older woman of about fifty-five or so, and she was wearing clothes that fit too snugly for her plump figure.

"You have a membership and ID, sweetie?" she spat out in a raspy voice.

"I have ID, but I need to purchase a membership. Oh, I have a friend meeting me here soon."

In the state of Utah, we do have some weird laws. There are misconceptions about polygamy and the Mormon Church, but most of what you do hear about the liquor laws is true. All bars and clubs that sell hard liquor require that one must purchase a membership for entrance into the establishment. Then there is a limit to what can be served to a customer. It is illegal to serve more than 2.75 ounces of liquor to a patron at one time. We have the worst Long Islands in the world here because it is mostly "mixer," so you are better off having a drink and a sidecar or bump. This would be like an ounce of vodka with my cranberry juice and an extra once of vodka for me to pour into my drink since it is illegal for the bartender to do so for me.

"What ya gonna have, sweetie?" The plump bartender asked. Her name tag read Babes.

"Stoli cod with a sidecar, please."

"You got it," she said with a wink. "What's the name of your friend, so I can leave it at the door? I'm heading out here in a few minutes."

"Paul, his name is Paul."

"Last name?"

"Oh, I don't know." She glanced at my wedding ring and gave me that "Oh I get it" look, and my eyes turned away from her as if to admit that she was right in her thoughts. I downed my drink and ordered a shot of tequila dressed with salt and lemon and chilled the way I like them (It is never good to give me a shot of warm tequila. It finds its way back up as soon as it goes down.)

I put five dollars in the video machine game and started to play strip poker. I was working really hard to get the fireman guy naked when my cell phone rang. It was my buddy Mike. He was twenty-five years old, and I sometimes partied with him. He was recently kicked out of my husband's club for some bogus reason, but I knew it was because he was someone my husband was jealous of because we hung out occasionally. Mike and I were actually only friends and nothing more, even though I was attracted to his clean-cut GQ-ish good looks.

"What up, Ter girl?"

"Hey, I'm sitting at Jake's Lounge, waiting to meet an architect who I may be doing some work for. What are you doing?" Mike had no idea of what I was planning to do, and he always knew that I was faithful to my husband.

"Cool, I was going to go out and see if you wanted to grab a few beers with me, but if you are meeting someone . . ."

"No! Come! Really . . . it's okay, he won't mind." *Did I just say that?* I must have been out of my mind. I was so nervous, and the thought of Mike being there soothed me.

"Okay, see you in ten minutes then." I had Babes the bartender make me another Stoli cod and sidecar, and by the time Mike got there, I was on my third round of doubles. I bought my buddy a few drinks, and he helped me get my fireman naked as well as the cop guy.

"What time's the architect dude supposed to be here, Ter?" I glanced at my watch, and it was seven thirty. He was late. Horrid thoughts raced through my vodka-laden mind. Maybe he was here and saw my ass, which would have been facing him as he walked in, and thought, *No way am I staying here.* Or maybe he saw me with Mike and thought I had picked up on someone. Maybe he just changed his mind and he's standing me up. Maybe, maybe, maybe. I went to the front door to ask the door girl to watch for him. She was a young, blond, thin thing, eating a huge sandwich and probably wouldn't gain an ounce in doing so.

"Oh yeah, some guy named Paul came in, saying he was meeting someone."

"Where did he go? Did he come in?" I was panicked and probably sounded a bit desperate.

"He didn't have his driver's license on him, so I told him I couldn't let him in. He said he had to go home and get it and that he would be back in twenty minutes." I wanted to slap her right about now as she took another bite of the sandwich while speaking with her mouth full. "Don't worry—he said he'd be back."

"How long ago did he leave, and was he cute?" I was for sure sounding desperate now. *Did I just ask her if he was cute?*

"He left about thirty minutes ago. He should have been back by now," she took another bite of her sandwich, and for some reason, she chose not to speak with her mouth full this time, keeping me waiting until she swallowed it before she answered, "Yeah, he was pretty cute."

I went back to my seat and ordered Mike and me another round of drinks. "He's on his way. He forgot his ID."

"What a dork. I'd be afraid to walk into a building he designed just in case he happened to forget to put one of those beam things in and the building fell down."

"Mike, shut up, you sound stupid. Don't even start to talk architecture when he gets here. I need a shot of tequila."

Someone tapped me on the shoulder, and I turned around, looking at a familiar face. It was him, and he did look like his photo.

"Teri? Hi, I'm sorry I'm late. I forgot my ID." He had the most amazing brown eyes, and I was flushed by either his smile or the tequila I just shot.

"I know, the door girl eating the great-looking sandwich told me. Oh, this is Mike, by the way. Mike, this is Paul."

"Hey, Paul, how's it going? I never met an architect in person before. You work with a lot of those beam things?" Mike was so dead. Paul looked puzzled, and it occurred to me that I forgot to tell him to pretend he was an architect if I happened to run into someone I knew. I would meet architects, builders, contractors, and clients often, so this was my cover if I were to be seen. He must have caught on, and he nodded to Mike, saying hello to him quickly before turning his attention back to me.

"Would you like to get a table? Or should we just sit at the bar?" I sensed that he was uncomfortable with Mike being there.

"Lets get a table," I said, "Mike, didn't you say that you had a date tonight?"

"No, but I get it. Nice to meet you, Paul. Ter, let's golf tomorrow, and this time, you don't get to drive the cart. She almost killed us last week, Paul. Damn women drivers." Mike gave me a wink, and I hugged him good-bye. I did "almost" tip the golf cart the week before, but it was not totally my fault. We were going down a hill, and the cart was at an angle. I meant to hit my breaks and straighten it out but hit the gas instead, and I think that maybe one of the tires was a bit flat, and the cart started to tip toward my side. Mike stood up in the cart, extending his leg and arm outward to help balance the cart with his weight so we would not tip. He looked so stupid in doing this that it was almost worth us tipping just to see. We made it down the hill when he yelled, "You fucking almost killed us!"

"No I didn't," I laughed. "We wouldn't have died, maybe broken a leg or two. Hey, I'm part Chinese, you know. No one said we are good drivers."

Paul found us a table in the corner of the bar. He was not a big drinker, I found out, but he drank one to every three I had. We talked for quite awhile, and I felt more relaxed and less nervous.

"Have you cheated before, Paul?" I blurted this out like it was a commonly asked question. "I have never cheated, you know. I mean I want to. I think. Or I think I want to." I was definitely wasted.

He smiled, knowing this. "Yes, I have cheated on my wife before, a few times. I got married for all the wrong reasons. We dated for two years and she wanted to get married and she gave me an ultimatum. I didn't want to lose her because I was comfortable with her, and I did care about her a lot. I knew she would make a good mother and wife, so I married her."

"Wow, that's sad." My head was resting in my hands by this time, and I was starting to slur my words. "You think you will ever leave her? I mean, I won't ever leave him, ever, ever."

"No, I won't leave my wife. Our children are young. My son is two, and my daughter is six months old. I'm in this for life or until they are grown." Paul had the most perfect teeth and smile. I found myself watching his mouth as he spoke, and because I was drunk, I probably did not try to hide that I was looking right at his mouth. I wanted him to kiss me.

"Wow, that's really sad," I said again. "I have to go. I have to go home before the bartender cuts me off here."

"Well, actually, you were cut off thirty minutes ago!" he laughed. "I will walk you to your car. Are you okay to drive?"

"I was? They cut me off? Wow, okay, then you can walk me to my truck. I'm okay to drive. I'm a very, very good driver, you know."

"Yeah, I heard." I watched him get up, and he looked good in his jeans. He had a great butt, and he was the perfect height at about five eleven. I always liked my guys a bit shorter because it made me look tall standing next to them when I would wear heels. He walked me to my truck, and I opened the door and got in.

"Buckle up, Speed Racer," he said as he reached over and helped me fasten my seat belt. His arm brushed against my breast, and I felt instantly aroused. Before he could snap the belt into a lock position, I turned to him and grabbed his head with my right hand, pulling him toward my face, and I kissed him. I turned my body toward him and he wrapped his arms around my waist and he kissed me passionately, hard at first, and then with soft gentle kisses. I wrapped and locked my legs around the backs of his legs tightly. His kisses tasted like I would imagine the forbidden apple must have tasted in the Garden of Eden, like sweet sin.

I can't remember for how long we made out, but I did know that it seemed like time had stopped. "I have to go, Paul. It's really late, and I'll be in trouble."

"Are you sure you are okay to drive, Teri?" He said to me as the lights of the parking lot hit his brown eyes and made them look like the color of honey.

"Yeah, I'm okay. Hey, thanks for making my first meeting the best ever."

"You're welcome, but I'm hoping that you will find that our second meeting will be even better." I could not stop looking into his eyes as he said this and wondered when I would see him again. I didn't want to ask this in fear of sounding clingy or desperate, so I just nodded.

"Okay, Paul, got to go here, so see you later." I was so playing it cool, or at least I was trying to. "Kiss me again one more time, bad boy." And he did.

CHAPTER FOUR

May '06

It smelled of *new car* and fresh linens. I opened the curtains to our new motor home and packed up the new pots and pans that I had just purchased for it in boxes. I cleared the cupboards and closets, packing up every thing that I had only just put there weeks ago.

"What the hell you doin?" my husband asked me.

"There are some refugee's from Saudi Arabia here. They have nothing. I'm giving them this," I said to him never looking up. One of my friends told me about a family who left Saudi Arabia and came to Utah. They had nothing and needed help.

"No you're not. Put it back. Damn sand nigger's aint getting my shit."

"Honey, don't say that word. You know it offends me. They have nothing. We can help. We have so much to give."

"Put it back now Ter! You aint givin my shit away to any rag heads!"

Ignoring what he said I called out for the children to help me finish packing blankets and towels.

"I told you to put the shit back where it belongs, now!" he screamed at me, infuriated that I was ignoring him.

"Fine. I will just go buy them what they need then."

"Why do you always gotta try and save the world? Last year it was two hundred backpacks for a shelter in New Orleans. That cost me enough dough. Teri to the rescue again! Fine, give it to them then but don't be buying anything," he pouted.

The children helped me load the things in my truck and we drove into Salt Lake to a dirty apartment building. I knocked on the door and waited.

"Mom, this is creepy. I want to go," my youngest son said to me.

"Sweetie, we will. We need to drop this off and we will go." My children were not happy about being here, yet I thought it was important for them to be. I asked for them to pack up toys that they didn' t play with anymore for the ten year old boy and they weren't too pleased with my request. The door opened and there was an older woman who was in her sixties who stood before us in the traditional garments of her country. She didn't speak English I soon realized as another similarly dressed younger woman approached us.

"Hello, I am Hanan. This is my mother. She does not speak English. Please come in."

We followed her instruction and took off our shoes, noticing that they had shoes lined up by the door There was a dirty mattress in the living room with a blanket on it and a television on the floor. That was about all they had, this and a few tea cups.

"Can I offer you some tea?" Hanan asked.

"No thank you. We can't stay very long but you are kind to offer."

Hanna shared her story about how she lost her six year old daughter and her husband. Both were executed in front of the family. Punishment for her husband denying the military. She was vague about the details of what this meant and I didn't ask. Tears swelled up in my eyes as I noticed that my children were also touched by her words. I was glad that I had brought them. We brought in the last load of things from the truck and it was Hanan's turn to cry now.

"Thank you. I don't know what to say to a stranger who brings my family so much. May your God bless and keep you," she told me as she grasped both of my hands in hers and kissed them. She did the same thing to each of my children next, asking that her God bless them this time.

On the way home, I thought of her words to me, *May your God bless and keep you.* I wondered if my God would forgive me one day, for the things that I knew I would commit.

"Mom, can I give the little boy my television?" my daughter asked, breaking my deep thoughts.

"Yeah, mom. We need to go back and get more stuff. Can we?" my eldest son added.

"You guys are great, but we already gave them a television. I think we gave them enough. Thank you for coming with me. Remember this always." I said to them, hoping that they would. Hoping that I wouldn't forget it either. That I would remember who I was, and what it would take to sustain me from losing myself when everything I knew would soon fall away.

For the next few days, I would find myself on the Cheaters Club site for hours during the day. I would chat with up to twenty men a day, thus adding to my "fan club" on the Yahoo account that I had created just for chat reasons. I had set up another meeting with Paul for the following night as well as meeting another local guy earlier that same evening. I had four meetings set up for the next week; I was on some kind of a roll. Scott and I continued to chat online in between my Cheaters Club chats. I was starting to form feelings for him which seemed so real. I found myself contemplating a trip to Florida to visit him. He was asked to model for some posters at his local gym, and one day he e-mailed me the photos.

MSN Chat:

Teri: OMG! These are HOT! I want a signed copy of one or twelve!

Scott: TY. I was really embarrassed to do this, but they have been asking me to for awhile now.

Teri: You could be the poster boy for all the gyms in the world! You make me want to go work out and I don't do that, it hurts. I don't exercise and I eat cheeseburgers.

I really do hate exercise; it is not my favorite thing in the world. I would later say to a few: "If I spent one twentieth of the time on the treadmill that I do online, I would be a skinny bitch!" There was something humble about Scott, and I recognized his insecurity. I tried to boost his ego, and because he was so perfect to me, I was actually telling the truth. I found myself beginning to learn how to flirt and tell little" fibs" to men online just to make them feel special, but with Scott I meant every word that I typed. He had low self-esteem, and I could not figure out why. He was always putting himself down in subtle ways and praising my graces, and I am less than perfect in my size six body form. His shyness was a turn-on for me, and the shyer he would become., the naughtier I was. He had a nickname for me because of some of the things I would spurt out of nowhere—he called me NUT. I called him SEXYHOT. We had only been chatting for a few weeks when one day he was really down on himself for some odd reason.

Teri: Sexyhot . . . know what?

Scott: What's that Nut?

Teri: You know that you are beautiful to me but if for some reason these photos that you have sent me are not really you, and you had bugged teethed and wore glasses, I would still want you.

No Response.
Still no response.

Teri: Sexyhot, you there?

Scott: Yeah, I'm here Nut. I have to go. I will chat with you soon babe.

He logged off, and it would be another week before I would chat with him again. I wondered what it was that I said that made him leave so quickly. I was trying to let him know that it was who he was on the inside which mattered to me, and then it occurred to me: What if those photos were not him? My perfect fantasy-man image of him shattered right then. I felt a bit betrayed and deceived at the thought of this, and I would never know if I was right or not, but I did know that he still meant something to me regardless of who I was really looking at when I viewed his photos.

My second meeting was with Travis. He was thirty years old and spoke Italian and French. He was well traveled and did well for himself. The photo that he had on the Cheaters Club site was a bit fuzzy, but he was handsome, with blond hair and a goatee, with a rugged look about him. We were supposed to meet in a parking lot not too far from my house and take a drive to the canyon. I was supposed to meet Paul later this same night, so my meeting with Travis was in the midafternoon. I had knots in my stomach and found myself just as nervous as I was the first time I had met Paul. It was exciting, and I would become addicted to the rush of adrenaline I would get with meetings to come. I had to calm my nerves, so I had a shot of tequila before I left the house. I took a bottle of wine and two glasses with me and drove to the parking lot. I didn't ask what it was he drove, so I sat there waiting.

Minutes had passed, and I was channel surfing on the radio when I happened to look up and noticed some guy walking toward my truck. He was about fifty pounds overweight, with a receding hairline. At first, I didn't think much of it, and then I froze. *That cannot be him! PLEASE GOD don't let that be him!* I instantly wished that I should have had two or three shots of tequila before leaving my house. I rolled down my window, "Hi, you must be Travis."

"Hi, Teri, wow, you are beautiful. Your photos don't do you justice. Can we take your truck? My car isn't running that great. You know how those foreign sports cars can be!"

"No problem, jump in." I thought to myself that I would make the best of this and that I would at least have made a friend who does own a chalet in France! He got in, and I started to drive. I glanced over at him, and he was staring at me grinning, and his teeth were crooked and yellow. I quickly turned away, focusing on the road again, and tried not to look at him as he was speaking.

There was an awkward silence as we headed up the canyon. Before leaving the house, I got online and looked up a phrase in French as to impress him. I had memorized it and felt that maybe I should break this silence and quote it to him now.

"Bonjour des Travis, je suis heureux de recontrer u," I said in French in the worst kind of California-girl accent. I glanced over at him after saying this, pretty proud of myself for remembering the words, however bad the accent was. He looked puzzled.

"What does that mean?" His one eye was squinting, and it was so not attractive.

"Hello, Travis, I'm glad to meet you. It's a simple phrase—I couldn't have fucked it up that badly!"

"Oh, yeah okay. No, you did pretty good."

"So how do you say that in French? That I did pretty good?" I laughed and thought at least I would be getting some lessons in the French language.

"My French is rusty. When I go visit my chalet, I normally get it back. I'm going next month, you know. Come with me."

I instantly thought bullshit. He was a fake. I glanced at his watch and clothing and noticed he was wearing a cheap Timex and Levi's. This dude was not who he said he was, and that bottle of wine was starting to sound good to me. I parked my truck and poured a glass of wine which I drank down like it was Kool-Aid. I got out of the truck and looked around me. It was beautiful. I grabbed my camera, which is always with me, and I started to take photos of my surroundings.

"What are you doing, Teri?" he asked as he followed me, hurrying to try to catch up.

"I'm trying to find my vision."

"What? Your vision—what's that mean?"

I had lost my ability to design the day that I joined the Cheaters Club. I could not see my designs, and my design vision was lost. I tried to find inspiration in nature as well as in anything really, but the harder I tried to see things, the more blinded I became. I would be able to walk into a space and *see* through walls and envision the new design I would see. I could only walk into a space now and see what was in front of me.

"I can't see my designs. I'm looking for inspiration here." I lay on a patch of grass and tilted my head back and studied the mountain and trees behind me. I was looking at this upside down, and the silhouette of the trees on top of the mountain cast the most amazing shadows. I snapped a few shots of this upside down.

"What are you doing?" He was standing beside me with his hands on his spare tire waistline. "What do you see?"

"Come look. Get down here and look for yourself."

He struggled to do this, but he lay down next to me, looking at the things I would point out to him. I noticed a patch of ugly weeds that resembled dried—up brown sticks which had a ball with pointy thorns on it. I went over and picked them as if I were picking daisies. I held them in my hand and snapped a photo. They were the ugliest weeds that I had ever seen, yet in a bundle they appeared beautiful. I pricked my finger with one of the pointy thorns, and it started to bleed.

"You're bleeding," Travis said, and before I knew it, he put my finger in his mouth and sucked the blood off it. "There, feel better now?" he kissed my finger, and I wanted to vomit.

"Thanks. Yes, much better now. Hey, I have to go though. I didn't tell my husband I would be gone, and he will be worried about me." I had several hours before I was to meet Paul, but I really needed to end this awful date.

"It's still early. Can't you stay for a few more minutes? Let's find some more inspiration. I bet I can inspire you!" he said as his spittle hit my face. I wanted to guzzle that bottle of wine, and fast.

"Really, I must go. I don't want to get caught." It took fifteen minutes of me convincing him that I did have to go, and he was persistent. We drove back to the parking lot, and I asked him where he had parked.

"My car is gone. Must have got stolen. It's not here," he stated this as if it were precontemplated, without any panic or real concern in his voice.

"What do you mean it's not here? Let's call the cops. This isn't good!" I wanted to believe him, but I knew he was lying, and he just didn' t want me to see what kind of car he drove.

"No, you go. I don't want for you to get into trouble with your husband. I will walk in the store and wait for the cops to get here. When can I see you again? Can you meet me tomorrow?"

"Just worry about getting your car back. We will work it out. Are you sure I can't call the police for you? I have my cell phone."

"No, better not do that. I don't want to get you involved. So do you think you can meet me again tomorrow?"

"I don't think so. Tomorrow's not good for me."

"Can I have your number, and I will call you tomorrow?" He was so pushy. "I can call you later tonight if you want me to."

"I don't give out my number. It's too risky. I have to go, okay?" As I said this, he grabbed my arm and pulled me towards him.

"Travis, I can't. Don't." I was not drunk enough to kiss him, and I don't think that I could ever be drunk enough, for that matter.

"Okay, I understand. It's just that you're so beautiful, and I have been looking at your lips all afternoon, wondering what they taste like."

"Good-bye, Travis, it was very good to meet you. I hope you find your car." I said this last sentence and thought to myself, *And I hope I find myself again, before it's too late.*

I drove off and didn't look back. I didn't want to see if he was really walking into the store or heading toward a Honda Civic. It didn't matter to me. All I wanted to do was to go home and shower before my meeting with Paul. I felt dirty, and it was not because I was lying on the grass. Being with Travis made me feel dirty, unclean.

Before I left the house, I finished the rest of the opened wine. I was extremely nervous again, and it was thrilling to me. My husband never asked me where I was when I was out, and often I would meet clients after they got off work, so it was not hard for me to get away. My husband was rarely home anyways, preferring to stay at the club at night and play video golf with his buddies instead of coming home. After enduring years of this, it wasn't anything which bothered me anymore. The loneliness never did get easier though and I never did become immune to that bug. I shared joint custody of my children with my ex-husband, so the days that they were with him were the days that I would meet men. Today was one of those days.

I got in my truck and drove to the same parking lot where I left Travis stranded. Paul pulled up next to me and told me to get in his BMW. We started to drive up the same canyon I was at only hours before, and I turned to look at him. He had a nice profile, and I smiled, thinking that this day was not so bad after all. The wine made my head feel fuzzy and my stomach warm. We drove in silence, yet there was nothing awkward about it as he held my hand tightly. The sun was setting over the mountains, and the color of the sky was the most amazing shades of burnt oranges and reds. We parked somewhere secluded, and he leaned over and kissed me.

"You taste like wine," Paul said to me as he pressed his forehead into mine and our noses were touching.

"Wine is good, isn't it? I could taste like Everclear or something nasty," I said as I rolled down the window and lit up a cigarette.

"You smoke too much. Ever tried to quit?"

"Once I did, and I was a bitch, so my husband went out and bought me a pack." I inhaled the next drag of my cigarette deeply as I pictured my husband's face, and by the time I exhaled, his face had left my mind.

I finished my cigarette and scooted closer to Paul. I brushed his hair gently with my fingertips and admired the curve of his face. He was so attractive to me, and there was this sexual tension between us.

"I love your dimples," he said to me as he poked a finger into my cheek.

"Thanks, but I only have one, see." I smiled wide with my lips closed as to exaggerate my dimple for a few seconds before saying, "And it's not real."

"How could it not be real?"

"Well, when I was eight years old, I was on a swing, and the chain broke. I landed on the left part of my face. I had this huge bruise, and when it went away it left behind this dimple!"

He laughed and said, "That's the sorriest story I ever heard! That's not true!"

"Yes, I swear it is! Really, it's nothing I was born with! You won't see it in any of my baby photos, and see . . ." I closed my lips and smiled again, this time wider. "My smile is crooked too because of it."

"That's crazy! It's still cute. I like it. You are so cute!"

I hated it when people would call me cute. Cute were babies and puppies and little fuzzy duckies, but I didn't seem to mind it when Paul called me this.

"I really want you, Teri. You know this, don't you?"

"I do know this, Paul. I'm really attracted to you as well, but this is hard for me. I have never been unfaithful to my husband, and I know that I will break my promise to him . . . but I'm not ready to do that yet." As I said this, I had tears in my eyes, saddened by the unambiguity of my words. "I don' t expect for you to wait for me to be ready, I just know that I'm not ready yet."

"It's okay, babe, don't cry. Just be sure that when you are ready, that whoever it is you are with is worthy of you. I hope that I will be that person. I won't ever hurt you, Teri." He brushed away my tears and kissed my eyes. I believed Paul to be worthy of me, and I knew that when I was ready, he would be my first.

The next day when I logged onto the Cheaters Club site, there were forty or so messages for me. I was overwhelmed with reading them all so opted to just delete them. I scrolled down the list of messages to delete, and there was one from Travis. It read:

Hi Beautiful, I had a great time with you yesterday and I really wanted to see your face today. I miss you already. Let me know when you can meet me today. Oh and btw . . . read my profile. It's just for you. I miss you and I want to help you find your vision. Travis

I clicked on his profile and his caption read: "FOUND INTELLIGENCE WITH VISION"

He was not serious; I was dumbstruck and realized that this was not a good sign. I knew that I would never meet him again and didn' t know exactly how to handle this. I felt as if I should just come out and tell him I was not interested and cut the ties with him now. I responded to his message with this:

Hi Travis, I will not be able to meet you today or any day. I have met someone and I want to concentrate on getting to know him. I think you are a nice person and I wish you luck in your search. Take care, Teri.

I deleted all of my messages and was going to log off when I saw there was a bull waiting to chat with me. I had become to think of these men as *bulls* because of all of the testosterone flowing! I clicked the flashing icon, and by now I was quick at clicking on to view their profile to see who I was chatting with. Dickboy1 was fifty-eight and from New York.

Dickboy1:   Hi design girl, are you feeling horny today?
Designgirl: Hi and good bye
Dickboy1:   Okay what do you want to talk about? What are you looking for?
Designgirl: I don't know what I am looking for; I just know that I haven't found it yet.
Dickboy1:   Have you banged any guys from this site?
Designgirl: Really that's none of your business now is it?

Dickboy1:   You women are all the same, just a bunch of cunt teases!

Designgirl: FUCK YOU!

Dickboy1:   NO FUCK YOU LITTLE BITCH!

Designgirl: You should be ashamed of yourself, you are fifty eight and guys half your age are better men than you are! You are a pig!

Dickboy1:   you are a stupid cunt and I bet you aren't even educated . . . fuck off!

I was shaking and could not believe this conversation. I blocked him instantly from ever contacting me again. There was another bull waiting, and I was so shook up I didn't know if I should even chat. I clicked on it anyways. Dickboy2 was from Calgary, and he was thirty-three. His photos were posted, and he was tall, with black wavy hair and blue eyes. In one photo, he was surrounded by mountains and he looked like he was camping. There was another photo of him on a four-wheeler and another one of him without a shirt. He was very handsome. I decided to say hello.

Dickboy2:   Hi there! (Smiley face) how are you today?

Designgirl: Hi

Dickboy2:   How's you day going so far? I love Utah! I used to be a Mormon you know!

Designgirl: Some major asshole just called me the "C" word so I' m a bit shook up, sorry

Dickboy2:   Hope he wasn't Canadian! Sorry to hear that, I bet there are lots of jerks here eh?

Designgirl: It's all good. I blocked him. It seems that most of the perv's on this site are the guys who are older which surprises me really

Dickboy2:   Doesn't surprise me. They probably can't get laid so all they do is cyber sex and have major load build up!

Designgirl: That's disgusting and wrong. Anyways, what is your name? I'm Teri

Dickboy2:   I'm Adam, and I like your name!

Designgirl: Thank you Adam, it's nice to meet you

Adam and I became fast friends. He was funny and musically talented. He played the piano and composed music. He would send me clips of it to listen to, and I was always in awe of his talent. It was Adam who inspired me to pick up my violin, which had been sitting so neglected in my closet for years now. "Music boy" and I would spend hours on Yahoo for the next several months chatting and playing online games together, such as Literary, similar to Scrabble, and it would become a favorite of mine. Adam became very special to me, and there would be nobody that I would meet who would be able to make me smile or laugh the way that he did. He became to me my best friend online for months to come.

I had three more meetings the next week. One was Paul. The other two were new meetings. I was on a fast ride here, and even though I was at the wheel, I could not put the brakes on.

I met Ron first the following week. He was from a town fifty miles away, and we had talked on the phone several times. His picture on the site was not what I considered *hot*, but I thought he was nice. After my meeting with Travis, I had learned not to expect a lot and to just hope for the best. We met again in a parking lot and drove to the canyon. I was nervous before the meeting, so I shot some tequila, about a half a glass or so. It was only three o'clock in the afternoon, and I was buzzed already and still hung over from the previous night.

The night before, something disturbing happened. I put the kids to bed and poured a coffee cup full of vodka and cranberry juice and logged online. I chatted with Adam, my music boy, who I challenged to a game of Literary and made a wager with. The wager was that the loser had to send a photo to the winner of anything the winner wanted to see. I was *not* going to lose, so I found a Web site where you could punch in the letters that you had, and it would give you all the words you could apply. Basically, I was going to cheat.

"Wow, Adam, I guess I won. Hmmm, let's see . . . I want a picture of your butt." I really did want a picture of his butt. "No hurry, you can send it to me within a week, but if it goes over a week, then I will collect interest on it, so you will owe me two of them. Rematch tomorrow night?" It would be a very long time before I would lose my first online Literary game, and my collections of "photos" were in the dozens. Adam had an early day, so he went to bed. Scott signed online almost as soon as Adam logged off.

MSN Chat:

Teri: Hey Sexyhot! How is the lust of my life for a minute doing?

No response for several minutes.

Scott: I'm ok
Teri: You are more than ok baby . . . .
Scott: Can I ask you something?

This is when I should have realized something was very, very wrong. Scott was acting funny.

Teri: Anything . . .

Scott: Who are you and how do you know my husband?

I froze, stupefied, and felt as if I were going to throw up. I didn't respond, not knowing how to answer this.

Scott: Do you work with him? Tell me who you are.

I logged off MSN and logged into the Cheaters Club site to leave Scott a message, knowing that he would know soon enough the event of what just happened. My message read:

> *Scott! I THINK I GOT YOU CAUGHT! I am so sorry! I thought it was you! Please forgive me, I am so sorry! Teri*

The following morning, he would respond:

> *Teri, it is not your fault. I was stupid and forgot to log off. I am deleting my profile on here and I don't know what is going to happen but I am not prepared to lose my boys so I need to try to see if I can make things work with her. Please take care and know that I will miss you and that if one day, down the road something changes . . . I will look for you. Be careful out there, there are a lot of bad guys. Take care, Love Scott*

This would be the last I would ever hear from Scott. I think of him a lot and hope that he is happy and has realized how special he is. This was a dangerous game I played, and it was never my intention to get anyone caught or to hurt anyone. You would think that this would have slowed me down, yet instead, I had a date with Ron the next day.

Ron and I drove to the canyon, and it seemed too familiar. Thus far, a trip to the canyon was a standard date for me, but it was safe, with little risk of being caught. I took a bottle of tequila with me, and we parked and hiked to a campground. Ron didn't look at all like his photos, but he was still cute. He was a bit older than I liked at thirty-eight years old. He looked taller in his photo, and in it he had a mustache. He was clean shaven, with dark hair and dark eyes and a stocky build. Always smiling no matter what, he was cheerful and pleasant to be around. I don't know for sure how he talked me into going on a hike, but I did warn him that I was not athletic. On his time off of his regular job, he would take people into the mountains to hike trails and camp out. He is some sort of a mountain man tour guide.

We started up the trail, and the shoelace from my hiking boot was untied and I tripped on it, falling on my butt only twenty feet up the trail. Normally this would be embarrassing, but the tequila made it seem funny. I walked another fifty yards and stopped.

"I can't do this, Ron, I'm starting to sweat like a piggy here, and I don't like it."

"Sweat is GOOD!" he laughed. "You can do this!" he said, beaming with all the confidence in me.

"I can't. My ass hurts already, and I need a cigarette."

"NO! That's going to kill you! I will help you, okay?" he stood behind me and put his hands on my hips and started to push my drunk butt up the trail. About one hundred yards later, I stopped.

"Ouch! Something bit me!" Something bit my lower buttocks, and it didn't surprise me because my shorts were very short. "I am sooooooo done! I'm not doing this anymore!" I spat out like a spoiled child as I reached in my backpack and pulled out my cigarettes. I lit one up and headed down the trail. He didn't argue with me; he just laughed at me, and I didn't care. I just wanted to get down the trail and shoot tequila. We sat on a picnic table and shared the bottle as we talked.

"Teri, you are my first meeting, you know—"

"SHUT UP! You never mentioned that!" I all of a sudden felt like the veteran for once. It was a good feeling, like I had hit some sort of a milestone and I was having a proud moment. "Well then, I guess I should be gentle with you!"

Before I could finish my sentence, he grabbed me by my wrists gently and laid me down on the picnic table. He spread open my legs and stood in between them as he lowered his face to mine. He stood over me, just looking into my eyes, and then he slowly kissed my lips. His lips were soft, almost too soft for a mountain boy, I thought. I felt myself getting aroused, and I wrapped my legs around him in a similar way I did with Paul on that first night. Something about the way I did this must have triggered a "Paul" memory because I stopped.

"Ron, I'm sorry, but I can't do this," I uttered quietly, "Paul . . ."

"Is Paul your husband? It's okay, Teri. I know this isn't an easy thing to do."

"Paul is not my husband. He is just some guy . . . well, he was my first meeting, and I don't know why I just called out his name . . . I am so sorry."

"Hey now, don't say you're sorry. It's okay, I will wait for you to figure things out. I' m not going anywhere. You will find out that I make a good friend."

We headed down the canyon, and the ambiguity as to why I said Paul's name danced in my mind.

Sadness chased me in the days to follow. I had several meetings ahead of me, my chats were going well, and my Yahoo fan club was growing. I was getting more attention now than I had in my life, yet I felt solemn and my heart heavy. I drank my cape cods to get me through my nights, and I chatted in the morning to get me through my days. I had a new meeting with someone named Ryan, who was thirty years old and supercute in his pictures. I was supposed to meet him a parking lot just to say hello because I had to get my children from school that day. Earlier before my meeting with Ryan, I received a phone call from my girlfriend Beth.

"Hi, Teri, Karen and I were wondering if you had time to do lunch today."

"Oh today is not good, sweetie, but how's the baby doing? I bet she's getting really big!"

"Teri . . . Karen and I are concerned about you . . ." Beth stated, and before I could respond, Karen was on the phone as well.

"Ter, we don't know what's going on with you, but you are different. We are really concerned, honey, and we want you to know that we are here for you," Karen said impatiently.

"Guys, why do I feel as if this is an intervention?" I answered. "Really, I am fine! I am just overloaded here, and my interns are flaking on me. I told Megan I would assist in design of the Sky Port offices, and I have so much other work I'm behind on!" They knew me so well, and I knew they knew that I was lying, but there was no way I would tell them or anyone.

"You know that you are the worst liar in the world, Teri? Don't lie to us. Tell us to fuck off and mind our own business, but don't lie to us!" Karen declared in her take-charge kind of voice. Beth was always more cautious in choosing her words.

"Teri, we are not accusing you of any misdoings, we are just very worried about your well-being."

"Beth, thank you, sweetie. Both of you, but really, I am fine! If you want to help me, then you can go slap some of my tripolar clients for me!" I joked, but they didn't seem to find this amusing. "Listen, girls, I have an appointment to go to before I pick up the kids. Love you both, and really, please don't worry about me."

I knew that I had to distance myself from my friends before they blew the whistle to my husband about their concerns. I checked the time and noticed I was supposed to be meeting Ryan in twenty minutes. I downed a few shots of tequila and headed to meet guy number who knows.

As he walked up to my truck, I had to smile. I unlocked my door, and he got in. He had to be the cutest thing I ever saw. Paul was more handsome, in a more mature way, but Ryan had a baby face and the all-American-boy look about him. He played college football, and he was well built. It is a good thing that I prefer brunettes over blonds because all but "lost car boy" had been brunettes, including this cute one sitting in my passenger seat. He had big brown puppy dog eyes and a great smile. But the thing I would like most about Ryan was that he was confident and took what he wanted without asking.

Hi was all he said before he reached over and kissed me. I am not just talking about a peck on the lips—he *kissed* me.

"Hi to you!" I gasped when I finally caught my breath. I liked this bad boy, and I could sense some fun ahead of me with this one. We talked for about ten more minutes before he was all over me again. He did this not in a threatening or overbearing way, but in a sexy way that I could not resist I let him touch me in ways that Paul did not, and it was the middle of the day in a busy parking lot. I agreed to see him soon, and I thought to myself, *This boy is TROUBLE.*

CHAPTER FIVE

June '06

"These are color pallets. Designers refer to these to help decide the color scheme of a space. How many of you have painted your room the coolest color in the world?" Everyone in my sons sixth grade class raised their hand but one little girl in the back of the room. It was the last week of school and career day. My son asked me to come and share with his class the profession of interior design. He was my biggest fan.

"Wow, you guy's are too cool, maybe I should hire you" I said to them. "Okay, looks like my times up here. I will be here for another ten minutes if any of you have any more questions. I will hang out for recess." I told them gathering up the samples I had brought to share. Several children came up to me, including my son and the little girl who didn't raise her hand.

"Mom, you did great! Thanks. Told you my mom is cool," he said to one of his female friends.

"Your mom is so pretty too! I want her to design my room!" she replied back to him as if I weren't standing there.

"No, she's expensive. You can't afford my mom."

"Can you help me design mine?" the little girl who didn't raise her hand asked in a small voice.

"No, YOU especially can't afford my mom!" my son said to her as the children laughed at hearing this. She turned and started to walk away. I threw my son a look and he knew what it meant.

"Hey, sweetie. Come here for a sec." I called to her. "What's your name?"

"Chelsea"

"Chelsea, that's a pretty name for a pretty girl." I said to her brushing back long bangs from her face. I noticed that the clothes that she had on were worn and dirty. I guessed that Chelsea's family probably didn' t have much money and that she most likely didn't have very many nice things. "Guess what Chelsea? I happen to have some extra pink and lavender paint and some really cool stuff that goes with it. Do you think that maybe I could design your room for you? I'd really like that a lot." Chelsea's eyes beamed up at my words.

"Really? You want to design my room?"

"Are you kidding me? I'd love to. Here is my phone number. Have your mom call me okay?" I gave her my number and then whispered in her ear "Tell her it won't cost her anything." She smiled and hugged me before running out for recess.

"Mom, why did you just do that? Chelsea's weird," my son said to me.

"Because she reminds me of someone I use to know," I told him, reminding myself to scold him later for his rudeness.

"Who?'

"Me. She reminds me of me."

In the week to follow, I had three more meetings, and my Yahoo fan club list was up to thirty men or so. Often one would pop up on my Yahoo, and I started to lose track of who they were, but I would always pretend to know who I was chatting with. Adam the music boy would introduce me to cybersex chats as well, and I felt comfortable enough with him to do this. I found myself enjoying it when only weeks before it was insulting to me when one would try to get down my panties online.

I would get bored with my Yahoo fan club and log into the Cheaters Club site to lasso in more bulls, and one night I started to chat with someone named Chas. He was twenty-five and from London. He had dark hair and dark eyes, a goatee, with a slim build, resembling Orlando Bloom in a way. Chas was the first single guy on the site that I chatted with, and he liked older women as I had come to conclude I was more attracted to guys between the ages twenty-five to thirty-four.

I didn't often give out my MSN but found that I quickly gave him my MSN address, and he met me there. We chatted for a few minutes, and something came across my screen and I was asked to accept some sort of invitation, then screen changed into a larger screen, with Chas sitting there smiling at me. I had heard about Web cameras but never actually saw one.

He looked into the camera and smiled a devilish grin that made me want to hop on the next flight to London. As we continued to chat, he took off his shirt and brushed his almost shoulder-length hair back with his fingers. This guy was *fine!* I told him to lower the cam so I could see more of him, and he didn't hesitate to do this. Before I could say, "Peter Piper picked a peck of pickled peppers," he was naked, exposing his pickled pepper, and I had to literally pull my face away from the computer screen because I was only five inches from it, studying his . . . form. He started to touch himself, and I felt as if I were watching a porn film made just for me as I watched the Chas show live. When he finished doing his "thing," I was amazed at how I could even watch this. He would cam for me on a regular basis after this night, and I was always eager to be his biggest fan.

I met Paul twice this week, once for lunch and once just briefly in a parking lot to say hello. I was ready to "go there" with him now, feeling both comfortable enough with him and mentally ready. I realized that when this did happen, I would need to be sober, with my wits about me, so that if I decided not to go through with it I could walk away. I wanted to remember it clearly as well.

One of my meetings that week was Tony. He was a handsome Italian guy of thirty-six. Tony and I agreed to meet in a parking lot, grab some coffee, and go for a drive. We took my truck, and I drove it up the familiar canyon road already knowing which way the road would curve and turn next. I could sense that he was nervous, and I was so hung over from drinking the night before as I watched Chas's new show that I didn't shoot any tequila before this meeting. I felt nauseated, and I looked like hell. I was wearing a short ruffled white skirt and a pink tank top that said "Pink Taco" with white wedged lace-up heels. I liked to wear white in the summer to show off my tan, and I smothered my legs and body with thick lotion to cast a glow on my skin. Tony was staring at my legs as I drove and put his hand on my leg and touched it.

"I'm sorry, I just had to feel your skin. It looks so soft," he said as he ran his hand up and down my thigh. "God, you have the smoothest legs, and they smell good too." He held his hand to his face to smell the pear-melon lotion that I chose to wear that day.

I laughed at him in doing this. "You have soft hands too, Tony. What is it that you do for a living? I'm betting you are not in construction!" His hands were softer than mine, and I noticed the way he was dressed in a preppy short sleeve button-down shirt, khaki shorts, and Birkenstock sandals. I guessed he was a computer geek before he could verify this. I liked this computer geek because he was so dorky and cute at the same time, and he seemed genuine. He told me about the affair he had which ended only a month ago when she got married and that he didn't have much luck meeting locals that he was attracted to since he was very picky. I nodded, listening to this, understanding his frustration.

"It's hard to establish a real connection. You can be attracted to them and not be compatible or really enjoy them but not be physically attracted." I stated this as if after one month now I was a pro. "It is hard enough, you know, to be married. I try to keep this thing I do here real, without games."

"That's always a good thing. Most women who are local on this site just want to have cybersex and not meet. Its sad how many lonely women are out there who are stuck at home with kids and are unhappy in their marriages. They seem to need attention, so they get it online, but a lot of them don't actually meet with men, sticking to only having online affairs."

"Wow, why do you think that is?" I asked.

"I think it's hard for them to get out of the house, and most have children. Then there are those who are into the fantasy of it all, never intending to meet whether it's because they are afraid of getting caught or they can't bring themselves to actually have an affair." He says this to me, and he was looking at my thigh while still stroking my leg. "There are twenty men to every woman on this site, and if you are actually willing to meet them in person, you will do very well. I had this one woman tell me: 'I can't meet you, I don't want to risk my marriage.'"

"That's insane. She put out that risk when she decided to become a member on that site and chat! Stupid bitch! I'm kidding . . . I don' t intend to judge why they don't meet. I can't even tell you why I agree to meet guys and not just keep it just an online thing." When I said this, I asked myself why it was that I chose to put the risk out there and actually meet them. I have always been a risk taker and a bit of an overachiever, yet this was destructive behavior, and I realized it.

We drove to a new spot in the canyon, somewhere I had not been. I lit up a cigarette and instantly felt sick because I was so hung over. I had to urinate, and there were no restrooms in sight.

"Tony, close your eyes. I have to pee," I blurted out as if I had known him for years. "Grab me a napkin in the glove box, please?"

"You can't do that here! Someone will see you. Let's drive to a restroom." He was so proper I wanted to belch just to see how he'd respond to that.

"Let em see, I have to pee, and I have to pee now." I got out of my truck and leaned against it and squatted. As I was relieving myself, a car passed by and the driver could clearly see what I was doing. He was an older gentleman, and I really believed that his car would go off the road as it swerved a bit while he was intently staring at me doing my thing. I gave him a little wave and pulled up my panties and jumped back in my truck.

Laughing, Tony said, "I knew that was going to happen!"

"Well now, I guess it's a good thing I'm not shy, huh? Probably got his blood circulating a bit, so I did my good deed for the day. Now he will have to go confess to his bishop here . . . oh, or better yet, maybe he IS a bishop!"

"You are a naughty girl, aren't you?" he said while I thought to myself, *You have no idea.* I drove us back down the canyon, and when we got back to the parking lot, I let Tony kiss me. I agreed to meet him again the following week, and my schedule was filling up fast, having made dates to meet Paul, Ryan, as well as two new guys. A feeling of emptiness came over me, and I wished I had made another date that day to help fill in that empty space. As long as I was with one of them, regardless of whether or not I was attracted to them, my *empty* feeling would go away for a bit. I had touched the center of my own sorrow and I could not sit with my pain. I could not be alone with the person called "Teri."

The day I met Paul in the parking lot of Home Depot it rained. I was dressed in business attire, having met with a client, and I fought the urge to stop and have a drink before our meeting. I got into his BMW, and he started to drive and pulled into a Hilton parking lot. I was not at all as nervous as I thought I would be; however, I still wished that I would have had at least one drink before meeting him. We walked into the hotel lobby, and he checked us into a suite, which I insisted be a smoking room. We sat on the sofa and talked for a while. and I felt amazingly at ease. I walked into the bedroom and left him sitting on the sofa as I undressed down to my bra and panties and sat on the edge of the bed.

"Come here, Paul," I said in barely over a whisper. "I need for you to hold me." He walked into the room and undressed, and as I watched him, I could feel myself starting to getting aroused, and my heart raced. He was averagely built and was hairier than I had expected, yet this did not matter to me because I had wanted him for weeks now. He stood in front of me and took my face into his hands and kissed me as I slowly leaned back, lying on the bed with the weight of his body on top of me.

He kissed my neck and unsnapped my bra. His lips found their way to my breasts as he sucked them, his tongue circling my nipples. His mouth traveled down my stomach as he spread open my legs to kiss my inner thighs and breathed his hot breath on the outside of my panties. I wanted to slide my panties off but fought the urge to do this. He sucked on the outside of my panties and softly bit me so that my legs started to shake. Sliding one side of my black lace panties over, I felt his tongue. I grabbed his head and pushed his face into me. Sliding his finger inside of me, I moaned and became dizzy within seconds.

"Stop, Paul, hold on, okay?" I said this having to catch my breath. "I need a cigarette." I lit one up before he could respond.

"Teri, are you okay, babe? We can stop if you want."

"I'm all right. I just need a smoke . . . I smoke a lot. Didn't I tell you that I smoke during sex?"

He laughed and said, "NO! And I wouldn't state that on your profile either because you will never get a date!" He took the cigarette out of my fingers before I could finish it, and he kissed my hand. "Teri, you need to quit. That's a nasty habit, babe."

"Paul, shut up and kiss me now." I remember the way he felt when he slid himself into me, doing this very slowly and deliberately. Somewhere in the first thrusts of him entering me, my mother' s words would enter my mind. My vase was now cracked. In the following hours, I continued to smoke during the sex, and he gave up trying to convince me not to. Paul had little odd phobias about germs. For instance, when I threw my panties on the floor, he quickly snatched them up, putting them under the pillow because the floor, he claimed, was dirty. He freaked when I pulled the comforter over us, stating that we didn't know who did what on it and so it could not touch us. This seemed "cute" to me, but later down the road I would find it to be more annoying than anything, oftentimes ruining the spontaneity of the moment.

When I went to bed that night, I did not say a prayer. It would be a very long time before I would be able to talk to the God that I once believed loved me unconditionally, so instead of praying, I closed my eyes and hoped to dream of Paul's touch. It was surreal how I felt no guilt whatsoever, but instead I felt myself longing to see him, if only for one more time.

It was early June, and I was designing a loft in New York and needed to go check on the progress. I panicked at the thought of not being able to chat online for five days, so I decided to buy a laptop to take with me.

"How do I turn this on?" I asked the salesman in the store. "It's my first laptop."

"It's not that hard. See, look—this is how it works." He showed me how to use it as well as how to get online with the wireless card I had purchased. I was all set to go, and as I walked towards the door, he said, "Oh I forgot—it has a built-in Webcam." *Uh oh*, went through my mind as I walked out the door, knowing that this was probably not a very good thing.

I met Paul again before I went to New York, and he had bought me a present, a lacy black bra that he would want me to wear for him. The sex that afternoon was even better than the first time, as I hoped that it would be.

"I have to go to New York, Paul, so I won't be able to see you for a few days."

"I'll miss you. I will call or text you every day," he said as he held me. "Teri, I know that this is fairly early on in our relationship as to ask this of you, but I don't want you to see anyone else for now, and I won't either. Promise me that you won' t sleep with anyone else?"

I knew the answer to this would be a lie before I could even finish thinking of how to respond, yet I blurted, "I won't sleep with anyone else, Paul." I lied with such ease, never intending to keep this promise. I had several new meetings set up, as well as ones with both Tony and Ryan.

When I got home that night, I put on the bra on that Paul gave me and took a photo of myself by holding the camera away from myself. I viewed it and decided to take another one, this time without the bra. I e-mailed it to him as a surprise and erased them off my computer, or so I thought.

New York was humid and hot. The loft project was hard to manage from two thousand miles away, and I was running into some problems with it. I was only too grateful that this was designed "before" I lost my design vision, knowing that the complexity of this design would be impossible for me to see right now. I spent my first day there meeting contractors and trying to work out the details of correcting the things that went wrong. I spent that first evening sitting in the lounge of the hotel with my laptop and chatting on the Cheaters Club site. I sat in a corner of the bar and logged in. It was only an instant later when the first bull popped up. Dickboy1 was thirty years old from Boston.

Dickboy1:   Hi, how are you today?
Designgirl: I'm doing well, and you?
Dickboy1:   Good! Did you read my profile? I love women who are older than I am!

His profile did indeed state this, as well as a few other things that made me raise an eyebrow, such as he stated he loved lingerie, especially thongs.

Designgirl: Yes I just saw that actually, good for me then
Dickboy1:   Can I see your pictures? Here are mine
Designgirl: Sure but I do revoke them ok? (This line became a standard line for me just in case they were not attractive, but if they were, I would always let them keep my key.)
Dickboy1:   WOW! You are sexy! Do you have a cam?
Designgirl: TY and maybe I do. You are cute yourself.

He was what I would consider to be average-looking, with a cute "boy" look and build. In his photo, he was standing next to a Renaissance painting in a museum, owning a haughty grin which made him look goofy.

Dickboy1:   Do you have MSN or Yahoo? I would love to see your cam
Designgirl: Do you have a cam?
Dickboy1:   No I don't. You are so hot I bet you look great on cam.
Designgirl: Well I don't turn my cam on for anyone, especially if they don't have one.
Dickboy1:   What if I get one? Can I see yours then?

This guy was way too eager and started to appear desperate to me with his overwhelmingly high energy which seemed to drain me. I needed to say good-bye to "eager boy" and move on to the next bull.

Designgirl: Listen, I have to go, so look for me next time ok?
Dickboy1:   I will! You are so sexy! I'm Alex too by the way!
Designgirl: ok Alex, I'm Teri and I look forward to chatting with you again. Kisses . . . .

I blew Alex off, and I ordered another drink from the waitress, asking her to make this one stronger. It was slow tonight on the Cheaters Club site because it was a Friday, but there was yet another bull. Dickboy2 was thirty-three years old from Kansas.

Dickboy2:   Hello, are you there? Would you like to chat tonight?
Designgirl: Hi, I'm here, how are you?
Dickboy2:   I'm good ty, just hiding from the wife and in-laws who are visiting.
Designgirl: Lol! I don't blame you there! I'm actually out of town tonight myself so I'm feeling FREE!

Dickboy2:   Lucky you, wish I were there with you. So how's this site treating
               you? Any luck?
Designgirl: So far it's been ok, and yes lots of luck really, but I'm a woman so it's
               probably easier for us. Do you have a key that I can see please?
Dickboy2:   Sure, trade you?
Designgirl: Ok you first, and oh, I do revoke it.

He sent his key, and when I opened it, I was instantly flushed He was
gorgeous! Think Rob Lowe, but better. The photo was a close—up of his face as
he looked intently at the viewer in the most seductive way. I found myself asking
him questions that would surprise me. "Do you have Yahoo or MSN?" I asked
him, and this would be the first time I would ask someone for this.

"I have MSN. Would you like to meet there?" he typed as I could only imagine
him sitting in front of his computer and looking so fine. "I will add you to my
MSN, what is your addy?" We met on MSN and chatted for another hour or so
as I ordered drink after drink, and the lounge was filling up with more people.
His name was David, and he was a professor at a university, teaching history and
English. I found him to be extremely sexy, funny, and intelligent, and we would
chat about things such as philosophy, God, and television shows.

MSN Chat:

Teri: David, do you have a webcam?
David: Nope, why do you?
Teri: I think they said I do . . . I just got this laptop, and I think this lens
               thingy here is the cam . . . . Should I try it? Should I see if I can
               turn it on?
David: Hmmm . . . well . . . . HELL YES! PLEASE!
Teri: Lol! Okay then, let's see how this works here . . .

I struggle for a few minutes and finally figured it out.

Teri: KK, see me?
David: No, not yet.
Teri: Hmmmm, well it says that it is on . . . this is weird.
David: It is up and working, I see the screen but it's black. Are you sure
               you have your lens open?
Teri: Oh, I have to open it? Okay then, its open, can you see me now?
David: Send it again ok?

I closed the screen and sent another invitation.

Teri: Ok, now?

Silence
I was really starting to get worried that he had seen my cam and thought I was some kind of ugly, but then . . . .

David: OMG Teri, you are stunning . . . really . . . wow.
Teri: (inserts a smiley) thank you, I wish I could see you too . . . hey I have an idea . . . are you going to be online for a few? I was just going to go up to my room. The lounge closes at ten o' clock and it's almost ten. I was going to my room and order a bottle of wine.
David: Yes, I will wait for you, are you going to slip on something sexy? JK
Teri: If you are a bad boy, yes . . . .

I went to the room and ordered my wine, not that I needed anything more to drink. I slipped into a lacy black tank top and panties since that was the sexiest thing that I brought with me on this trip, not intending to see anyone. I logged online and he was waiting for me.

Teri: I'm here; let me turn my cam on
David: Can't wait . . .

I turned on my cam, and we chatted for another hour as I drank my wine and continued to get really wasted. I stared at David' s display photo and asked him to send me more photos, and he did. He was super hot, and I was super horny. For Teri, super hot plus super horny equals JACK.

Teri: David, want to meet someone?
David: Who's that?
Teri: Jack
David: Jack? Is someone there with you?
Teri: Yep, my best guy. His name is Jack. He's purple and has a silver ball that travels up and down his shaft and the has the best bunny ears in the world!
David: YES, YES, YES! I want to meet Jack!

I went to get Jack and checked my image in the bathroom mirror. I was drunk for sure, my face was flushed, and my eyes glazed over. I fixed my hair, and as I walked out of the bathroom, I practiced sucking in my gut. *Why did I have to drink myself into bloatation tonight? My first night on a Webcam and for Rob*

Lowe's twin at that! I sat down very slowly and deliberately, making sure that he would see my lacy black panties, and I hiked the lacy tank up just a bit. I slowly scooted my chair back and threw one leg over the arm. I pulled my panties to the side and licked the tip of Jack with my tongue. I could only hope that he was enjoying the Teri show, and from what he typed, I guessed right.

David: MMMMMMMM .... GOD THAT IS SO HOT! You are so sexy!

The strap on my tank top slipped off one of my shoulders, and I didn't make the effort to fix it. Rather I squeezed my breasts together so that it dropped further down, almost exposing one. I slid my chair up to the computer and started to type.

Teri: Call me, call me now.
David: What? I can't, my in-laws are here, and I am hiding as it is.
Teri: I won't do the rest of my show unless you call me and I can hear your voice.
David: You are so bad . . . and I want you that much so okay, what is your number?

It was as easy as that. He called me within one minute.

Teri: What do you want to see me do David? Tell me, tell me now and I will do it for you.
David: God, I can't believe I want you this badly; my wife and her folks are upstairs. God Teri! I WANT TO SEE EVERYTHING!
Teri: Tell me then, how badly do you want me? Tell me. I want to know how badly.
David: God I want you so badly you have no idea. I'm so hard here looking at you.
Teri: If I was in your class, I'd sit in the front row in a short skirt without panties and spread my legs open . . . would u give me an "A" Professor?

This was the power that I had come to possess over men. It did not matter who I was chatting with. I had chatted with doctors, attorneys, contractors, models, and even a judge. The way I structured my chats was all the same regardless of what they did for a living. I became a tease girl. I became the biggest tease girl, not afraid to push limits as to what I wanted at the time, regardless of what I thought may be acceptable to them. It was now just all about me.

David: God yes! And I don't think I would be able to speak! You would have me stuttering Teri.

I wanted to control everything that would happen now. It was in my power to make this professor want what he could not have. I claimed ascendancy over what I was to do and relished in knowing that he would give this to me. The Webcam became all about power and control to me at this moment, more power than chatting had ever been.

Teri: I want you to beg me to do Jack for you. Beg me Professor
David: Teri, I have never begged anyone for anything in my life, but I will say this . . . PLEASE! PLEASE! PLEASE!

That was sufficient, I decided, as I took one last look at his photo staring at me in the most captivating way, not letting on that I was enticed by him as well. That would be rule number one from here on out. RULE NUMBER ONE: Never let them think you want them more than they want you.

I slid my chair back again, and this time I leaned back and lifted up my tank only to the bottom of my breasts. I lifted one leg up on the chair and leaned back. I touched the outside of my panties with one hand and grasped the arm of the chair with the other hand. I slowly slipped off my panties and let them drop to my ankles. I ran Jack up my thigh slowly and slid him into me. I made a moaning noise when I did this, and David moaned as well. We didn' t speak much at all in the next few minutes, but we ended up having an orgasm at the same time. I would have to practice being on the W ebcam and talking on the phone at the same time; I made a mental note of this.

Teri: Wow . . . how was that cowboy?
David: God Teri, one day, I'm going to meet you and do that to you.

That day has never come even though we chat regularly to this day. Yet one day, he would purchase a cam and show me what I had suspected all along—that he was so much hotter than Rob Lowe.

CHAPTER SIX

June '06

I was learning a new design program called Revit, which would help me to construct my furniture designs in perspective drawings. I had to hire a tutor to show me how to use it since I always wanted to convert back to the other drafting program that I was comfortable with. A few weeks earlier, my tutor, Glen, was coming at eleven o'clock in the morning to give me a lesson. I was chatting online and did not realize the time and the doorbell rang; he was early. I woke up that morning and logged online, so I was still in my tank top and panties, so I hurried and threw on a skirt but forgot to put on a bra.

The whole time Glen would be staring at my chest, and actually this would have been a turn-on for me, loving the attention; however, this kid was a young married Mormon guy with a brand-new baby. I did not want to entice him. I knew that I was probably going to hell, but I didn't want to go there any sooner than I would be, so I tried to cover up as much as I could without being conspicuously obvious that I was doing this This happened about two weeks ago, as I said earlier, and the day after I got back from my New York trip, Glen was coming over to give me another lesson. This time, however, I was prepared, and I woke up that morning and showered and dressed with proper undergarment attire before I got online that day.

The session went well that morning, and I learned more than I had the time before. I needed to move my files over into a master folder, combining both drafting programs that I used, and I asked Glen to help me do this. All went smoothly until I realized that I was missing a drawing that I needed for New York and I had to find it.

"Glen, it has to be here. I know that I saved it, but I can't remember where I saved it to. I have to find it. Maybe it's in my other document or picture files? I can't imagine where I would have saved it to," I said, a bit panicked and sickened by the thought of having to recreate it if I could not find it.

"Don't worry, Teri, if it's here, I will find it," Glen said assuredly, and I wanted to believe him. "It may take me a bit. Hold on, I will scan through some things here. How do you like this program so far? It's really going to serve you well once you get it down. Just remember that the commands are the opposite of AutoCAD so you have to take yourself out of that mode of thinking . . . I . . . oh, what's this?" He asked this, and then when he realized what he was looking at, he did his best to not blush and continue to finish what he was saying, but I was mortified. There it was, not the drawing that we were so feverishly looking for, but the photo of my *boobs* that I had sent Paul several weeks ago and thought that I had erased from existence. I rarely blush and don't consider myself to be shy, but at that moment, I think I wanted to die, and by the look on Glen's face, he already did and went to heaven.

"Oh hold on, this is a joke. It's not me either, by the way," I managed to say, biting down on my pencil nervously, giving away the lie I just told. I erased it again, this time for good, I hoped, and then I promised myself that I was done taking photos of myself and sending them from at least *this* computer. That promise would last for only a month.

June was the month I would turn forty-two, and I was drawn to guys even younger now. Never realizing why, I tended to chat and meet more with men who were between twenty-five and thirty now.

There was one in particular that I will call Sam, who was local and twenty-six. Sam was what I would call a "pretty boy," tall and fit, with the bluest eyes and dark wavy hair. We didn't chat online but rather sent e-mails back and forth, exchanging stories of how our day was going, and his was never as interesting as mine. We decided to meet. This was his first meeting and my fifteenth or sixteenth, making me the veteran. Nonetheless, I still required several shots of tequila before each meeting. Sam's wife was out of town, and so was my husband, but he was watching his children, so after he put them down to sleep, he met me in a parking lot two blocks away from his house. He was, by far, the most like his photos and actually better in person.

Out of all of my meetings, Sam and just one other—the one that would become for me several months from now "the *only one that would matter*"—would be the only two that upon seeing them for the first time I would have to tell myself to *breathe*. He climbed in the back of my truck, and I uncorked and poured the wine that I brought for us to share. We didn't have a lot of time, neither of us feeling really comfortable with leaving his small children asleep and alone, something that I would have deemed neglectful and extremely irresponsible only months earlier. We drank our wine quickly, and then he had to say it:

"This is so strange to be here with you, Teri. I haven't even kissed another girl but my wife since I have been married. I was a virgin when I married her, you know."

"No. You were a virgin? Sam, please tell me you are not a good Mormon boy? Or rather, please tell me you are!" I was having fantasies of Mormons and all of their goodness and potential badness lately.

"Why, are my garments showing? Can you tell?" he laughed. "I thought I told you that I was Mormon. Hey, this is good wine too, by the way." I was so going to see how bad this good boy could be.

I sat on his lap sideways, with my legs stretched out on the backseat of my truck, and wrapped my arms around his neck. I was careful not to kiss him rather than to get real close so that he could smell my perfume and feel my breath on his face when I talked to him.

"I won't be first woman you kiss besides your wife," I lied, with the undertone of innocence in my voice, and he didn' t notice it.

"Maybe I want you to be," he said as he ran his hand up and down my upper thigh as my skirt was hiked up, exposing just a glimpse of white thong panties.

"No."

"Why? Aren't you attracted to me, Teri?" I had Pretty Boy in the palm of my hand, and I was going to close my fingers now and gently squeeze. He was very bright and held a job as an executive, but just as I guessed, he was naive when it came to women and their games.

"Sam, yes, I am attracted to you! You are amazing!" I also learned to stroke egos. Men' s egos were fragile despite of the physical strength of the man and needed to be handled with care. It was amazing how I could throw them a compliment of some sort, either sexual or not, and they would soak it up as a sponge does to water. I was the water, fluid and sometimes solid, able to take on different forms or fit into any container. I moved around men as water sometimes does, in a gentle, tranquil flow and would pull them into my river.

"Can I kiss you then?" he asked. "I would really like to kiss you."

"Then do it," I said in a mere whisper.

He leaned into me, and I opened my mouth slightly as to invite his kiss. He tasted of sweet wine, and by the way he pressed his lips into mine, I could sense that he was nervous. Sam grabbed my hair and closed it in his hand and pulled me even closer to him. His other hand gently slid up the back of my skirt. His hand was cold, and I could feel him start to tremble, so I took his hand and held it. He kissed me harder and moved his other hand under my skirt.

"God, Teri, this feels way too good," he said, and I could feel his body trembling all over. "I' m not going to lie and tell you that I'm not nervous because it's only obvious that I am."

"Are you okay with this so far? It's all right if you aren't—I understand how hard this can be."

"I'm more than okay with this—that's what scares me. I would like to see you again, if that is something you may want as well."

"Sam, let's play it by ear, okay?" I really did like him, but I knew that this good boy was not ready to be bad, and I was not going to be anyone's regret.

When I got home that night, there were several e-mails that he left for me. The first one read,

> *Teri, it was amazing to meet you tonight and I'm sorry I was so nervous. To tell you the truth, I didn't think that I would be that nervous and don't take this personally but I didn't think that someone your age would have this kind of effect on me. That had to sound bad; I didn't mean it that way. Anyways, when I got home my daughter was at my neighbor's house because she had woken up and could not find me. Don't worry I made up something and told my neighbor I had to run to the store so it will be okay. I would like to see you again soon . . . .*
>
> > *Sam,*

The next one read,

> *I know that I just sent you an email but I can't seem to stop thinking about you. Do you always have this effect on men? I can smell your perfume on my shirt and I know that I should put it in the wash before I forget and my wife comes home and smells it, but I want to remember the way you smelled tonight for just a few more minutes. I must sound like the biggest loser here! So in just admitting this I will add: I have imagined what it would be like to kiss someone else and you have more than exceeded my expectations as to what this would be like. I know that you must be popular and can have you pick of guys so I'm ready to send you a resume if you want! Just don't make me wait too long to see you again, I promise I won't shake so badly (I hope)*
>
> > *Sam,*

He did send me his resume the next day, and as impressive as it was, I knew that I would not see Sam again. We would message to each other for months, and I always had a reason why I could not see him, and then one winter day, many months later, he would send me this e-mail:

Hi Teri,

> *I have thought of you a lot lately and I received the email about your new boyfriend. I just can't believe that someone actually TAMED you! How the hell did he do that? And why would you let yourself become tamed? That's not like the girl I met that night in the parking lot who made me shake! See what happens when you fall for a cop? They are bad! I'm glad you have found what you are looking for, as for me, I have given up my search. I'm off the site and I realized that I am not ready to go through*

with this so you were right. There are too many people who do this and mess up their lives. I should just get a divorce and be happy I guess but this site just isn't for me. Keep in touch and let me know how things go with your young cop. Take care and continue to be good because I'm betting the bad girl will resurface again one day.

Best of Luck, Sam

That would be the last e-mail I would get from Sam. I spent many days in June at my local hiding place, drinking by noon and hiding in the corner of the bar with my laptop, chatting. I stopped eating and lost ten pounds. The more I chatted, the lonelier I became, but that did not seem to stop me. Not that I even realized at that time that the reason I felt this way was because of my chat addiction and the emptiness I felt in my marriage. Often, when one of my "fans" would log on, I would turn on my cam and blow them a kiss. I continued to see Paul throughout the month of June, several times a week, and I knew that I would soon have to end things because he was becoming attached.

It was the day before my birthday, and I was struggling with the fact that this would be the last day I would ever be forty-one again. I had seen Paul the day before, and I wanted to be alone for the rest of the week without any meetings. I was at my hiding place when I got a text from Ryan.

Text Message:

Ryan:	Hey sexy what u doin?
Teri:	Hi babe getting wasted I hate today
Ryan:	Why?
Teri:	I'm turning 42 tomorrow I'm OLD
Ryan:	Naw just a number
Ryan:	Where are u?
Teri:	At my hideout
Ryan:	Cool

Ten minutes later, Ryan walked in the club, and I was too drunk to be stunned.

"What the heck are you doing here, Ryan?"

"I'm coming to save you. Get up, let's go." This was the bad boy I was attracted to in the parking lot that day who took what he wanted without asking.

"One more shot."

"No, Teri, we are going. Get your shit and let's go now. You are not going to sit here and feel sorry for yourself. Get up." Ryan was valiant, and I really liked that about him. He worked as one of the heads of security at the airport, and he possessed this knack for dictatorship which impressed me. I gathered my belongings, and he walked me to my truck. I don't recall how it happened, but I do remember that we ended up having sex right there in the parking lot. It was my second sexual encounter. It was the first time that I had sex with Ryan, and he would later joke as to how romantic it was. Really, we were lucky that we didn't get a ticket for lewd behavior, especially because he was in law enforcement. Ryan hated that I sat in the bar and drank during the day, and he often would come to *rescue* me, making sure that I got home safely. I would stop telling him that I was at the bar, knowing that he would probably come save me from myself, and eventually he stopped asking me where I was.

That was the good part of that day. Later that night, I would lose my first Literary game online with my music boy, Adam. We turned on our Webcams for the game, and I had my Scrabble word cheater Web site up to assist me. There should have been no reason I lost that night except for the fact I was still very intoxicated.

Yahoo Chat:

Teri: Adam, did you know it's my birthday tomorrow?
Adam: Yep you mentioned that five minutes ago babe and no I'm not throwing the game because it's your birthday, you asked me that too five minutes ago.
Teri: God . . . it's so hot in here. Do you mind if I take off my . . .

I bent down and took off my shoes.

Teri: Shoes?
Adam: Not working Ter, sorry.

It would take more to distract Adam, and I was becoming desperate not to lose and have to produce my first "loser picture." I stretched out my arms, leaned back in my chair, and yawned, exposing the white tube top I was wearing. By the look on his face, I could tell I was getting warmer.

Teri: Your turn bad boy

I took a sip of my drink and purposely dripped some on my chest so that I had to wipe it off and then lick my fingers.

Adam: You cheat you know. That's not nice.
Teri: What do you mean Adam?

This time I shifted in my chair to one side, and my tube top slipped a bit, almost exposing myself.

Adam: That! I mean that! What you are doing now.
Teri: Good God, are you going to ever take your turn here? You can pass if you need to, it's ok.

He didn't pass, and he ended up winning despite my drunken attempts to distract him.

Adam: Well, let's see. I think I would like a photo of you on your truck.
Teri: No way. How am I to do that? It's not like I can hop on my truck and say to my husband *hey Hun snap a quick one of me okay?*
Adam: I'm sure you will figure it out, and oh you have a week. After a week I get two, interest of course.
Teri: FINE.

My birthday was a dark day for me. My children were out of town with their father, and when I woke up that day, I popped a Valium and went back to bed. I woke up later that afternoon and called my husband.

"Hi, Honey, are you coming home soon?"

"What do you want to do?"

"Did you forget what today is?" I was already depressed, and I knew that he was well aware of the date, but I also knew he was extremely unhappy with my behavior and late nights on the computer. "Can we go for sushi? I know you hate sushi, but I really feel like it." He came home, and we went for sushi and he hated it. I almost relished in the fact that he did hate it because he never did wish me a happy birthday. I didn' t hear from my guys that day because I gave them specific orders not to call or text me on my birthday so that I could feel sorry for myself all alone. All of them complied but one. Ryan sent the text during lunch with my husband, wishing me a happy birthday and promising me lots of spankings to come. I went home and took another Valium as my husband decided that he was going to hang out with his friends for the night. I went to bed early so that when I would wake up again this day would finally be over.

CHAPTER SEVEN

July '06

Dara, my other sister was eighteen months younger than I. She was visiting with her family for the Fourth of July holiday and would stay with me for half of the time. Our mother who lived five miles from me made her crazy at times. I was the one who had patience for our mother. Kirstin and Dara as well as my younger brother would try to understand our mother' s ways, not that I really understood her. I only had more patience for her than they did. Our mother grew up in China and had lost both of her parents by the time she was ten. She was living on her own at the age fourteen and suffered a hard life, always reminding us how lucky and spoiled we were. I forgave her harsh words, understanding that she never really had a mother and so she didn't have an example. While growing up, she would tell us of the things *she* didn't have in her childhood and tell us how spoiled we were for having food. She should want more for her children I would think, but that' s my mother. I also never bonded with her, having to be separated from her at birth. I was born in Vietnam during the war and she had to leave me there for several months. If she didn't flee she would risk having to stay in the country and they would not let me out. It would take my father many months and a case of Johnny Walker Red to finally reunite me with a mother that I didn't want to go to. That I didn' t recognize or want. We went to the mall one day, Dara my mother and I.

"You look so sad Teri. Are you okay?" Dara asks me. Before I can answer my mother replied.

"She smokes too much and doesn't sleep. Look at her. She never tells me anything so don't ask me," I ignored my mothers comment.

"I'm okay. I just smoke too much and I don't sleep," I laughed.

"You look like you've lost some weight. You need to eat," Dara said.

"She looks better now. She was getting fat," my mother said. "She needed to go on a diet. Your husband should go on one too," she said the last sentence looking at me.

"Mom!"

"It's okay Dara, she's right. And if you really want to know why I look like crap mom, it's because I'm having an affair and I drink too much," I blurted out. I had desired to tell someone, anyone. It felt good to finally say it.

They both just looked at me without saying anything. Moments passed and my mother decided to be a mother.

"You cracked the vase?" she asked sounding as if I had just robbed a bank. "It's okay. I know you aren't happy Teri. I know my daughter. It will be okay."

"What vase?" Dara asked. I guess our mother never had the "vase" talk with her.

"I'm unhappy mom. I'm so sad and my heart hurts all the time. I can't leave him. But I don't know how to stay. Tell me how to stay mom?"

"I cannot tell you how to stay. I cannot tell you to leave. But I can tell you that I love you. Be the strong girl you are. You are my strongest child. Never could tell you what to do. You will do what is right. You are a good girl with the biggest heart, always thinking about everyone else first."

"I' ll be strong mom. I promise. Please don't think I'm weak," I cried, as she held me for a brief moment. There were tears in my mother's eyes. I had cracked the vase. I had become weak in my mother's eyes and I saw this through her tears.

July was here and it was time for me to end things with Paul. He was getting too emotionally attached, and every day I would get a text from him, saying, "H ow many dates do you have today?" He would do this pretending to be joking, but I knew that he was upset that I was still meeting guys. I had stopped trying to conceal this from him weeks ago in hopes that he would be okay with it, concluding that I lie to my husband, but it was ridiculous that I had to lie to my lover as well.

The thing that I regret most is that I didn't tell him in person. He deserved at least that, but I was never one who liked confrontations, so I took the chicken way out and called him.

"Paul, I'm not saying I never want to see you again, I just know that I want to see other people and slow things down between us a bit." I was for sure a chicken because this is not what I intended to say to him, yet I couldn't find the words to say anything else.

"You aren't slowing down at all, Teri. You have a problem." I could hear the anger in his voice even though he never raised it once. "When is it going to be enough for you? Are you that insecure that you need attention from all these guys?"

I knew what he was saying was true, but I would not admit to this, and becoming a bit defensive, I said, "It's not that I' m at all insecure, Paul, I'm just looking for something that I haven't found. I don't want to hurt you because you are great, and I do care for you, but what we have is not enough for me for some reason. It's not you, it's me. One day I will kick myself for letting you go, but you do know that I still want to see you, don't you?" I was becoming weaker by the minute and knew I would have to end this conversation before I ended up promising him something that. I knew I would not be able to give him.

"Let's meet for lunch next week, okay." Like that. I didn't make quite a clean break, but it was a start. I would continue to see Paul for lunch or over drinks, but we would never have a sexual relationship after this day.

The week was almost over, and I didn't have the picture that I owed Adam. I could not ask anyone to take it, and I was too stupid to figure out how to delay my digital camera and take it myself. A deal is a deal, and I knew that I would have to figure out a way to take it soon.

Tony, my Italian computer geek, called me that day.

"Hi, Teri, I was wondering . . . if you aren't going to do me, then will you help me find a girl?"

"Tony, you are not serious. You so did not just ask me that"

"Um, let's see . . . yeah, I so just did."

"Fine, meet me at the park in thirty minutes, okay? I will bring my laptop and see what I can do" We met at the park, and I had him log in to the Cheaters Club Web site on my laptop.

"Let's see, what about this one?" I said, searching the local women who, surprisingly enough, were few and not very attractive. "No wonder I'm so popular—look at some of these women."

I started to chat with one who was twenty-eight and was online. She went by the name Kat.

Teri:	Hey kitty kitty . . . how are you today?
Kat:	that's original. I'm fine.
Teri:	Great, I'm fine too now that you are here!
Kat:	Great
Teri:	Are you working or playing?

No response

| Teri: | Your profile says that you like tall guys; I'm six foot is that tall enough? |

Still no response.

This chick was tough, and she was starting to irritate me with her curtness.

Teri:	So what brings you here today?
Kat:	Nothing I'm just here

"Tony, if I could slap this girl, I would. She is so incredibly RUDE!" I said to him as he chuckled at me with an *I know* look on his face. "I' m dumping this one. NEXT!"

There was one more local online, who I will call Amber. Amber was thirty-two, and her profile didn't say a lot.

Teri: Hi sweetie, care to chat?
Amber: Hello, how are you?
Teri: Good thanks, how is your day going?
Amber: I'm at work so it could be better
Teri: alright beautiful, will try to brighten it up for you a bit then . . . want me to tell you a joke?
Amber: Lol . . . sure why not?

The only joke which came to mind was the stupid attorney one, so I told that to her.

Amber: That's not funny at all, but know what is?
Teri: No, tell me
Amber: I work in an attorney's office, I'm a paralegal

Strike two, but then:

Amber: Do you have a key? I would like to see what a bad joke teller looks like
Teri: Yes, here you go. Can I see yours?

Her photo was not good. I could tell by the look on Tony's face that it was a no-go. I was just wondering now how to get out of this conversation without being an ass, so I told her another attorney joke and it worked.

"It's not easy, is it?" Tony said to me. "Women are either bitches, or the ones who aren't are fuglies."

"Hey, I'm neither, so don't get all negative on me here. Hold on, Mr. Impatient." Another one came online, and before I could check her profile I was chatting with her out of desperation. This was definitely not as easy as chatting with men, who were more than eager to listen to my bad jokes and even pretended to think that they were funny. I will call this one Mary.

Teri: Hi, please tell me that you are in a good mood and will be nice. They are brutal here today!
Mary: LOL! I'm very nice and I will only be brutal if you want me too (inserts a wink)

Teri: Nice . . . what do you look like babe?

My patience was running out, and I found myself cutting through the chase and getting down to business here. We exchanged keys, and she was what I would call *acceptably cute.*

Me: YOU ARE GORGEOUS!
Mary: TY . . . I like your photo as well
Me: Good would you like to meet for lunch or coffee maybe?

"Teri, um . . . that's coming on a bit strong, don't you think?" Tony said, in his negative way of being negative today. I threw him a *shush now* look, and he got the message.

Mary: I would, yes

Bingo. I hit the jackpot and wore the proudest of smiles. I glanced at Tony, and his smile was absent.
    "What is wrong now? She's not that bad. I'd do her if I were a guy." I was over this hunting for women here, and Tony was being overly picky in my opinion.
    "Nothing. She's okay, I guess. Set it up then, Miss Make-the-girls-hot. Thanks too, by the way. I owe you one." As he said the last part of this sentence, I knew how I would get that photo that I owed Adam.
    "Tone, can I collect on that favor now?"
    "Will this scare me? What is it?"
    "I need for you to take a picture of me on my truck. I always have my camera handy, so will you?"
    "Yeah, all right. Go get it then." I grabbed my camera out of my truck and handed it to him. I was wearing a short brown skirt and tee shirt with high heeled brown sandals. I hopped on the hood of my truck and leaned back on my hands with my knees bent and spread open my legs.
    "Okay, I'm ready now, and don't look at my panties."
    Tony stood there for what seemed minutes and looked straight at my panties.
    "OKAY, ANY DAY NOW! This isn't really comfortable, and this hood is hot on my ass. If I scratch my truck with my heels, I'm not going to be happy. Tony, take it already!" He snapped a shot, and I jumped off my truck, not even caring if the camera goddess liked me that day or not. Adam was getting whatever that shot would be.
    "Can I have a copy?" Tony asked. "Need any more favors, by the way?"
    "No and no. Thank you, though." I would send Adam the photo that night, and my debt would be paid in full. The next time I would lose at Scrabble and

continue to always lose would be with the one that I should have *run* from, but I would have no way of knowing this until it was too late.

It was a Sunday afternoon, and my children were with their father that weekend, my husband had gone somewhere, so I was alone. I logged on to the Cheaters Club site and checked my messages. I was getting up to fifty or so a day now, and after fifty my mailbox would not hold any more, so I would have to log in and delete them in order to receive more. I never read through most of them unless one caught my eye or if it were one from one of my "guys." I noticed two of them were from my local meetings. One was from Ron the Mountain Boy asking when we could meet again and promising that hiking was not required this time. The other was from Travis, the one whose car was "stolen" from the parking lot. Travis's message read something like this:

Hi Beautiful,

It has been a long time since I have seen you and you keep blowing me off. I have decided to take off my profile here because I can' t seem to find anyone who is close to what you are. You have ruined it for all the other women! I will be in touch with you through emails and remember that you promised to see me again. You promised. I have missed you and I have been waiting patiently and I think you owe me another date at least. I'm going to Africa tomorrow to aid in some charity work but when I get back I expect to see you and this time no excuses. Remember that you PROMISED me another date and you don't seem the kind to lie. Stay safe Beautiful and I will see you when I get back.

Love and thinking of you always, Travis

This guy for sure required meds. He was out of his mind if he thought that I would meet him, and there was never a promise on my part made to see him again. *Unstable* and *delusional* came to mind when I thought of him, he was dangerous. I quickly deleted that message with a Godspeed. There was a bull waiting to chat with me, so I clicked the flashing button to check it out. Dickboy1 was another Canadian from Vancouver, and he was thirty-eight, with no photo displayed.

Dickboy1:   Hi, care to chat? How's Utah today?
Designgirl: Hello, It's a beautiful day here actually; I should be lying out by my pool
Dickboy1:   Yeah, you have a pool? I wished that I had one but there aren't many pools here
Designgirl: Too bad, so what do you do? I'm Teri by the way

Dickboy1:   I'm an architect. I like your name! I like names that end with "I"s, I'm Will

Designgirl: LOL! Will, why's that? The names ending in "I" thing? That's very interesting and a bit quirky.

Dickboy1:   I don't know, I just think it's sexy. I was seeing a girl and her name was Toni and I liked it.

Designgirl: Phew . . . good! I made it into the "I" club. Nice. You are an architect? I have a thing against architects and pilots you know . . . but I will make an exception with you! Unless you are not cute, JK

Dickboy1:   Oh really? Why's that? Why don't you like architects or pilots?

Designgirl: Well, architects irritate me because many think they are designers and tend to look down on us, and pilots are cheap butts.

Dickboy1:   Lol, oh yeah, that's funny, why are they cheap?

Designgirl: Don't ask me, when I was a flight attendant I would tip the driver a buck for them when we would get shuttled to the hotel because they never had any cash on them and they only made ten times more money than I did. Then they would hit happy hour with free hordourves instead of having a meal somewhere. And forget about tipping, they don't know the meaning of the word. All the pilots that I flew with were like this however it is logically possible that there are one or two out there who I aren't I suppose.

Will and I chatted a few more minutes before we exchanged keys. His photo was a black-and-white one, a close-up of his face, and he was extremely handsome. He had short dark hair and a goatee. I liked his face, and he had a sexiness about him that instantly allured me into wanting to know more about who he was and what he was looking for.

Designgirl: What color are your eyes? Blue?

I already had made a guess they were blue, not being able to tell in the black-and-white photo.

Dickboy1:   Yes, how did you know?

Designgirl: Lucky guess

It would only be minutes later when we would meet on Yahoo Messenger and he would turn on his Webcam for me. He was in his office, and he was wearing a sweatshirt and baseball cap. The camera goddess loved this boy. He demurely looked into the lens and smiled for me for the first time. We chatted about architecture and design and relationships. He would tell me that he was married, with two young daughters, and not actively pursuing an affair, especially one with someone who lived far away. Toni, the woman that he saw for almost a year, lived in the States, and he explained to me the strain of a long-distance affair as well as pointing out the positive sides of it. Regardless, he was not looking for another long distance friend. This didn' t really bother me when he mentioned it because I was certain that he would want to meet me if we continued chatting.

Yahoo Chat:

Teri: So Toni was single? Wow, aren't single people dangerous? They don't have anything to lose. Weren't you afraid that she wound become attached or flip out and tell your wife?

I had established rules to abide by, and one of them would be *no singles*, so it intrigued me to find out as to why married people would "go there" and put out that risk. Besides, single people were not a part of our "club."

Will: No, not really, she had a boyfriend but she did start talking about wanting children with me, she's only thirty and that's when I ended things because I couldn't give her what she wanted.

He typed this, looking cute in his baseball cap as he did this. Will would go from sexy to cute in seconds. He would become bashful, yet I had to wonder if his vague shyness was only an act because then he would become extremely composed and confident. Besides Toni, Will had been chatting with another girl from the States named Vicky for the past two years and only met her once in this time.

Teri: How do you have the patience to chat with someone that you can't see or meet when you want too?

This long-distance thing sparked my curiosity. I was becoming more intrigued with the thought of it.

Will: I don't know, it was hard. We would chat online for hours as day and talk on the phone and text. It was draining at times and it takes effort and time to get to know someone but I was really into Vicky. She probably knows me better than my own wife does.
Teri: That's insane! I would just fly down there and meet her every month if I were you! But I don't have any patience. I want what I want and I always get it. Beware, I may want you.
Will: Lol oh really?

I could see on the camera that I had just made him blush.

Will: Do you have a cam?

Teri: I do, but I haven't showered yet so if you give me like forty five minutes I will be back.

An hour later, I turned on my cam for him, and I could tell by the look on his face that he wasn't disappointed in what he saw. Will became my focus for the next month. I would still meet some locals, mostly Ryan, but the prospect of meeting someone not only from a different state but a different country was too delicious for me. For much of the month of July, I would find myself online with Will every night, and often we would turn our Webcams on as well.

A week later, I logged into the Cheaters Club site and there were several messages from Alex, the eager boy from Boston. This guy didn't give up. He must have been looking for me because I didn' t finish reading the messages he sent before I noticed that he was online and requesting a chat with me.

Alex: I'm so glad you are here! Did you get my messages? I got a web cam just for you! (Smiley face inserted.)

Teri: Oh, no, I haven't read them yet. Wow, you did get a cam? For me?

Alex: Yes! So can I get your Yahoo or MSN? PLEASE???????

His efforts in pursuing me paid off because I found myself giving in even though in the back of my mind I hoped I would not regret it. We met on MSN Messenger, and he turned on his cam. I was taken aback at first. In his photo on the site, he was standing next to a painting in a museum, looking a bit dorky, but he was anything but dorky—he was extremely attractive, sporting messy sandy blond hair and hazel eyes. He resembled more a surfer from California rather a Bostonian to me.

MSN Chat:

Teri: You are cute Alex

Alex: TY . . . can I see your cam now please?

He smiled and reminded me of a little boy. I found myself lured into a faint fascination with him, which surprised me because for the past month I had been avoiding him. I turned on my cam and his expression froze.

Teri: Alex, you ok?

Alex: Teri, you're beautiful. I mean it. I' m so glad I finally got a cam!

I talked him into meeting me on Yahoo and kicked his butt in a game of Literary, and he would owe me a photo to add to my fast—growing library of pictures.

Alex: Instead of a photo I can show you the real thing now
Teri: You are a bad boy . . . that you can do, but I want my photo as well

He stood up and unbuttoned his jeans and pulled out his already hard penis, never once asking to see me do anything. When Will was not online at night, Alex would be who I spend my time with, not logging onto the Cheaters Club site as much. I had enough men to juggle, and I was still meeting a few locals, but it would only be with Ryan that I would do anything sexual with.

One day in mid-July, I was sitting on the back porch with my husband. It was hot that day, and I was a bit sunburned from lying out by my pool. He rubbed aloe vera on my back and asked me something that I was not prepared for.

"Why are you getting calls from Canada?"

Without hesitation, I calmly answered, "The architect who is helping me with the loft project in New York is from Canada."

"Why would he call you from Calgary and then from Vancouver several hours later?"

"He has two phones, Honey. One is his business one, and the other is his private one, and he calls me from both, depending on his battery charge." I was amazed how composed I could be under pressure, and I lied so very easily. I did however decide to get another private cell phone the next day and have it billed online so there would be no statement mailed. I would call this phone my "BGC," standing for Bad Girl Cell. From this day forward, my guys would call or text on the BGC, and I had over thirty of them programmed on this phone.

Will was online, working late from his office one night. I had been drinking that night and was in a flirty mood. I turned on my cam and took it into my closet and locked the door. I asked him to call me on the BGC, and I introduced him to Jack. This would be the first time that he would expose himself to me as well. After our cam/phone sex session, I asked him something.

"Will, when are we going to meet in person?" I was intending to ask him this soon, and it seemed to be the right time now.

"I don't know. What is your schedule like in August?"

"Let's meet on the first of August then. It's a Tuesday. We can meet in San Francisco if you want because I was intending to go there that week anyways—unless that's too far for you to travel?"

"No, that sounds good, but I can't stay for more than a few nights," he said. "My wife will be out of town that week, so it should be fine."

Right then and there in my closet, I booked my flight, and he did as well. He booked us a room at the Marriott in Union Square.

"Should I get two beds or just one?" he said as he booked the room.

"One is good, unless you hog the covers." Will was always a gentleman, and I wasn't surprised that he asked this question.

"You aren't gonna pull a Vicky and cancel on me at the last minute, are you?" he asked.

"No way, after what you just showed me. I sooooo want a piece of that! Not a chance I'm going to back out, babe." Vicky would do this to him in the past. He would book a ticket to go see her, and she would cancel, finding some lame excuse to why she could not see him. This did not happen once but several times, and I could sense in his voice the concern of me doing this to him, plus I really did want to meet him.

San Francisco was beautiful in August but chilly. I borrowed my sister's BMW and picked Will up from the airport later that day. I recognized him immediately and gave him a hug. He looked bigger than he did on cam, taller and a bit stockier, but his face was the same in all the expressions that I had come to associate with this past month. I drove us to the hotel in the city and only almost hit just one pedestrian in doing so. Driving in the city was something that I should not be allowed to do, and the drivers on the road with me would agree to this. We checked into the hotel, and he showered before we went to dinner. The restaurant that I wanted to go to was supposed to be close, but we could not find it, so we decided to just walk until we found something

"Oh, there is the Starlight Room. I love it there! It's on the twenty-first floor. We should go there after dinner to dance," I said to him as we walked by it.

"The twenty-first floor? Aren't there lots of earthquakes here?" As he said this, he had a look of concern on his face that I had to laugh at because it was too funny.

"Naw, not for a while. It's okay, you will be fine, I promise. No earthquakes tonight."

"On the flight here, I was thinking to myself, 'What if the plane goes down, or if there is an earthquake.' My wife is out of town, but she thinks I'm still in Vancouver. How would I explain that one?"

"Pretty sure if your plane went down, you'd be dead, and if there is an earthquake, you'd most likely be squashed, so I wouldn't worry about having to explain anything to her in that case." I don't think that I should have mentioned the "squashed" part if I was hoping to get him up to the twenty-first floor and take me dancing later. We found a place that seemed nice for dinner We were seated, and I ordered a cape cod and he ordered a berry martini.

"I can't believe I brought you to a place that serves fried chicken gizzards," I said, mortified at what I saw on the menu. "How's that martini?"

He took a sip and squinted his eyes "It tastes like cough syrup, really bad cough syrup."

"Let me taste." I took a sip, and it was more than awful. It was death to the taste buds. "Send this back. It will make you sick if you drink it, and you're already starting to turn green."

We had dinner and joked about how awful the food and décor of the restaurant was. He was easy to be with, and I found myself wanting to slide closer to him in the restaurant-style booth we were sitting in, but I refrained from making the first move. I told myself before I picked him up earlier that I would let him make the first move and for once be submissive. I fought the urge to sit closer, but seducing him with my cleavage was something that I didn't tell myself I couldn't do. I was wearing a short white miniskirt with a black lace camisole and sweater. I took off my sweater even though it was a bit cold in the restaurant, and his eyes went straight for my cleavage. Men were so easy. They didn't even try to hide their desires, and if they did, they did it badly. I smiled at him and batted my eyelashes as I said, "So, what do you think? Take me dancing and show me what you got?"

We went to the Starlight Room, and it was almost empty. I was carded at the door and pretended to be offended as usual. We took a seat by the window overlooking the city, and the night was clear, with all the lights of the city lighting up the sky like a Christmas tree in August. The band was good playing R&B and eighties music, and after two drinks, I couldn't wait for him to ask me to dance.

"Dance with me, bad boy," I demanded. I got up and took his hand and led him to the dance floor. I was really feeling the music and practicing my sexy hip moves when I noticed him dance. He danced like the worst kind of white boy, and I tried so hard not to laugh, but I did anyway. I don' t think he realized I was laughing at him, but he was so incredibly cute at that moment it took everything I had not to grab him by his blazer jacket and pull him into me for a kiss. We danced all night, and it was amazing how his clumsy moves turned into something incredibly captivating to me by the end of the night. I just wanted to get this boy back to the room, and the club was closing now.

We walked into our room, and I stood by the bed. Forgetting that I was going to be submissive, I wrapped my arms around his neck and kissed him for the first time. He tasted of cranberry juice and vodka, which made him delicious to me. His lips were warm on this chilly night, and it would only be seconds before I would start to undress him. The room had two beds in it, and I lay down on the bed closest to the door sideways and pulled him down on top of me

He kissed me and slid off my panties and moved his head down to taste me. His tongue was warm. He was for sure talented in doing this, and I wanted to explore what his other talents were like. I returned the favor orally, and I could not wait any longer to feel him inside of me. He put on a condom, and when he entered me for the first time, I moaned. He felt good as he gently slid in and out of me in slow movements. I came almost instantly and was very pleased to find that he had great stamina and would become quickly aroused soon after having an orgasm. I don't recall how many condoms we went through that night, but I do remember that we didn't get much sleep. When we woke up the next morning, he left the room to call his wife.

"Teri, she said that she called me all day yesterday and wondered where I was." I could tell by the look on his face he was a bit worried. "I know my flight doesn't leave until this afternoon, but would you be upset if I took the earlier one? I just feel as if she calls me again and I don't answer, she will know something is up."

"No, take the earlier flight if you have to. It's okay, I understand."

We had time to grab some breakfast before I took him to the airport, so I drove us to a small place on the way. My BGC kept beeping as text messages were coming in already, and it was only nine o'clock in the morning.

"Will, I don't do well with texting and driving—well, I don' t do well with driving in general, and do you mind seeing who this is?" I asked, handing him my phone.

"It's Adam. He says, 'Hi sexy, what are you doing?'" Will pretended to respond back and said "Hi, Adam. I'm with a hot Canadian and just had the best sex of my life." He looked at me and said, "I'm kidding. I wouldn't say that."

"Do it!" I replied. "He knows I'm with you."

"Oh there's another one coming in. This is from Tom." Tom was a local attorney that I had met and I golfed with.

Tom and I and were just friends, and after meeting, we concluded that we would rather have a long—lasting friendship rather a sexual relationship. He was one of the few that after meeting I would still talk with. He would often ask me for advice on women and pick my brain on how women think, and I would share with him stories of the meetings I had with men. He would come to call me the "goddess of lust."

Golfing one day, he asked me, "Teri, how do you keep all of your men straight?"

"I don't know, I just do. I guess I need or want something different from each of them."

"Yeah, like their penises."

"No! I don't want nor need your penis now, do I?" I snapped. "I just need for you to play golf with me because you stink at it like I do! I' m just a wee bit better at it than you are, so you make me feel good."

"Yeah, 'cause you cheat."

"So? You never said I can't throw my golf ball."

"You throw like a girl too, by the way. Let me show you how to throw a ball." Tom always made me laugh, and I trusted him. There were a few local guys who were in the same category as Tom in only just being my friends, and I liked this. I could go to these guys with my troubles and know that they would only tell me the truth, with no intent to get into my panties. It was like having a bunch of gay guy friends to talk to except for that they were not gay.

I drove Will back to the airport, and I felt sad. I didn't want him to leave, and the past seventeen hours had gone by too quickly. I felt a connection with him in a way that I had not with anyone before. I felt as if I had known him for years, and if I never did have sex with him again, that would be fine as long as I could keep him in my life as a friend. He kissed me good-bye, and I felt as if an old friend were leaving to get on that plane. It happened that later this night there would be a small earthquake, and Will and I would laugh about the irony in this for a very long time.

I drove back to my sister's house after dropping Will off.

"This is destructive behavior. I don't understand why you risk everything like this," Kirsten said to me. She was nine years my senior and she practically raised me. My sister was a flight attendant and beautiful, looking more like she was in her middle thirties. "You've always been impulsive in your behavior but this scares me," she added, clipping up her long black hair in a clip.

"Tell me what you ache for Kirst. I want to know if you dare to dream for your hearts longing. Would you disappoint another to be true to yourself?" I asked my sister. She studied me for a few seconds and then applied a shade of red lipstick.

"You're being true to yourself?" she asked me, ignoring the questions that I presented to her. "I don't think so. You never should have married your husband to begin with. We both know this. You have never been true to Teri," she said as she sat on her bed. "Come here. Sit with me," I reluctantly sat on her bed, not really wanting to have this conversation anymore. "These guys that you meet online don't give a shit about you. If you are this unhappy then do it the right way. Get yourself established, get your household together and *then* leave him. You are a wonderful, smart girl. You have talents I wish I had. You are a loving, generous person Teri. But when I look at you now I don't see my sister."

"I don't see me either Kirsten. I'm lost within myself. And I don't know how to stop this."

"You don't want to stop it, or you would."

"No, it owns me right now. I fight the urge to get online, I do. But then I lose the battle. Really though, I feel as if I'm starved for *joy* and it feeds me. I can bear the accusation of betrayal Kirst, but I betrayed my own soul. I'm a bad person," I sobbed on my sister's bed, knowing that I was defeated.

"Then stop. Stop this behavior now. Save yourself. Trust in yourself again."

"I am faithless. Therefore I am not trustworthy. Don't give up on me. I can live with failure, but I can't live without my sister by my side." She wouldn' t say much more, knowing that I was broken. But it would be many months down the road when she would try to save me, in her own way.

Will and I would not chat online every night as we had in the past, and I would move on to the next potential meeting. He would ask me about my guys and who I was meeting next, always amazed at how quickly I moved from one to the other. After meeting Will, someone who lived far away, the local meetings did not hold their appeal to me anymore. The focus for my meetings shifted from the adrenaline rush of the meetings themselves to meeting men who lived distant to me. My next focus would be both Adam the Music Boy from Calgary as well as my newest cam buddy, Alex the Eager Boy from Boston. I wanted more now. Will had introduced me to a new kind of anticipation of meeting men. Men I would have to wait for.

I would spend the first few weeks of August online with Adam, Alex, and Will and planning future meetings with both Adam and Alex, who were both eager to meet me. I only needed to decide who to meet with first and when. It would be the middle of August when I would log onto the Cheaters Club site to browse for new bulls. This would be a turning point for me, and I did not know at the time what was in store for me. If I had known, I would never have logged online that starry night in mid-August.

Chapter Eight

August '06

It was the middle of August, when the moon is the most full in its entirety. The stars were exceptionally bright as I glared up at them, wondering if another king would be born on this perfect night. I counted shooting stars but dared not wish upon any of them, knowing that my wishes don't come true and hoping that someone else in this world would wish upon them. I tried to remember what a shooting star was. Tiny bits of dust not any larger than a piece of sand falling into the earth's atmosphere and burning up, leaving a trial of light which only lasts seconds. I remembered something about how it could have hit the atmosphere hundreds of years ago but only now be visible for those few seconds—as if it were just a ghost and not really there.

It was a Sunday night and getting late. I decided to check out who was online on the Cheaters Club site. I had changed my profile name from Designgirl to Sassypants because I had come across a few stalkers who would not leave me alone, and they were starting to scare me a bit, both of them locals. I was also getting some hate mail because I had stated in my profile that I was only interested in men who were thirty—five or younger. One nasty message I had recently opened read something to the effects of this:

> *For a designer you have short sited vision! I'm sixty and my girlfriend is thirty one and weighs 115 lbs to your 135 lbs and I bet she is hotter than you are! She doesn't mind that I'm sixty and says that I'm better sex than her thirty three year old husband.*

Normally I don't respond to these nasty messages, but I was in a mood, so I replied back:

> *Hooray for you and your girl friend! I'm happy for the both of you. Not that I owe you an explanation, but since your britches are a little twisted here, my husband happens to be your age and we have no sexual relationship hence the younger guy thing. We are all on here looking for*

whatever it is we are looking for and this happens to be what I want. If it offends people that is not my intention, however maybe you should not be so concerned by what it is that others are seeking and focus on yourself and your hot girlfriend.

He did respond back, apologizing, but I did not respond to his apology and changed my profile name anyway. My feedback remark numbers were getting too high, and it made me seem like a tramp (not as to incriminate myself), so it worked out that I started fresh with a new name. I did state that I was interested in men younger in the new profile, knowing that I would still receive hate mail, but I was getting used to it, and it didn't bother me much.

I logged onto the Cheaters Club site, and instantly I had many bulls waiting, but I sifted through them as if they were garments on a rack at my favorite store.

He caught my eye at once, and I would find myself not accepting any other chats on this night. He was twenty-six, single and from New York, and my only hope was that he could at least spell. Dickboy1 would say to me for the first time:

Dickboy1:   Hi, how are you tonight?
Sassy: Good thanks, and you?
Dickboy1:   I'm good as well
Sassy: So, do you have a key?

I had learned by now not to waste my time or theirs and to be bold in asking for what I wanted. We exchanged keys, and the first thing I noticed was *blue*. In his photo, he was shirtless, and the background he was standing in was blue. He stood there in all of his perfection as if I was viewing Michelangelo's statue of David. His hair was dark and cut short in a militarylike way, and his eyes were blue. I imagined my fingers touching his skin and running up the contour of his abs. It would be impossible for me to know that this twenty-six-year—old would eventually be all that I would want or hope for. On this night, however, he was just another hot young guy who would have to take a number and wait in line for my attention

Sassy: So, what do you do?
Dickboy1:   Do you really want to know?

He was too young to be an architect, and he most definitely didn't look like a pilot, so I considered this question to be safe.

Sassy: Yes
Dickboy1:   I'm a State Trooper
Sassy: You are a cop?

Dickboy1:   Nooooooooooo . . . I'm a Trooper

I needed to do my homework on this one. I knew how irritated I would get when people would call me a "decorator." I would instantly correct them and say I was a "designer."

Sassy: Oh, ok, so have you met anyone in person on this site?
Dickboy1:   Yes I have
Sassy: I have met lots too, but the locals are boring me here. How did you find me tonight?
Dickboy1:   I did a search for who was online and read your profile. It said you like younger guys so I decided to take a chance and say hi.
Sassy: Ohhhh, I didn't think many read profiles. Well I'm glad you found me. I'm Teri by the way, what's your name?
Dickboy1:   Jason
Sassy: Nice to meet you Jason
D1:   Nice to meet you as well
Sassy: I used to live in New York when I was a flight attendant, have you always lived there?
Dickboy1:   Yes I have

Jason was short with his answers and comments but very methodic in his speech. I didn't know how to take this wondering if he was at all interested in me or if that was just the way he chatted. I was too tired to care, and it was getting late, so I decided to say good night using the standard excuse I always did when I wanted to leave in a hurry.

Sassy: Well I have to go, he's up. Add me to your favorites ok? Look for me
Dickboy1:   Ok, I will. Good night Teri
Sassy: Kisses (lips inserted)

The next night, I put my children to bed and poured a stiff cape cod. I played a half of a game of Scrabble with Adam, but he had to get up early, so I waited for Alex to get online. He had called me earlier that day, saying he had a baseball game to play, so it would not be until late that he would be able to get online. There was no one on my Yahoo list that I cared to chat with, so I stayed invisible and decided to log onto the Cheaters Club site while I was waiting for Alex to log online.

"What you doin Ter?" my husband asked coming up from behind me and grabbing my laptop. He had been asleep in his chair for hours and I didn't hear him wake up.

"Don't do that. I don't grab your remote control from you. I'm chatting with Lisa." I told him as I closed my laptop.

"Oh really, how is Lisa? Let's see. Open it." He demanded. I had it in my arms with a death grip and there was no way he was going to pull it from me. I was so busted and we both knew it.

"Okay. I lied. I'm not talking to Lisa. I have been gambling online. I didn't want for you to know because I knew you would be mad." Before he could ask to see my laptop I got up and put my arms around him and reached one hand into his boxers. I was desperate. "I won't do it anymore. Can we do it honey? It's been a year. Don't you want me?" I asked him as I touched him with both hands now. He pushed me away.

"No. I don't want to do it and stop spending my money gambling! You need to find a younger guy Teri. Do what you have to do. I'm tired. I'm going to bed now. Try not to break me okay?" he said as he walked downstairs to our bedroom. *You need to find a younger guy.* Did he just say that to me? If he only knew. I logged back online to the Cheaters Club when I was certain my husband was asleep.

It was busy for a Monday night, and I sifted through my chats quickly because none them were very attractive, and I wasn't in the mood to be nice just for the sake of being nice. I poured myself another drink and made small talk with the less-than-cute bulls on tonight. I glanced at the time, and it was midnight, which meant it would be one in Boston. He should have been here by now, but there were times when he would have to wait for his wife to go to sleep and would sign in as early as one in the morning his time just to blow me a kiss. *Where are the hot guys tonight?* I thought to myself as I was about to log off in frustration, and then he appeared.

Cheaters Club:

Jason:	Hi Teri, how are you tonight?
Sassy:	Oh Hi! Thank God you are here! Save me from all these boring guys!
Jason:	I will try to
Sassy:	Hey, do you have Yahoo?
Jason:	Yes I do
Sassy:	Why didn't you tell me this last night? Let's meet there ok? I want to log off here, there are too many guys trying to chat with me and I can't type that fast and get my conversations confused.

I remembered back a few months ago when I was chatting with Paul. I was being a bit naughty in our conversation, and I was multichatting with several guys. One of the guys that I was chatting with was there for the first time; it was his first chat, making him a "virgin."

I was trying to hold three different conversations and be sexy with Paul at the same time. My spelling was suffering, and I was having trouble typing fast enough for all of these conversations.

I thought I was chatting with Paul when I typed: "Unzip your pants baby and take it out for me . . . Mmmmmmmmmmmmm . . . I bet you are hard aren't you? God I so want you right now." Then what I received was this: "Um, you want me to take it out and do what?" I was mortified as I realized it was the virgin guy I had typed this to. I responded: "NOOOOO! Put it back, don't take it out! I'm sorry; I thought you were someone else."

Needless to say, virgin guy was one of my fans from this day forward, and he wasn't at all someone that I would have asked to "pull it out for me."

I met Jason on Yahoo a few minutes later, and he turned on his cam for me. He was lying in his bed, and the room was a bit dark, yet I could still see him clearly—as if he were in the same room as I. My fingers froze on the keyboard, and I couldn' t move them for a few seconds. He was perfect in form, but there was something about his face that captivated all of my senses.

As he looked into the cam, I could feel the blood rushing to my face. His face reminded me of a Botticelli painting with features almost to perfect. It was oval in shape, with a strong jawline and a cleft chin leading up to heart-shaped lips, but it would be his eyes that would spin me into fixation. They were big and blue, the most amazing shade of navy blue. The corners of them would tip downward, and I could see that he had thick dark lashes that lined his eyes. This would be the closest thing to love at first sight for me, even though I don't believe in love at first sight—lust, perhaps.

Yahoo Chat:

Teri:	Hi
Jason:	Hi
Teri:	Hi. Hi. Hi there.

I was feeling like a "dorkess" by now, trying to break away from the spell he just cast upon me. I don't know if it was the vodka or him, but for the first time ever in any chat I was at a loss for words, either intelligent or not.

Jason:	Can I see your cam?
Teri:	Oh, yeah. Hold on okay? brb

I went to pour myself another drink, and by this time, I definitely didn' t need another one. I turned my cam on and hoped that I was still not flushed. I don't remember exactly what was said this night because of how much I had to drink, but I do remember taking him to Morocco.

My guest bedroom is Moroccan in design. Sometime later that night, I would take him to the guest room and lock the door and introduce him to Jack. Besides David, my first cam experience in New York, I NEVER had cam sex with anyone that I just started to chat with on the first night, not even Alex or Adam; they had to wait patiently until I was ready and felt comfortable enough with them. I knew it wasn' t the alcohol which guided me to Morocco that night because on several occasions I was just as intoxicated with Alex and would not show him my cam even though he would show me his. I felt an instant connection with Jason which made me both trust and want him at the same time. I would never feel a connection this strong with anyone again.

The room was cold and the lighting bad, but I turned on the ceiling light as well as the lamps. I lay on the bed with my panties and a tank top and set the laptop in front of me and spread open my legs. It was hot on this night, and the alcohol seemed to make it feel ten degrees warmer than it actually was.

I pulled my shoulder-length hair to one side, wishing I had a clip to tie it up. When I glanced at the camera, he had taken off his shorts, and he was stroking himself. I had seen several of my guys do this before, but I was transfixed upon what he was doing as if I were watching someone do this for the first time. He never smiled and kept a straight face. It would be weeks before I would notice him smile and wonder why he didn't smile more because he was most beautiful to me when he did.

His strokes were slow and deliberate, and his gaze didn't shift from the camera once. He had a large penis, and I tried not to seem fixated on just that part of him, forcing myself to look at his face and hairless chest as well. I could tell he worked out by the way the muscles in his stomach and arms were defined. I wanted him so badly, more so than anyone I had seen on cam thus far.

I slipped off my panties and touched myself, circling my fingers in big circles. I wanted to hear what he sounded like and what sounds he would made when he would make. I typed: this is my number can you call me?

A minute later, he was on the phone. He had a New York accent, and by the way he was almost whispering, I sensed that he did not live alone.

"Do you like my friend Jack?" I said, holding my vibrator up to the cam so he could view it.

"Yes I do," he answered without hesitation.

"Do you want to see him slide into me?"

"Yes." He said this while exhaling, and his breathing was getting a bit heavier.

I slid Jack into me, and as I did this I moaned softly. "Ohhhhh, God this feels good," I said slowly in almost a whisper. I pulled my tank top over my head, exposing myself, and I touched my breasts for him to see. His gaze still did not shift from the camera, and he was still except for his stroking movement. I closed my eyes and imagined him inside of me as I glided my vibrator in and out of me. I moaned as my heart raced, and the phone slipped out of my hand and slid down in between my breasts

I turned around on the bed and leaned up against the headboard so that he could view me from behind as I slipped Jack into me again. I held the phone in one hand to my ear and held Jack with the other hand, thrusting him in and out of me, slowly at first, and then faster as I said, "God, I'm sooooo!"

My hips started to move back and forth in rhythm to the thrusts, and I forgot for a minute that I was on cam for him until he started to breathe heavier and said, "God, I have never had an orgasm so hard like that on cam before." I had missed seeing him do this, but I was certain that I would get my chance to do so soon.

I met with Jason online again the following night after my husband went to sleep. I introduced him to Literary, and he was winning.

Yahoo Chat:

Teri: God, it's so hot in here . . . . Do you mind if I take off my . . . .

I removed my shoes.

Teri: Shoes?

He didn' t seem to flinch at all as he concentrated on making another word as to kick my ass a bit harder here. I resorted to the stretch that had once worked with Adam. I leaned back into my chair and stretched out my arms and shifted in my chair, exposing my cleavage. I noticed him glance quickly, and then he continued to concentrate on his letters. I didn't have a drink in front of me, so I couldn't do the dribble trick, spilling a bit of it on my chest and licking it off with my fingers as I did that night with Adam, which seemingly worked as well, so instead I grabbed my pen and put it in my mouth, gently sucking the tip of it.

Jason: It's not going to work babe, nice tactics though

He said this as he laid down the word "sonnet" on a triple word score, putting him in the lead by at least sixty points now. I could not believe that he was winning here, and by a lot, really. This didn't happen to me.

Teri: Jase, do you even know what a "sonnet" is?
Jason: I believe it is a song
Teri: It's a verse
Jason: It's a word though and I'm ahead, your turn babe

I was already losing but was going to ask if he would like to try to distract me anyways, but before I could do this, Alex logged online.

Alex Yahoo Chat:

Alex:	Hi baby, I missed you so much today! I'm sorry I couldn't get online last night, we went for beers after the game and I pulled out my knee.
Teri:	Hi babe, that's ok, I was tired anyways
Alex:	Hope you didn't wait up for too long, what did you do?

Jason Yahoo Chat:

Jason:	Your turn babe
Teri:	I know, hold on k?

Neither of them knew that the other was online, and I was trying to be coy about it.

Alex Yahoo Chat:

Teri:	Oh nothing, when I didn't see you online I went to bed at ten thirty but couldn't sleep. I missed you too babe.
Alex:	Where is your cam baby? I need to see your face.
Teri:	Hold on k?
Alex:	Ok, but hurry, I'm really hard here thinking about you. We don't have to play Literary first tonight do we?
Teri:	Yes! You know the rules bad boy! But I will make it worth it. Brb

Jason Yahoo Chat:

Teri:	Jason, I have to go. I'm sorry
Jason:	You don't want to finish the game?
Teri:	You won. Listen, Alex is here online and I missed him yesterday so I need to spend some time with him. I'm sorry. I have to go; if you are still here later I will say hi.
Jason:	Oh, ok. Ttyl then bye
Teri:	Kisses

Alex Yahoo Chat:

Teri:	Sorry babe I'm back

Alex: Where is your cam?

I turned my cam on for him, and we played our game, and I won as I always did with Alex. The word "sonnet" kept passing through my mind during our game, and I wondered what Jason was doing right now. I don't know why it was that I would let everyone know about Alex, yet Alex believed he was the only one that I was chatting and camming with. Even Adam and Will knew of Alex, but Alex was more sensitive, and without ever asking me not to chat with others, it was only obvious that he would be upset if he knew I had. He was needy, and I liked that he needed me.

I took Alex to Morocco that night, and after he logged off, I found that Jason was still online.

Jason Yahoo Chat:

Teri: Hey are you still there?
Jason: Hi, yes I am
Teri: Whatcha doin?
Jason: I just cammed for some woman and her husband was there and he knew
Teri: Nice, was she cute?
Jason: I don't know, she didn't have a cam
Teri: She what? No way! You cammed for her and she didn't have a cam?
Jason: Yes

I could now see how Jason was a bit naive in these things, so I felt the need to educate him.

Teri: Jase, NEVER cam for anyone who doesn't have a cam! You could be camming for a guy or a group even! And even if you are on the phone with her, she could be some COW! You must never do that. Actually, don't cam for anyone that you don't trust. You know that they can record it and you may find it on some trashy web site one day, unless you are into that.
Jason: Oh, ok, I never thought about it like that. I won't cam for anyone who doesn't have a cam from now on.
Teri: Good boy, now, turn on your cam for me please . . .

CHAPTER NINE

It was a Friday night and I was bored and without my children. I decided to go to my husbands club and have a drink. He was sitting at his usual table with his buddies, the "A" table is what they liked to refer to it as. I called it the "D" table because all the babes with size D cups who would usually surround them. Sitting on my husbands lap was some blonde Barbie with ample boobs and big hair. I approached the "D" table, a bit irritated that Ms Barbie didn't move from my husbands lap.

"What are you doing here?" my husband asked me.

"I thought I'd come have dinner and a few drinks. Maybe sing some karaoke. What's up guys?" I asked his friends who were sitting with Barbie's of their own.

"Hi Teri, you look gorgeous. It's hard to trim a perfect rose. Get off his lap, show some respect to his wife here Jennifer," one of his friends said. Barbie girl jumped off my husbands lap as he slapped her butt. His friend pulled up a chair for me to sit in next to my husband. Really, I was used to seeing this, as well as my husband give "kisses" to his customers. It never got easier to view, but something I'd seen a thousand times. "Good customer relations" he would call it. I called it "bullshit."

"I need a drink! What ya got in this place?" I asked my husband. He threw me a look that wasn't favorable. "Did you eat yet? Are you hungry?" I asked him.

"No. We can order dinner. Hey, my wife needs a cocktail here! Ordering!" he screamed to the waitress. I hated it when they did this, it was so rude. He and his buddies would scream their orders to the help as if they were the only ones who mattered. "Do you need smokes baby?" he asked me. I wondered as to why he was being nice to me all of a sudden.

"No, I'm good thanks. How was your day?" I asked my husband as I lit up a cigarette. His buddies started to laugh.

"I bought a new bar. I need you to design it," he said to me. I choked on my cigarette.

"Excuse me? What did you say? You didn't tell me you were thinking of purchasing a new club. Is this wise? Why would you not tell me this?"

"Don't get negative on me. I don't need this from you. Don't design it then. Just sit back and do nothing. I got it under control." I glanced around and his friends were staring at me, grinning.

"No, I will help you design it. I just don't know why you didn't tell me. This is a big deal."

"Just drink your cocktail and enjoy life." I drank my cocktail and another one and four more after that. But I wasn't enjoying life.

Between Alex, Adam, and Jason, I had little time to log onto the Cheaters Club site. Alex and Adam would only be online in the evenings, and depending on Jason's schedule, he would be on some mornings and afternoons. But it was never an easy thing for me when they were all three online at the same time. I had to juggle them, and they all wanted my cam, so I would have to spend an hour or so with each one individually—with the exception of Alex, that is. When Alex would come online, I would always say my goodbyes to anyone I was chatting with. Adam was the one who made me laugh the most, and Jason was the most sexy and attractive. But there was something about Alex that drew him to my attention. The good thing was that he would only go online about two nights a week, so I would be able to spend time with the others on the nights he was absent. It was getting trickier for me to make up reasons to why I was always online. My husband was becoming more suspicious, and the false gambling addiction was wearing thin. I promised him that I would limit my spending, and he left me alone, well for a while.

Paul called me, wanting to meet for a drink at this place downtown. I arrived early, at around four o'clock, and ordered a cocktail. I brought my laptop with me and logged onto the Cheaters Club site to check messages. Kyle was online and started to chat with me. He was someone that I had been chatting with for a while now, and he lived in Maine and was thirty—two years old. Kyle was a pilot for a freight airline, another exception to my no pilot or architect rule yet worthy of the exception. He was stocky and muscular, with blue eyes and blond hair which was cut in a buzz cut similar to Jason's. Kyle was ex military, and that was where he learned to fly, and he looked every part an ex-Navy boy.

Cheaters Club Chat:

Kyle:	Hi sexy, I was hoping you would be online today, I have a surprise
Teri:	Oh yeah, what's that?
Kyle:	I'm in town today, and I was going to let you know but you changed your Yahoo addy and I couldn't get in touch with you, did you get the message I left here for you? It said I would be here today.
Teri:	Oh no, I haven't logged in for awhile. I had a few stalkers so I had to change my Yahoo addy and forgot to tell you! You are in Utah now? Where are you at?

Kyle:	I'm staying at the Marriot in Salt Lake City, wanted to meet up with you. I have my captain with me though if that's okay
Teri:	Wow, okay, I wish I had known, tell you what . . . . Can you meet me at this club later? I have things to do now but if you would like to meet there and bring your captain we can have dinner.
Kyle:	Okay great, but we should decide now what to tell him. How did we meet?
Teri:	You are an online stud who seeks out women to have cam sex with and you seduced me into chatting with you, you man whore.
Kyle:	Ha-ha that's really funny Teri, but really, what should we tell him?
Teri:	Tell him that I'm a friend of your cousin who lives in New York and we all went out one night when you were there. Tell him I told you that I would take you out if you ever came to Utah. It's not that hard babe.
Kyle:	But I don't have a cousin who lives in . . . .
Teri:	KYLE!
Kyle:	How's seven o'clock then?
Teri:	Works for me, see you then stranger

Kyle had purchased a cam about a month ago, and I had cammed with him on one occasion. He was incredibly sexy and very shy, which I found appealing and intoxicating. He would display a subtle shyness on cam, not to be confused with insecurity, which he was not. Kyle grew up in the South and was truly a Southern boy, exhibiting all of the characteristics of what you would expect to see in true S outhern boys. I never really intended to ever really meet him in person. We talked about it a few times, yet Kyle was never a focus for me like Will was, I really wanted to meet Will.

Paul would be here any minute, so I decided to log off and try to figure out what to say to him so that he would leave before Kyle got here. I called my husband, telling him I had late appointments in Salt Lake and might go to a movie later with a friend.

"Hey, you," I said to Paul as he walked in.

"Hi, Teri, you really look good." I did look good that day in my jeans and a tight lacy blouse "I have missed you."

"Missed you too, babe," I lied. "Are you hungry at all? I ordered you a mai tai. They are strong, so take it easy, bad boy." Paul didn't like to drink much, and I wondered why I had ordered him such a strong drink. I definitely didn't want him to get too tipsy, or he wouldn't want to leave when I needed him to.

"No, I'm not hungry. But order something if you are. I just can't stay too long tonight. We have friends coming for dinner. I just found out right before I got here."

"Oh, that's okay," I said as I imposed a rather disappointed look upon my face. "When do you have to go then?"

"Not until seven, so I have some time," he said while sipping his mai tai and squinting his eyes a bit after tasting it. I needed to think of something to get him to leave before seven. I went to the bathroom and called my best friend, Charlotte. She had covered for me in the past and had been urging me to leave my husband for years, now knowing the extent of my unhappiness.

"Shar . . . you have to do me a favor. Call me in like ten minutes and tell me that you need me that you need me to come to your house 'cause you are breaking up with Duke." Duke was a chick. Charlotte decided several years ago that after a long string of abusive relationships with men, she was going to switch teams. I often wondered if she missed men—well certain parts of men, that is, but never asked her. I was more building up the courage to ask about the lesbian thing, which intrigued me to know.

"What and who are you doing now?"

"Paul, and I'm not *doing* him, I want to do someone else actually, so can you help me out?"

"Teri, I hope you are making them wear condoms . . . hooker."

"Shar! Mom! This isn't the time for lectures, sweetie, but YES I am being safe."

"Good. Okay then, I will call you here in a few minutes."

"Better make it like thirty minutes. I don't want him getting suspicious."

Charlotte called, and Paul believed that I had to go. He walked me to my truck and kissed me a quick good—bye as you would a friend. I drove around the block and then went back into the bar. It was almost seven, and Kyle would be here anytime.

I recognized him immediately when he walked in, and he was wearing shorts and a button-down shirt. His captain was in his late fifties or early sixties, and not the happiest of fellows. He was a frowner, the type that you tried to avoid when you could because they just suck the life out of you. I sat next to Kyle and across from his captain. It would take some effort, but I eventually landed some smiles on the grumpy captain and won him over. All the while Kyle sat there, stealing glances at me and turning away when I would look at him. This boy was shy beyond what had I originally thought. I knew that he liked me—women can just tell these things, but I found it easier to reel in the attention of the captain more than Kyle. He was bolder with his chats online, probably because it's easier to be when the person is not actually in the room with you. It's easier to say things that you wouldn't say in person.

The music started, and it was too loud for the captain, so we decided to go to the lounge at the hotel they were staying. After we had several drinks, the captain went to his room. Kyle invited me up to his room, and it surprised me to how bold he was in doing this. I realized that he was holding back only on the captain's behalf.

The room was cold. He had left the air conditioning running, so I grabbed the extra blanket out of the closet and wrapped it around me.

"You don't need that to keep you warm," Kyle said to me as he slipped the blanket off my shoulders as he kissed one shoulder softly. He turned me around and wrapped his arms around my waist and started to kiss the back of my shoulders and neck. This felt divine, and I was no longer feeling cold in his arms. His hands felt warm on my stomach as they found their way to my breasts. I leaned my head back, resting it on his chest as he fondled me until I slowly turned around, grabbing him gently by the by the belt loops on his shorts and pulling him close to me.

I looked into his eyes to see if he would falter, but instead he brushed my lips with his finger and pressed his lips to mine as he kissed me for the first time. I looked into his eyes once more, and still he did not falter. I lifted my blouse over my head to remove it and wrapped it around his neck, slowly pulling him toward the bed with the leash I created with my blouse. The next time he would kiss me I would respond to his kiss with all the passion that I had within me which would lead to a night of sweet lust.

I wondered on the drive home that night why it was that I could do what I did and still look at myself in the mirror. Who was I? Who was this girl that I had become? I wasn't at all sure that I liked this bad girl, but I did know that for the first time in years, I felt alive again, whoever it was that I called "me" now.

A few days later, I would find myself setting up yet another new meeting with a local guy who was single. He had been chatting with me for months now, and I avoided meeting him for several reasons. The first reason was that he was single, and that was a rule that I had established—to not meet with singles. Another reason was his age—he was thirty-nine, and that was older than I preferred them to be. Lastly, in his photos, he wasn't my type. In one photo, he was standing next to a Disney character at Disneyland, looking rather dorky. He was semiattractive, but he worked out and had an amazing body. Ryan was visiting his family in Atlanta, and I found myself craving a meeting, so I settled by agreeing to meet him, breaking my "no single" rule. I met him at a restaurant for lunch, and I was pleasantly surprised that he was just a tiny bit more attractive than in his photos.

"I am free during the days if I were to start an affair with you," he said to me. "W hat is your time like during the day? Are you flexible?"

I didn't know how, or even *if*, I wanted to answer this, feeling as if I was on a job interview and not wanting to give any kind of impression that I was interested in starting an affair with him.

"My days vary, really, but no, I don't have lots of free time," I lied. I tried not to stare at the white crusty stuff that had gathered and settled at both corners of his lips. My salad didn't look that great to me anymore, so I pushed it away and took another sip of my wine.

"Can you get away then in the evenings? Would that work out better for you? I can meet you in the evenings too." He said as the white stuff around his mouth appeared to be growing larger with every minute. I found myself wiping the corners of my own mouth and had to stop myself from doing this. It reminded me of one of my earlier meetings with this guy who was extremely hot and young, but when he talked, there would be a string of thick saliva between his lips when he spoke. It was just disgusting and wrong, with that date ending in the same handshake that this date would as well.

"No way, there is no way I can get away in the evenings," I said without it being a lie. If I ever did get out in the evenings, I was usually home by eight o'clock, and that was pushing it. There were some occasions as with Kyle that I could be home later, using the "movie excuse," and I only saved that one for a few.

"Then when are we going to meet?"

I never did answer this question and quickly changed the subject. He walked me to my car, and I shook his hand, thanking him for lunch. These meetings were losing the nostalgia from what they were in the beginning. I was starting to wonder if the risk was worth meeting the local guys anymore. Local guys proved to be disappointing since Paul and Ryan.

Jason had just returned from the shore house that he and some friends rented for the summer. Jason was single and without a girlfriend, but that didn' t seem to bother me because he lived two thousand miles away, and it was actually a nice change that he could text me or call me in the evenings and weekends, unlike the married guys. He had more time for me than Paul and Ryan, and I was becoming more needy lately, requiring more attention, for a reason I didn' t know at this time. I would figure it out much later when I would finally seek help.

It had been two days since I last chatted with him online, but we had texted on the phone back and forth for those few days. I was astonished that I would find myself excited now that he was home and could be online. It was sometime in the afternoon that he logged in and I received a request to view his cam. I immediately accepted the invitation, and when he appeared, he was in the same position that I was accustomed to seeing him, lying in his bed without a shirt.

The first thing that I noticed was that he was sporting a deeper tan. It was a good thing that I was on my desktop where I did not have a cam because he would have noticed that when I viewed him, the expression on my face probably read "I missed you"

Yahoo Chat:

Teri: Did you have fun?

I asked this hoping that he would say he had a horrible time hanging out with his buddies and all the young girls in bikinis and that he missed me terribly, but instead:

Jason: Yes I did
Teri: Good then, glad you are back. Summer has passed by too quickly
Jason: Yes it has.
Teri: September is almost here and it's really my favorite month of the year. It is so amazing here in September
Jason: It is?
Teri: Yes, when I was based here as a Flight Attendant I had never been to Utah before but when the plane touched the ground for the first time, it felt like home to me and I knew I would never leave, and that was in the month of September many years ago.

I rambled this. It was easy for me to do this with him because he would listen to me ramble about anything and always seemed to be interested in what it was that I had to say, even it was nothing interesting. What amazed me, however, was that he retained everything that I would say to him, remembering things such as my favorite flower or song that I mentioned in a chat long ago.

I don't remember which one of us mentioned it first, or maybe it was both of us who brought up the possibility of me flying to New York in September to meet. I do know however that once it was mentioned, it didn't take me long to decide that I was going.

Teri: I can come on the sixth which is a Wednesday and come back on Sunday.

I said this looking over my schedule and thinking that maybe I could meet Alex there too.

Jason: That works, I can stay with you Wednesday and Thursday but I have to work on Friday. I can come back to see you on Saturday though.
Teri: That works then; I will hit a play or go out clubbing on Friday then.

I would say this, but I would really be thinking that I would invite Alex to come to New York. We had been talking about meeting there now for a month. I wondered how to tell Jason that he might be coming up and that I would need to spend Friday and Saturday with Alex. I would figure this out if Alex did plan on coming.

Teri: Great, should I book it then?
Jason: Yes, book it. And when I come to your room, be wearing a short skirt.
Teri: Hmm . . . . What if you meet me in the hotel lounge and I'm in a mini skirt without panties and you can sit next to me and . . .
Jason: That I can definitely do. And I'm not going to wait to kiss you. I will walk up to you the first thing I will do is kiss you and slide my fingers into you.

With just these words, I would find that I wanted him so badly right at that moment. Just one mention of him telling me what he would do to me sent me into this fierce desire for him which I had never experienced with anyone else. The connection that I had with Jason was so powerful in many ways, more so than with anyone before him, and I wondered if he felt it as well.

Teri: Have you been with an older woman babe?
Jason: Yes I have, but it wasn't good.
Teri: How old was she?
Jason: Forty eight and she didn't look that great.
Teri: Wow, that's not good. Was the sex good at least?
Jason: No it wasn't. One of my buddies told me that I needed to be with an older woman because they can teach you a lot, but it wasn't good with her.
Teri: I bet I can teach you a thing or two, and you won't want "girls" after this.
Jason: Oh really? What would you teach me?

He asked this with a look of amusement on his face.

Teri: Depends on what you already know.
Jason: Give me an example then.

He was not going to let me get out of explaining to him what I just claimed to be able to do.

Teri: Okay, have you ever had someone get on all fours and grab their ankles as you locked their hands behind their back and inserted a piece of ice in them and took them from behind?

Jason:	No that I have never done. What else would you teach me?
Teri:	How about I teach you the way I like to be touched. We can start with that. And take notes too, I hate to repeat myself. You seem to be a quick study though.
Jason:	I am and I won't need to take any notes.
Teri:	Good boy then, I just booked my ticket and hotel. It's set. Wow that's only a week away.
Jason:	Yes it is. What are you going to tell your husband?
Teri:	That I'm going to New York

That was exactly what I would tell him, not that he cared. When I thought of this, I became sad for a few seconds before looking up and smiling at the screen in front of me. He looked at me with his beautiful blue eyes, and I knew *it was going to be okay.* I was going to be okay. Everything was going to be okay

Ryan had just got back from Atlanta, and I was supposed to meet him that afternoon. I almost didn't want to tell this to Jason, especially after just booking a flight to go see him in a week, but I decided that I didn't want to start a chain of lies that I had done with Paul. I was determined that I would be honest with these guys, with the exception of Alex, who still did not know that I was chatting with other men. I would find that the *truth* would be something that I would hide from Jason as well very soon, and a crop of countless lies would blossom into something that I would lose control of.

Teri:	Babe, Ryan is back and I'm supposed to meet him here in an hour so I have to go.
Jason:	Where are you meeting him? For lunch you mean?
Teri:	No babe. I'm meeting him at the Hilton.
Jason:	Oh. Okay.

The look on his face told me he was not okay with it. I instantly regretted telling him, but it was too late. I should have known it would bother him to know this. It would bother me to know if he were going to be with someone. Neither Paul nor Ryan saw anyone else but me; however, it would not have bothered me if they had. The thought of Jason being with someone else, however, put a knot in my stomach. I instantly felt like the biggest ass.

Jason:	Don't go babe. Stay with me here. Don't do this.

I wanted to stay with him, I really did, but I knew that I could not cancel on Ryan this late without upsetting him. I had to decide what was more important—to not hurt Jason or not to upset Ryan. They were both important to me, and I hated to have to make a decision *Ryan is my local guy*, I thought. He was someone I trusted and who cared for me, and he was also *here*. I trusted Jason as well, and I did feel as if he was starting to care about me, but the bottom line was he was not here, and Ryan was. If only he lived closer.

Teri: Babe, I have to go. He won't understand if I cancel on him this late. Listen, I will only be a few hours.

Jason: Call me when you are on your way then.

That was the most awkward call. I was talking to Jason the whole time I was driving to meet Ryan, and he was well aware of what I would be doing in the hours to come.

"I'm here babe, I need to go in."

"Okay, I will talk to you later." Disappointment was clearly heard in the tone of his voice, making me feel like the biggest ass in the world. I didn't want to go in, and I wanted to turn my truck around and go home, but I said good-bye to him.

"I will call you later, okay?"

"Sure."

The next time Jason would cross my mind would be when I called him on the way home several hours later. I didn't think of him when I was with Ryan, but he was the first thought that came to mind as I left that room. I envisioned him in his bed without his shirt as I last seen him and wondered what his touch felt like and how his kisses would taste. In one week, I would know this, and this would be the first time of many times to come that I would think to myself, *How many days until I see him? That seems so far away* . . .

CHAPTER TEN

September '06

"Yay! Is it pusghetti night?" my youngest son asked as he came into the kitchen dripping wet from being in the pool.

"It most certainly is pusghetti night, wanna grab the garbage bags and put them on the table for me please?"

"Sure mom," he answered, carefully laying down several large plastic garbage bags on the table.

"Thought today was *around the world* day?" my fourteen year old son asked, seeing his brother do this. Once a month we would go somewhere *around the world* to try a new restaurant.

"Nope, we're going to Thailand next week remember? When the new place opens."

"I don't like Thai food mom, can we visit Japan instead?" he asked.

"Nope, we had sushi the last time, we are always visiting Japan. We go to Thailand next. Go grab your dad and sister please, dinners ready." I asked him as I dumped the pot of very hot spaghetti over the garbage bags on the table. My daughter looked at the large pile of spaghetti that I dumped in the middle of the table and rolled her eyes.

"Can I use a fork this time? Aren't we getting too old for this?

"You know the rules; only daddy gets to use a fork. And no one is ever too old for pusghetti night. Who wants to say the prayer?" I asked as my husband took a seat at the table, tossing a disgusting look at the glob of spaghetti.

"I will mom! Pick me!" my youngest son asked, raising his hand in the air.

"He always gets to say the prayer, no fair," my eldest son said.

"Would you like to say it then?" I asked him.

"No, but he always gets to say it."

"I don't either! You lie!" my youngest son screamed.

"Boy's! Shut up!" my daughter yelled. Before I could scold her my husband was laughing. I didn't see the humor in what she said but I knew not to say anything to him.

"Go ahead baby, say the prayer then please," I told my youngest son as his brother angrily crossed his arms and bowed his head.

"Thank you God for the lovely pile of pusghetti my mom flopped on the table. I hope no kids starve today and that everyone in the world will be happy. Amen."

"Amen," we all repeated after him.

"I have a houseboat lined up for Labor Day weekend. Invited some people to go with us," my husband said as he moved the pile of spaghetti sitting in front of him around with a fork.

"We're hosting a party, remember? I invited people over for a barbeque."

"No, I don't remember that. Well cancel it."

"I don't want to cancel it; it's been planned for weeks now. Why didn't you tell me about this earlier?" I asked him.

My youngest son grabbed another pile of the gooey pasta with both hands and flicked a meatball at his brother, which actually hit my daughter in the chest.

"This is disgusting! I don't want to eat with my fingers and have meatballs thrown at me! I'm done!" she screamed getting up from the table.

"Stop flicking your meatballs baby, its bad table manners," I said to my son as I grabbed a small portion of spaghetti with my fingers and attempted to get it into my mouth.

"Fine, don't cancel it then. Life revolves around Teri. I'm done too. I'm going to the club," my husband said as he got up from the table.

"You didn't eat anything," I said to him.

"I'm not hungry. Bad stomach again."

"You've been having that a lot lately, maybe you should go see the doctor," I told him.

"No, I just need to start enjoying my life. With or without my wife. See you later," he said as he walked out the door. I wondered if my husband was well. Lately he was having problems with his stomach and would not go see a doctor. I'd make an appointment for him and he wouldn't show. He stopped taking his diabetic medicine and I was curious if he had a death wish. *Go enjoy your life baby.* I sadly thought as I heard his truck pull out of the driveway. *However much of it you have left.*

It was Labor Day weekend, and Jason was at the shore house for what would be the last time this summer. He had mentioned something to me about a girl that he had his eye on all summer who would be there. I pretended that this didn' t bother me and reminded myself that I was just with Ryan and he knew about it, wishing now I didn't tell him because I was about to ask him something.

"Babe, how old is she?" I asked, knowing that she was probably close to his age.

"She's twenty-five and a teacher. She has a good job, and I like her, so we will see what happens."

"Can I ask you something? I know that I don't have a right to ask this, but will you not sleep with anyone this weekend? We are meeting next week, and really, I don't want you to be with anyone this weekend." *Where* was this coming from? I had never before displayed any ounce of jealousy or possessiveness with any of those that I saw, and especially with one that I had never met before.

"Okay, I won't then," he said without even bringing up that I was with Ryan recently. He made this promise and he kept it, but one night when he was there, he would call me late at night. He had been out at a bar and admitted to making out with her.

"Did you think of me when you did this?" I asked, not really knowing why I did. I wanted to see how deep in my pocket I had him.

"Honestly, no, Teri, I did not think of you."

"I didn't think of you either when I was with Ryan!" I wanted to say to him but thought better of it.

"You like her lots, don't you? Do you still want me to come there?"

"Yes, come. I do like her, but she's still talking to her ex-boyfriend, and I'm not into games."

"Great, good luck with her then, and I hope it works out between you two," I lied.

"She's close to my age, and you know that one day I want to have kids. Don't you want me to be happy?"

These words stung like a bee. Closer to his age? I would never fit into his world because there would always be the element of age. I did know that he wanted children, and we had talked about this on many occasions. He always asked about my children, which was a topic that I never indulged in with any of the guys that I met or chatted with. I kept my children private, guarded from this other life I led.

The day finally came. This was the day I would meet Jason for the first time. The flight was long, and I found myself wedged between two heavy people, which was no fun when I had to use the restroom. It literally took the guy sitting in the a isle seat plenty of effort to get up and let me out. I felt bad for him when he had to get up for me and decided that I would not have another diet Coke this flight.

We landed at John F. Kennedy Airport at five o'clock, and it would be a forty—five minute cab drive into Manhattan. When I arrived at the hotel and checked into the room, I was not too happy. The room was about fifteen feet square, with a full-size bed that barely fit in the room.

The bathroom was even worse. It housed the tiniest toilet I had ever seen as well as a small pedestal sink and a bathtub that only a child could fit into comfortably. This was so not good. I called the front desk, asking if there were any rooms that were larger and was told I was in the largest room. Jason called me a few minutes later.

"Babe, the room is BAD!" I said in my dramatic way of freaking out.

"How bad?"

"BAD! You will see. This is by far the worst room I have ever stayed in, and I have to be here for four nights! It didn't look at all like this when I booked it online."

"That's not good. Is the shower small?"

"Um, YEAH! It's tiny, so forget what we were going to do in it!"

"It's okay, babe. I'm just glad you are here. No ones has ever traveled to see me."

I needed to tell him that Alex was still possibly coming to see me Friday and Saturday and after he said this I couldn't. Jason knew that Alex might be here that weekend because I told him several days earlier. Alex had taken on more projects at work and this was short notice, but he really did want to come, if at least for just Saturday night. Before I even finished this thought, Jason asked,

"Is he coming then? Because if he's not, I want to come back on Saturday night."

"I won't know until later, but really I doubt that he will be able to come. I told him that I was going to be here at the end of the month originally so that is what he planned on. When are you going to be here?"

"I will be there at about eight o'clock, is that all right?"

"It's perfect. See you at eight then."

It would be a little after seven o'clock when I poured myself a huge shot of tequila. I was so nervous, more so than on any meeting thus far. It was ridiculous that I was since I had virtually either been online camming or on the phone with him every day for almost a month now. I put on a short black miniskirt and blue camisole and poured myself another shot. By the time he would arrive, I would be feeling very buzzed but not drunk.

There was a knock on the door, and my heart jumped. I opened the door, and before I could say hello or get a good look at him, he walked toward me and kissed me before he even dropped his bag. His kiss was forceful yet passionate, leaving me literally breathless. No one had ever kissed me like that, and I felt myself instantly losing control as he pressed his opened mouth to mine, moving his tongue gently in slow circles. He leaned me up against the wall, and his hand moved under my skirt as he slipped his finger inside my panties and slid it inside of me, causing me to softly moan and catch my breath again.

The room seemed to be spinning, and it was not the tequila but the effect that he had on me which had me bewildered. I walked to the bed and sat on the edge, trying to gain some composure. I looked at him closely, and he was everything and more that I knew he would be. He seemed taller in person and not as stocky as he was on cam. His hair was jet black, and his eyes were the most intense shade of navy blue, but it was his mouth that I could not stop looking at. His lips and teeth were perfect, and he had a dimple on his chin that was sexy. As I studied his face for these few seconds, he approached the bed and kissed me again.

He slipped my camisole over my head to remove it as I unzipped my skirt and slid out of it, leaving on only my panties and heels. I reached for his belt and unfastened it. It was as if he were in slow motion as he started to undress himself in front of me. He was transcendent in all of his perfection, unmatched by all those before him. He was so beautiful to me, and I found myself becoming a bit self-conscious of my C-section scar and stretch marks, something that never bothered me to show in the past. I would wear these marks with pride for being a mother.

He didn' t seem to notice or care about this as he pulled my panties off slowly. He moved his head between my legs. As I moaned in pure pleasure, my legs straddled his head, squeezing it and I felt them start to shake, something I never did.

I wanted to feel him inside me, and I could no longer wait to know what he felt like.

"Come here . . ." I said, as it was no more than a whisper

He moved up towards me and kissed. His lips were wet and delicious. I pulled him closer to me, and when he entered me I could feel myself tense from his manhood, which was larger than I had expected it to be. His body inside of mine felt like the uppermost part of heaven, as if it were the very first time. The movements were slow at first, and as they became faster, I came instantly, screaming his name. This did not stop him from continuing in a slower rhythm now.

I rolled over and shifted myself on top of him without him ever slipping out of me, and I straddled him, riding him slowly. I moved my hips in a circular movement, which was slow at first and then becoming faster as I thrust deeper into him. I could feel his body tense and knew that he was close, so I slowed my movements down to a slower thrust. I bend down and kissed his mouth and held his head between my hands, and I started to move my hips faster now. I could no longer wait as I knew I was close, so I arched my back and thrust as deep as I could so that he could not be any deeper inside of me as we both came for the first time together.

I poured myself another shot of tequila and lit up a cigarette. We ordered room service, which was delivered in a brown paper bag. This hotel was bad, and if it were not for the tequila, I would have been more embarrassed by it, but Jason didn' t seem bothered. I logged online to check messages from clients, and up popped several of my guys to say hello on MSN and Yahoo. I should have gone invisible, but it was too late, and he had seen that they were there. I would tell them all good-bye except for one.

"Jase, how do you feel about having sex on cam for one of my guys?" This came out before I even realized what it was I was actually asking. Had I gone mad?

"We can do that if you want."

"Wow, that was easy. Really? This is Chas. He was the first one who introduced me to a cam. I was thinking that it would be really hot if we did this, and I trust him."

Chas watched us on cam as we would go for round two that night, and afterward I turned off the cam, yet the rest of the night left us sleepless and in a state of lust in its purest form.

"OH MY GOD!" I screamed out as I looked at myself in the mirror the following morning. "My eye is red!" A vessel in my left eye had broken, leaving two thirds of it the color of crimson, a color that up until now I considered beautiful. "OH MY GOD!" I repeated, freaking out literally by now. "How did this happen?"

"I don't know," Jason said. "I noticed it last night and mentioned that your eye was red."

"I can't go out like this in public! Does it look bad?"

"Um, yeah, it looks pretty bad," he said without lying as he probably should have done.

"I must have had one hellava orgasm last night."

"Is that what happened?"

"I don't know! I really don't know. I can't look at it, it's making me crazy." I would wear sunglasses for the next two weeks until the redness would fade and my vanity would once again find me as these would be the longest two "ugly" weeks of my life.

We spent Thursday in the city as I never took off my sunglasses, even in the dark lounge that we went to for drinks. Alex started to text me; however, I was becoming agitated with Jason, who was receiving and sending texts to the girl he had made out with at the shore house several days earlier. I panicked as one of Alex's texts came in saying that he would be flying into New York the following day to see me for a few hours. He could not stay the night and was going to meet with a client before he would meet me and have to fly home.

I made a decision right then not to tell Jason that Alex was flying in. This would work, I thought to myself. Jason would leave on Friday morning because he would have to work that night, and then he would come back on Saturday. I could have my cake and eat it too; it was too perfect.

We decided to stay in the room that night and have drinks. Alex called me, so I took the phone into the bathroom so I could talk to him in private.

"I'm so excited to see you, baby," he said.

"I'm excited too, Alex. I just wish you could stay the night."

"In a few weeks we can meet again for the weekend, and I want to take you ice skating and to the Metropolitan Museum." Alex, like Jason, was a hockey player, and he loved the ice, always telling me that he wanted to share the things that he loved with me.

"Let's go to the museum tomorrow. Would you like to meet me there? I can meet you at the airport, and we can ride together." I was getting excited just thinking about it as I remembered the fist photo that I saw of him standing next to a painting in a museum. "I would love to show you the painting by Botticelli that is there, and babe, I told you that I can't skate, remember? I would fall."

"I would catch you if you fell. We can go to the Met tomorrow if you want to. I just want to see you and hold you in my arms."

As we said goodbye, excitement filled within me. I lost track of how long I was in the bathroom and knew I needed to get back to Jason.

"Who was that?" Jason asked.

"Oh it was Adam. He's fighting with his wife. Sorry about that," I lied. "He's been texting me all day. He's not having a good day here."

I wondered if he actually believed this, considering the previous night Adam had called me and Jason talked to him briefly. Would he wonder why I would now hide in the bathroom to talk to him? My lies would catch up with me one day, and there were so many men in my life that I could not even manage to untangle these lies when the time would come. I was in over my head, and even though I realized this, I would move forward with full speed until one day I would crash and burn. Crashing didn't scare me as bad as the thought of stopping what I was doing did. Control over these men was intoxicating to me, even if it meant that I had lost all control over myself.

I lay next to Jason, and he held me in his arms. We fit together like two pieces in a puzzle. Never before had I felt so comfortable in anyone's arms, and for the first time it hit me that I was really starting to fall in love with him. This scared me because I was losing control here. I had to keep my feelings under control and not fall in love with him. It would become a pattern that I would push him away from me emotionally, starting on this night.

He kissed me, and before I knew it, I was lost in his kiss, and all thoughts of pushing him away or Alex coming the next day escaped me. I opened my eyes as I felt him slide inside of me and I started to quaver from his touch. The sex lasted for hours on this night, and when we were finished, what I said next came out of nowhere, surprising even myself.

"I think that I'm starting to fall in love with you, Jase. That's not good, is it?"

"No, it's not at all," he said as I wished I could just sink through the bed and disappear into the cruddy carpet.

Embarrassment turned into animosity within seconds, however, before I said, "Well, I think that you should probably go now. This wasn't a good idea after all."

"What? Why?,"

"Get out of my bed and go."

"Fine. I'm out of here." he said as he got up and started to dress.

Everything in me wanted to pull him back and tell him that I didn't want him to leave, yet instead I added, "And lose my number."

He took out his phone and erased my number right then, and I felt as my heart was going to break right at that moment, but the look I gave him was bitter and cold. I said nothing as he walked out of the room.

It was a very long night, and I found myself lonely, and instead of thinking of Alex, who I would be meeting in only just hours now, I was thinking of how I wished to hear a knock on the door in the hope that Jason would come back.

Friday was sunny and warm, but I felt cold and despondent as I got up from the bed and headed toward the bathroom. I said a silent prayer that my red eye would have vanished or at least transitioned into a shade of pink, yet it was just as red as it had been the previous day.

When I got to the airport, I was surprised at how I was not at all nervous or even very excited anymore to meet Alex in person. The events of the night before played through my mind as I tried to figure out why I had said the things I said to Jason. I would never probably see him again, and I knew that I needed to put myself in a happy mode before I met Alex. I was concentrating really hard to do this when I felt someone tap me on the shoulder.

"Hi, baby! God I'm so glad to be here!" Alex said, and he put his arms around me and drew me closer to kiss me on the cheek. "You look amazing, but you always do." He looked exactly like he did on cam except I never really noticed that he had a bit of a beer belly going on. My Eager Boy was looking more eager now than ever as he smiled hugely, and I realized that it was the demeanor of his gleeful disposition that drew me to him and that I found to be so sexy.

"Hey, you, you scared me! I'm glad you are here as well. Should we get going? When is your appointment with the frozen chicken guys?" Alex was working on a marketing contract for a frozen chicken company. The month before, it was a baby blanket product that had taken him to England to stage. He was young and ambitious, with much drive for many things in life, including his work, which I held much admiration for.

"Not for hours still, so we are okay. Teri, let's just go to your hotel. W e can always visit the Metropolitan in a few weeks."

"Alex, really, let's just go to the Met today."

"What's wrong, baby? We've been waiting a long time to be together. I want you, you know that."

I did know this, and up until a few nights ago, I thought that I wanted him as well, and as he stood before me, I realized that I couldn't take him back to my room, the room that Jason had been only several hours ago.

"This is really embarrassing, but it's that time of the month, and . . ." I said very convincingly as I looked down, faking my best bashful performance.

"Oh. It's okay. That doesn't bother me, but if you are uncomfortable with it, I understand."

"I'm very uncomfortable with it. That's something that I never do, it's gross."

On the way to the museum, he talked nonstop, as he always did, and my phone beeped, letting me know that I had an incoming text message. My heart stopped for a moment as I hoped it would be Jason until I remembered that he erased my number from his phone. It was Ryan, asking me how my day was going. Alex still did not know that I had other "bulls," so I decided not to respond to Ryan's text and closed my phone. The museum was busy that day, and we walked around as I showed him my favorite paintings and explained the iconography behind them. I was excited to see that he was interested in art, and he held fast to every word as I explained the symbology of the different works.

"Baby, we are inside now, why are you still wearing sunglasses?" I didn' t tell him that the vessel in my eye had burst, and I had forgotten that I was still wearing my glasses. "Let me see you, take them off."

"Alex, I can't. I broke a vessel in my left eye, and it's so red and ugly, you really don't want to see it, trust me."

"Take off your glasses. I don't care about your eye. Let me see you, baby," He didn't get his way. There was no way I was going to take them off, and after ten minutes of trying to persuade me, he gave up.

"You're a stubborn girl."

"Not me. There is not a stubborn bone in my body," I said, batting eyelashes that he could not see, but I did it anyways. "I'm just vain. You're the Taurus. You are the stubborn one, Alex."

When it was time for him to leave, I walked him to the front door of the museum. I was grateful that it was busy with little children everywhere so that he could only just hug me and kiss my cheek.

"I'm looking forward to seeing what's behind those glasses and what's under . . ." he said as he traced his fingers over the neckline of my shirt. "Can you meet me here in two weeks like we planned originally?"

"I'll try to. I have to think of why I will be coming back in two weeks. Let me see what I can do."

"I will call you tomorrow, baby. I really am glad I got to see you today. I wish I didn' t have to leave you right now. I will see you in a few weeks then."

"Yes you will. Oh, and good luck with the chicken guys," I said, and as I watched him walk away, I knew that I wouldn't see him in two weeks. I knew I would never see him again.

I should be out tonight. It's Friday, and I'm in the city, I thought to myself as I settled onto the lumpy mattress pad in my hotel room. I poured a huge shot of tequila and logged online. Chas was there.

MSN Chat:

Chas:	How's my sexy girl tonight?
Teri:	Not good Chas
Chas:	Is he still there?
Teri:	Jason? Nope. He left me last night.
Chas:	He did? Why?
Teri:	I don't know babe, he got mad and left.
Chas:	Why did he get mad?
Teri:	Who knows? He's a hot head.
Chas:	What a dumbass. I'm sorry baby, I wish I was there, I wouldn' t leave you. Do you want to cam tonight?
Teri:	Not tonight babe, I'm really not in the mood.
Chas:	One day I'm going to marry you . . . . you're a goddess . . . .

This was the standard "Chas line." He always told me this when he knew I was down. My Orlando Bloom look-alike tended to be overly nostalgic for being twenty-five years old, yet he was an artist, so it made sense.

Teri:	Naw, you don't want to marry me, I snore. Whatcha working on now?
Chas:	I'm sketching a scabia in charcoal
Teri:	What the hell is a scabia?
Chas:	It's a lamb's ear
Teri:	Never heard of a scabia, you're such a weirdo.
Chas:	That's because I made it up. It's just a lamb's ear.
Teri:	You scare me baby.

I chatted with several of my bulls that night, giving them my sob story of how I was abandoned by Jason, gaining the sympathy I intended to from them. I drank tequila, played a Nirvana CD and listened to the somber songs of a ghost. I played it over and over until I was numb and my pain left me. My pain would leave me alone with myself, numb and empty in this moment.

The following morning, I would get up and log online again, this time logging onto the Cheaters Club site to find a date on this last night I was here. I started to chat with many local guys in New York, and it was extremely easy for me to find three dates for that night in only an hour. Before I chose to commit to one, I had an incoming bull waiting to chat. My heart jumped when I saw that it was Jason.

Cheaters Club Chat:

Jason:	Hi Teri, do you hate me?
Teri:	Nope, not at all.
Jason:	Good. What are you doing?
Teri:	I'm looking for a date tonight actually.
Jason :	You are? Have you found one?
Teri:	A few, but I don't know if I will meet any of them, I'm going to see a play and it may be too late to meet up with anyone afterward.
Jason:	Okay. How did I do in my lessons? Did I pass?
Teri:	You did okay, but you haven't graduated yet I would have to say. There are a few things that I didn't get to teach you.
Jason:	Such as?
Teri:	Guess you will never know unless you come back.

There was nothing that I needed to teach him I just wanted to see him again before I left. I manipulated the conversation, making him want to know what was left for him to "learn" until he suggested that he come back to see me that night. He would come by after my play, so I told the other bulls that I could not see them.

I lit several candles and turned out the lights so that in this lighting my red eye was not very noticeable, gaining me the confidence that I needed. It was about eleven o' clock that night when I heard him at the door. The second he came in, I could not contain myself as I kissed him immediately, realizing how I had missed him and thankful that we would have just one more night together, a night of "firsts" for both of us.

We didn't speak a word as we tumbled onto the bed, never releasing our embrace or kiss. I wanted him more than I had ever wanted anyone, and my passion ran wild, casting me into a dreamlike spell that I never wanted to wake up from.

I struggled to gain composure back, aspiring to be the teacher that I had set out to be. I claimed control by rolling on top of him and undressing him slowly, kissing his body as I did this. His skin was soft and moist as my tongue traveled to his most private parts and his taste was sweet. This would be the first time that I would succumb to swallowing as he unleashed his semen deep into my throat. I thought that I would gag, yet instead I was found it pleasing and gratifying.

He gently rolled me over onto my back as he slid off my panties and positioned himself between my legs. I closed my eyes and moaned quietly as his tongue trailed up and down my inner thighs. It felt divine, yet I remembered I was supposed to be tutoring him so I suggested to him certain pressures. I needed to feel him inside of me, and as I pulled him up to me, he was hard again.

As he entered me, I came instantly for the second time in only minutes. I wondered now if he was the "teacher," gliding effortlessly in and out of me as if this was a dance that he had mastered He would remain inside of me as we finished and rolled over onto our sides facing one another.

"How did I do?" he asked me.

"You are amazing. Consider yourself graduated. Although . . ."

"Although what?"

"Never mind, you did really good."

"No, tell me. I won't be upset or angry, Teri. That's why I came back—so you could teach me what I don't know," he said, and I knew that he was sincere in saying this. I, on the other hand, was not as sincere in my reply as I needed to assume the control I believed I was losing with him.

"You could work on your oral technique some. You aren't really very good at it, babe. I'm sorry, I don't mean to sound harsh here." Everything about the "evil" I had written so long ago for my final paper passed through my mind, flashing its ugliness in my direction.

"Okay, what else?"

"Really that's it. You are great otherwise. You get an A."

Before I knew it, he became hard again as he was still inside of me. I had never known any man to be able to get an erection so quickly after intercourse several times, and then something magical happened in the next hour. It is hard to describe, and Jason and I both would later discuss what it was that happened to us on this night, both of us still not fully understanding it. But I think that I would describe it as "feeling" the instant that one falls in love.

He started to kiss me softly as I could feel him growing inside of me again. I straddled him, moving my hips in only small back-and-forth swaying movements, taking him as deep inside of me as he could go. Holding both of his hands above his head and balancing myself as I did this, I leaned down to kiss him, never closing my eyes. We moved together in a slow rhythm as our lips barely touched, and I could feel his breath on my face. He never closed his eyes, nor did I, as we came together, holding each other so tightly and closely it felt as if we were only one person. On this last night in New York, he had become to me the essence of my being.

CHAPTER ELEVEN

September '06

"Trust me, I will catch you" he said to me as I was stuck up in the tree. I was five years old and my father was annoyed that I had climbed up so high, and that we didn't have a ladder.

"Daddy, don't drop me. Please, don't drop me."

"I won't sweetie, jump. I will catch you." This was the last thing my father said to me before I jumped. I woke up on the sofa with a bump on my head and a small concussion. My father had dropped me.

I dreamt it again. I hated having this dream, I could always feel myself dropping, and it hurt. I woke up with a headache, almost feeling the bump on my head from falling from this tree.

"Wake up mom! Surprise!" my kids screamed as they came into my bedroom with a tray of food.

"Is it my birthday? No, what's this for guys?"

"Cause we love you! And you're the best mom in the world!" my youngest son screamed. I grabbed him and pulled him onto the bed with me giving him kisses and tickling his ribs.

"Hmm, what do we have here?" I asked viewing the interesting items sitting before me on the tray. My daughter had created some kind of gooey ice cream dish with gummy worms and candy sprinkles. My eldest son made scrambled eggs, smothered in ketchup with what appeared to be parsley flakes sprinkled heavily on top. My youngest son who was creative like me made some sort of sandwich consisting of mini hot dogs, tomatoes and pickles "This looks fabulicious. I love you guys! Thanks!" I said taking huge bites of each dish, acting as if it were the best food I had ever tasted and making "yummy" noises.

Somewhere between bites I started to cry.

"What's the matter mom?" my eldest son asked me. My daughter moved closer to me and wrapped her arm around my shoulder.

"You guys are my world. You bring me so much happiness. I'd be lost without you. I love you so very much. Come here." I gave each of them hugs, embracing them as I cried tears of joy and tears of sorrow. My children were everything to me, yet I could not stop myself from self destructing. And for the first time, I felt truly afraid.

It would be another month before I would see Jason again, and even though I realized what I had begun to feel for him was real, I found myself still searching for something. I logged online to the Cheaters Club site one night after I got back from New York. It was late and a slow night, with not too many hot bulls online, so I was about to log off when I decided to check out just one more incoming bull.

Dickboy1 was twenty—five and from New Hampshire. In the photo he posted, he was sucking on a red Popsicle. His hair was dark and wavy, and he had dark brown eyes. This photo was taken outside as he posed looking away in a forty-five—degree angle, sucking on the melting Popsicle dripping onto his naked chest. He looked more delicious than the Popsicle that had stained his full lips my new favorite shade of red.

Dickboy1:	Hey sexy
Sassy:	Hi sexy boy . . . I wanna lick your Popsicle . . .
Dickboy1:	Lol! Is that all you want to lick?
Sassy:	Oh no, that's just a start.
Dickboy1:	So CUM here and I will share my pop with you!
Sassy:	Are you sure? I eat twenty two year olds for breakfast, twenty three year olds for lunch, twenty four year olds for dinner, but save twenty five year olds for desert and then some . . .
Dickboy1:	Oh really? Should I be afraid?
Sassy:	Yes, I'm the kind of girl your Mother warned you about, so proceed at your own risk . . .
Dickboy1:	Damn! Do you have MSN? You are damn sexy, do you know that?
Sassy:	Yes I am. Here's my MSN addy if you want it.
Dickboy1:	Are you there now? I will add you, hold on.

Popsicle Boy and I chatted on MSN, and I found out that he was from London and new to the S tates. He claimed to have an accent, and he invited me to hear his voice, so we turned on the MSN voice messenger.

MSN VOICE:

Popsicle Boy: Can you hear me, Teri?

His accent was thick and British, yet he sounded older than twenty-five to me, but it was probably the connection here, I figured.

Teri: I hear you! This is cool. I have never used this feature. Say something for me, say "Hi, you sexy sweet thing."

Popsicle Boy: Hi, you super sexy sweet thing, you make my Popsicle melt.

Teri: YUM! You have a sexy voice! I love it! Did I mention that I have a thing for Hugh Grant? He's not a manly man, more like a sexy dork, but his accent makes me crazy.

Popsicle Boy: That old fart? He's a dried-up crumpet.

Teri: Don't be mean to my Hughie . . . that's not nice. I'd butter up his crumpet any day.

He laughs

Popsicle Boy: Okay, my puppet, I will be nice to your Hughie. Anything for you.

Popsicle Boy seemed very mature for his age, and he made me laugh. I liked his British humor, and I agreed to meet him online the following night, hoping that Jason would have to work that night. I could tell he was starting to get irritated when I chatted with other guys while chatting with him, even though he never came out and said this.

I ordered takeout that night for the kids as I did almost every night lately. It had been weeks since I cooked a real meal for my family I had become someone who they didn't recognize or probably didn't even like much. My daughter was becoming suspicious of my behavior. We lay out by the pool while we waited for the dinner to be delivered.

"Mom, you are acting really weird. Are you going through a midlife crisis?"

She was only fifteen, but older than her years. She was brought up Mormon by her father, holding strong to her values with an immense faith. My mother would always say to me when I would give her problems growing up, "I hope you have a daughter one day and she is just like you!" I thank the good Lord that I was blessed with a daughter who would grow to be nothing like me.

"Naw, I'm way too young to be going through a midlife crisis, sweetie. Mommy's just tired, that's all. I am burnt out from working so hard last year."

"Mom, you are different. That's not it. You are always on the computer, and you text more than I do! And I'm a teenager, they say we're text monters . . ."

I knew that everything she was saying was true, and I had to turn my head from her as not to let her know that I realized this.

"Wonder if our food is here. Didn't you say that your friend was coming over tonight? What is his name? Jacob?"

"You're changing the subject, Mom, and his name is Josh. Yeah, he's coming over. Mom, can you like go inside when he comes?"

"Oh I see, you don't want your mom hanging out with you and your buddy. I'm not cool enough, huh?"

"Ummm, it's more like your bikini is like . . . skimpy? Just cover up and go inside when he gets here, okay? And don't try to be funny and tell one of your stupid jokes again. It's so embarrassing when you do that."

"Okay, but can I crank the music and sing?"

"Mom . . ."

"Kidding, I was just kidding. Mellow out, Sis, I won't embarrass you. I will even go put on a nice floral print prairie dress and bake cookies for dessert." I said with a wink.

"Now I know you are going crazy."

I had become one of those mothers I used to heavily judge. A mother who was selfish, who didn't pay enough attention to her children. My heart hurt as I thought of myself as one of these mothers, always striving to be the best mother to my children. I decided that from now on, when they were with me, I would not go online until they were asleep. That I would start to make meals again, and that no matter how unhappy my marriage was or who this wicked person was that I had become, my children deserved the mother they once had.

Later that night, after my children were asleep, I logged online Jason logged online, and I had the most exciting idea that I wanted to share with him. I didn't know what his reaction would be, but I decided that I would just come out and ask him.

MSN Chat:

Teri:	Babe, have you ever had a threesome?
Jason:	Umm, no. Why?
Teri:	Would you want to?
Jason:	Do you mean female/male/female or male/female/male?
Teri:	m/f/m
Jason:	Where are you going with this? Are you asking me if I would fuck you with some other guy?
Teri:	Yes, would you?
Jason:	Honestly Teri, I don't think so.
Teri:	Why not?
Jason:	Babe, I just don't think I would want to.
Teri:	You wouldn't do it at all? Or just not with me.
Jason:	Not with you. You aren't the Eiffel tower type.
Teri:	What the hell is that?
Jason:	It's when a girl is standing between two guys and they give each other a high five.
Teri:	That's not right . . . . you are right, I'm not an Eiffel girl.

Jason:	No you aren't.
Teri:	Is it because it would be hard for you to see me with another guy as well?
Jason:	Honestly, I don't think I would want to see you with another guy babe. I'd probably want to punch him.
Teri:	Fair enough. So what about a girl? Would you be with me and a girl?
Jason:	Let me think . . . ummmmm . . . YES
Teri:	I have never been with a girl before. Really I don't know what I would be able to do with her . . .
Jason:	Do you want to be with a girl? And let's think about this here, what would you allow me to do with her?
Teri:	I think I would want to experience that yes . . . and really I don't know what I would feel comfortable with you doing
Jason:	We should determine what the rules are before we venture into this.
Teri:	You can't sleep with her.
Jason:	Then what would you allow me to do with her?
Teri:	Nothing
Jason:	Um, ok . . . that sounds like lots of fun
Teri:	Okay, how about you can go down on her, but you can't have sex with her or you can't kiss her
Jason:	I can't kiss her?
Teri:	Nope
Jason:	Okay, but why?
Teri:	Kissing is too . . . Intimate
Jason:	How so?
Teri:	You can fall in love with just a kiss . . .
Jason:	Okay, so I can't kiss her or do her but I can go down on her and can she go down on me?
Teri:	Yes, she can

After we established our agreed rules, I logged onto the Cheaters Club and created a "couples profile" seeking women. I downloaded photos of both of us, and the username I came up with was *SweetNasties*. We were ready to catch some "fishies" as I called them. I referred to the women as *fishies* as I had referred to the men as *bulls*.

Teri:	Okay, its ready, do you want to look first or should I?
Jason:	You go ahead
Teri:	Okay, hold on

I logged in and browsed to see who was online. It was strange for me to seek out women. It was different from when I was trying to find them for Tony because I was actually looking for them for myself now. There were many really pretty women on here, and I was surprised by this. I was expecting to see what I called "she-men," but most seemed very feminine. I started to chat with Fishy1, who was thirty-four, from Canada. There were only body shots of her in her photos, but I could see that she had long dark curly hair. She had an amazing figure, and all of a sudden, I felt a bit intimidated. Did I really want Jason to be with someone so hot? Was I crazy? Tomorrow would be the day I would give up cheeseburgers and get my butt on the treadmill, I promised myself. I started the conversation:

SNasties: Hi, how are you tonight?

My hand was shaking as I typed this. I was incredibly nervous, unlike how I was as Designgirl or Sassypants when seeking out *bulls*, when I was probably more overly confident than I should have been.

Fishy1:   Hello, I'm good thank you, how are you?
SNasties: Good as well, just joined here tonight, so we are new.
Fishy1:   We?
SNasties: Yes, me and my boy friend, we are a couple. Is that a problem?
Fishy1:   I don't do guys. But he can watch us
SNasties: Fair enough

I messaged Jason to let him know that I had hooked our first fish.

Teri: Babe, I hooked a fishy
Jason: Who is she? How old is she?
Teri: She's thirty four and from Canada, she's really pretty, well, she has a killer body, I don't know what her face looks like.
Jason: Are you sure you want to do this?
Teri: No, but its fun fishing
Jason: Does she know that we are a couple?
Teri: Well, yes I told her
Jason: Did she say anything about me?
Teri: Well, she doesn't do guys. She said you can watch. (I insert a frown face)
Jason: Oh, okay. Who else is there? Are you chatting with anyone else?
Teri: No, just Lori, that's her name. She wants my MSN, what do you think?
Jason: That's up to you babe, give it to her if you want to.

So I did give Lori my MSN addy, and it would only be weeks later that I wished that I hadn't. Lori would become the worst kind of "guy," always requesting my cam. There weren't many fishies online that night, unlike the hundreds of bulls that were always online, so I logged off.

Teri:	Why don't you go look tomorrow and request some keys?
Jason:	I can do that
Teri:	Just make sure they aren't ugly fatty's babe; I don't do ugly fatty guys so I wouldn't do an ugly girl
Jason:	Teri, I don't do ugly, fat girls either, relax.
Teri:	Okay, just making sure. Wanna play a game of Literary? Can you not kick my ass so badly this time?

He kicked my ass badly, but I would get the best kind of booby prize afterward when he would turn on his cam for me. I loved watching him on cam, and I missed him terribly. After we would cam that night, I knew that I needed to arrange our next meeting, so we decided it would be the nineteenth of October.

Teri:	That's so long away babe.
Jason:	Its not that far, it's only a month
Teri:	It's going to be a very long month
Jason:	It will go by quickly babe.

I knew that I would probably not make it a month without seeing Ryan, but I didn't want to think about that. All I knew was that I was wishing away the days until I would be in Jason' s arms again. Something that I dreamed about almost every night. And I dreamed about it on this night too.

I woke up and my husband was still home. He didn't go to work.

"What's up? Why are you home? Are you feeling alright?" I asked him.

"I'm going out of town for a few days with the boys. A Harley ride. Can you pack me an overnight bag?"

"Who you goin with?"

"The boy's."

"Are they bringing their wives or girlfriends?"

"Don't know. Pack a bag for me? We want to get out of here soon. I thought you were going to book the trip for us in Cabo, what ever happened to that? Do it today before it gets too late." He had been asking me to book this trip for a month now. The thought of not having my computer for a week was frightening. What was even more frightening to me was spending a week with my husband. I shuttered at the thought. I knew I wouldn' t book the trip.

"You don't know if any women are going?"

"Baby! Don't do this now! Just pack me a bag okay? We need to get on the road." I complied with my husbands orders and wondered who was going on this road trip with him. I didn' t really care actually, I was glad that I would have the house to myself for a few days.

Popsicle Boy was online the following evening as he said he would be. Jason was working, so it was perfect. I had started to drink, and I was feeling a bit tipsy and bold.

MSN Chat:

Teri: Wanna play a game with me bad boy?
Popsicle Boy: What kind of game?
Teri: Truth or dare
Popsicle Boy: Sure, sounds like fun
Teri: Okay, you go first, truth or dare?
Popsicle Boy: Truth
Teri: bock, bock, bock, I smell an English chicken here . . .
Popsicle Boy: LOL! I'm no chicken, okay, dare
Teri: Good boy, hmm, let's see . . . do you have a web cam?
Popsicle Boy: No, do you?
Teri: Yep. I do. Okay, do this, go get your camera, and take a picture for me and send it now
Popsicle Boy: Now? Okay, what is it that you want a photo of?

This was like setting me free in my favorite store during a clearance sale. I contemplated asking him for something naughty, but I really wanted to see his face as I pictured him sucking on that red Popsicle.

Teri: I want a picture of your eyes, only you eyes.
Popsicle Boy: Lol! You want a photo of my eyes? I could take one of something much more appealing for you
Teri: Nope, I want your eyes

Minutes later, the e-mail came in. I opened up the photo, and there it was. Only one eye, and it was blue. I sat there perplexed for a minute, thinking back to his photo. Didn't he have brown eyes? I had been drinking, so maybe I was mistaken. I looked at his one blue eye that didn' t really seem at all sexy to me but dismissed it, and it was my turn now.

Teri: My turn. Dare

Popsicle Boy: Well, that was easy. You said you have a cam? Turn it on and show
        me your tits.
Teri: Hmm . . . Okay then

I turned on my cam, and it seemed really weird to be camming for someone who
I could not see as well. I remembered the advice I gave to Jason many weeks ago about
never camming for anyone who does not have a cam. I chose to ignore my own advice,
so I quickly flashed him my boobs for a few seconds and turned off my cam.

Popsicle Boy: OMG! Where did you go? Come back! Don't do that to me . . .
        your tits are perfect!
Teri: I know. Ok, truth or dare?
Popsicle Boy: Truth
Teri: Okay, I dare you to take another picture, this time of your mouth . . .
        Only your mouth.
Popsicle Boy: Lol! Did I say dare? Okay, you win. Hold on

It would be another few minutes before the second e-mail would come in.
I opened it to view a set of thin lips that didn't resemble the one in the photo
covering the tip of the Popsicle. *I must be drunk tonight*, I thought to myself. He
was so much hotter in the other photo.

Popsicle Boy: Did you get it?
Teri: Yes, thank you,
Popsicle Boy: I dare you to turn on your cam and drop your night gown
Teri: Did I say dare?
Popsicle Boy: Bock, bock, bock, do I smell a sexy hen?

I turned my cam on without even responding to his comment. I was wearing
a white eyelet lace baby doll nightgown. I stood up and looked into the cam with
a devious smile as I slowly turned around removed the straps off my shoulders,
allowing the gown to drop slowly to the floor. I stood there for fifteen seconds
before I reached down and gathered my gown and turned the cam off.

Popsicle Boy: No, that wasn't fair! You didn't turn around!
Teri: You didn't say I had too, you asked for me to drop my gown and so
        I did.
Popsicle Boy: Damn! You are a tease!
Teri: Yes I am. Now, I would like for you to take a photo of . . . .
        Hmmm . . . Let's see . . . your whole face this time.

There was no response.

Teri: Hello? Are you still there?
Popsicle Boy: I'm here Love; don't you want a photo of something more?
Teri: No, I want your face.

Minutes went by, and then I received the e-mail. Before I could pull it up, he said, Teri, are you mad?

Teri: Why would I be mad?

Before I typed in the last word, I understood why he said this to me. There before me was a photo of his face. It was not the sweet young Popsicle Boy in the photo. He was in his fifties and heavy. I felt as if I were going to be sick.

Teri: Why? I don't understand?
Popsicle Boy: If I posted a photo of myself tell me, would you really be here with me tonight?
Teri: No, but you robbed me of making that choice for myself. I trusted you. I cammed for you.
Popsicle Boy: I'm truly sorry Teri, I really liked you, you excite me and I haven't felt this way in a long time.
Teri: Where did you get the photo of that guy? Who is he?
Popsicle Boy: I saw him on a MYSPACE page so I took his photo and downloaded it.
Teri: That is so wrong. I never want to hear from you again. Don't you think it's hard enough to be here, and do what we do? I try to keep it as real as I can, but you have deceived me and how many others? How would you feel if I had turned on my cam tonight and I was not who I proclaimed to be? Don't you get it?
Popsicle Boy: Yes, I do, and I promise you I will change that photo out and post one of me. I will be honest and I won't bother you anymore.

I logged off, having had enough fun for the evening; I went to the bathroom and vomited. I wasn't sure if it was the tequila or the fallacy of what just happened, or maybe a combination of both, perhaps. Days later, I would log into the Cheaters Club site and notice that Popsicle Boy's photo was still there in all of his cuteness. Whoever this person really was made me sick, and as I looked at the young guy in the photo sucking on the popsicle, I knew that he was being exposed in the worst way I blocked him from my profile and hoped that whoever he might charm next would be smarter than I was. For the first time, I felt the evilness of this site hovering over me, and for just one brief moment, I considered deleting my profile entirely until a new bull messaged me and I was sucked right back into the hell of it:

Dickboy1:   You are hard to get a hold of! I have been waiting for you to log on. I sent you some messages but never heard from you.

Sassy: Hi, sorry, I get so many of them I really don't respond anymore, no offense.

D1:   I understand. So I'm twenty five, and intelligent and good looking, would you meet me?

Sassy: Lol! Well, I don't meet people blindly, do you have a photo? Not that I'm not taking your word for it.

D1:   I don't have a photo on here, it's not safe. Just meet me and if you don't like me then you can just drive off and I wont take offense.

Sassy: Really, I haven't met anyone new for awhile; I kind of gave up local guys.

D1:   Just meet me for fifteen minutes

Sassy: I will think about it okay?

D1:   You won't be sorry baby; I can rock your world, which is a promise.

He was arrogant and very sure of himself. After a few days of chatting with him, I did agree to meet with him in a vacant parking lot. I allowed myself only fifteen minutes with him, and Jason called me as I was on my way.

"Teri, why are you meeting him? You don't even know who he is," Jason said.

"It's just for fifteen minutes, babe. I guess I'm still addicted to the rush of meeting new guys. I will only stay for fifteen minutes at the most." I could hear the disappointment in his voice as I composed my lame excuses for why I was doing this. I knew that if Jason were local to me I would not meet with anyone new or anyone in any respect. But he wasn't local, and there was a burning desire for me to search for something that I didn't even understand. "I'm here, babe. I have to go. I will call you later, okay?" I said this, feeling guilty that I was meeting this guy. Not because I was married—the guilt was not directed toward my husband, rather Jason. I felt as if I were betraying him in some way.

He got out of his truck and walked over as I unlocked the passenger door so he could get in. He was attractive but looked much younger than twenty—five, sporting a baby face looking more like he was twenty one. He was nicely built, and I could tell that he took care of himself.

"Hi, I'm Teri, are you sure you are twenty-five?" I said with a small laugh.

"Yes, I promise you I am Wow, you are more than I expected you to be."

"Good, glad to hear that. Do I look forty-two?"

"Hell no! You look great for your age. I would have never guessed you are forty-two. So let's go for a drive?"

"Oh, I can't. I told you I only had fifteen minutes, remember?" As I said this, my BGC beeped. I had a text message from Jason. He asked me if I was okay, and I said that I was fine. I told him that I would text him when I was leaving.

"It's really busy here on this road Let's just get into my truck, and we can drive over there in that corner where it is more private." He pointed to the corner of the parking lot, which was only hundreds of yards away. This seemed like a good idea, so I got out of my truck and into his. He started to drive but passed our destination, heading around the vacant building.

"Um, where are you taking us? I thought we're going to park over there?" I said as I started to get a bit nervous and uncomfortable.

"Let's go around the building. It's more private."

"No, let's not. I think you should take me back to my truck now. I have a meeting in thirty minutes."

He ignored my request and parked his truck around the back of the building. He turned off the engine and started to unzip his pants.

"What are you doing? Don't do that," I said with panic in my voice. He reached over and tried to kiss me as I scooted as far away from him as I could. I tried to open the door, but it was locked.

"Let me out now! This isn't funny. I want to go."

"No you don't. Tell me that you aren't attracted to me. I know you are. Don't you want this?" he said as he pulled his penis out of his pants.

"No, I don't want that. I want to GO!" I was freaking out now, and my phone beeped again. It was Jason again, asking how much longer I would be. I decided not to freak him out and tell him that I was anything *but* okay, yet I knew that this was going to be what would save me from this situation.

"Listen, that's my boyfriend again, he knows I'm with you and he knows where we are meeting. He's also a cop. You need to take me back to my truck NOW!"

"Your boyfriend knows you are meeting me? Why would he allow you to do that?"

"Because we had a fight, and I threw this in his face. He knows where we are, and he knows about you. Now please drive me back to my truck, and I will see you later."

"Will you meet me next week?" he asked. I thought for sure he was crazy now. I decided to lie to him so that he would take me back to my truck.

"Yes, I should have more time next week." I lied, praying that I sounded convincing, more so than any other time I had told a lie.

"Don't tell your boyfriend next time."

"I won't," I said with a nervous grin.

He drove me back to my truck and reached over to kiss me, but when he had turned on his engine, I had positioned my hand on the door handle ready to make a quick escape. Before he could move any closer to me, the door was open and I was out.

"Okay, I will be late. I have to go."

"When are we seeing each other next week? Can I get your number?" he asked.

"No, I can't give you my number. Just send me a message on the Cheaters Club site, and we can figure it out then."

"Will you answer my message this time?"

"Of course I will. Got to go. See you later."

I was shaking all the way home. How stupid was I? What I was doing was dangerous, and for the first time I realized how much so. Usually I would meet them for coffee or in a restaurant. I realized that what just happened could have turned into something tragic. I called Jason and told him I was leaving and explained what had happened, thanking him for his texts, which seemed to have saved me. He was angry, and I didn't seem to hear his lecture as I thought silently of the horrid situation I had just put myself in. When I got home, I poured myself a drink to calm my nerves, and the first thing I did when I logged online was block this guy from my profile so that I would never hear from him again. I would just pretend this never, ever happened. It never really happened. The world was a happy place, with happy dancing flowers and pink and yellow skies.

CHAPTER TWELVE

September '06

My husband was having a birthday in a month. I remembered the big deal I made of his last birthday, hiring people to come to our home and staged a "casino" night. I invited sixty of his friends and had it catered. I decided that this year I would just throw him a surprise party at his club, remembering that he did nothing for my birthday and that I had to ask him to come home and take me to sushi. It didn't matter really. I wanted to do something for him, and I loved throwing parties. I made phone calls to his friends and started to plan his party. I didn't know what to get him. What do you buy someone who has everything? A delicious idea came to my mind. What if I learned to do a lap dance for him? What a splendid idea! I only hoped that he would like it because I loved the idea of it. I loved the idea of who I was becoming, someone he couldn' t own anymore.

It had been a little over a week since I had come back from New York after meeting Jason. Ryan texted me, asking to meet me. I agreed to meet him at our usual hotel later that day. I contemplated not telling this to Jason but decided that I would be honest with him and not lie as I did with the others. This attempt at honesty would fade quickly, as I would find myself eventually lying to him the most. Jason was online that morning, and we said hello as we did every morning.

Yahoo Chat:

Teri:	Morning Pop Tart!
Jason:	Morning babe
Teri:	Whatcha doin? Did you just wake up?
Jason:	Yes. Just relaxing and watching TV.
Teri:	OMG! Lori is online and asking to see my cam again! She wants to know what I am wearing today; I swear she's a dude babe.
Jason:	You think so? Maybe.
Teri:	She's worse than most men are about asking for my cam, and she's always wanting to cyber all the time, horny bitch.
Jason:	Yes she is.

Teri:	Did you get the video of the forty year old from Albany that I chatted with the other day on our profile? She sent me a video of her using her vibrator.
Jason:	Yes I did.
Teri:	It wasn't pretty was it? I tried to warn you.
Jason:	Yes you did warn me and no, it was not good.
Teri:	Well, she's a definite no. But she's nice. Did I tell you her boyfriend called me?
Jason:	He what? You gave him your number?
Teri:	Yes, why is that bad?
Jason:	Why would you want to talk to him?
Teri:	I don't know, he was online on her messenger and we started to chat. He asked me for my number so he could call me and I gave it to him.
Jason:	What did he want?
Teri:	He wants to meet me.
Jason:	You mean with her? The three of you?
Teri:	No, he wants to just meet me. He really doesn't like her that much.
Jason:	R U KIDDING ME?
Teri:	No. Jase, Ryan texted me today and . . . .
Jason:	Wait, this guy wants to meet you and Ryan texted. Where is this going?
Teri:	I'm meeting him today
Jason:	Guess I didn't fuck you good enough last week if you need to meet him today.
Teri:	That's not it. I don't know why I feel as if I need to see him. It's not about the sex Jase, it's more about attention and affection.
Jason:	I must not be enough for you; first you meet this guy you don't even know in a parking lot, and now just only a week after you see me you are going to go fuck Ryan. Good job.
Teri:	That's not true, you are enough for me. You know that I see Ryan occasionally. I didn't know that it bothered you.
Jason:	Honestly, I don't like it when you meet locals Teri. You are going to get caught here someday. Every time you meet them you put out a risk.
Teri:	I think that's what I'm addicted to though; it's the excitement of the risk. I promise you I won't get caught, that would mean I wouldn't be able to see you again.
Jason:	No, you would not.
Teri:	I have to get ready here, I need to go soon.

Jason:	Fine.
Teri:	Text me later from work okay?
Jason:	I will.

As I was driving to meet Ryan that day, Jason called me from work. He was on patrol, yelling and cursing at passing drivers as he was speaking to me. His mood was foul, and I knew why. I felt badly for the drivers that would be on the road with him that day.

"Are you really going to meet him? YOU FUCKING JERK OFF! This fuck head just pulled right in front of me!" he screamed.

"Babe, calm down. You are in the worst kind of mood here. That's not good."

"These people drive like fucking idiots! They have no consideration or respect at all! And no, I'm really not happy. Teri, I wished you wouldn't have even told me that you are going to meet Ryan today. If you do this, then don't bother calling or texting me later. I will just talk to you tomorrow."

As I pulled into the hotel parking lot, I felt a bit sick to my stomach, something I never had felt when meeting Ryan. I sat in the parking lot, trying to calm Jason down and stalling my entrance. I said goodbye to Jason and walked into the hotel, taking my time. I knocked on the door to the room, and Ryan stood there without a shirt on and quickly embraced me.

"It's about time, sexy. Come on in," he said as he released his embrace. I sat on the bed and took my shoes off and then lay on my stomach. Thoughts of Jason passed through my mind as I wondered if he were screaming obscenities at some driver at this very moment or ticketing every mildly speeding car he could see. Ryan sat on the bed next and started to rub my back.

"What's wrong? You seem tired, old lady."

"Babe, I hate it when you call me that."

"But you are."

I wasn't laughing at his humor today. He always teased me about my age since I had my last birthday in June. He did this not to be mean, rather to help me realize that I tended to overdramatize having turned forty-two. My age was never an issue with Ryan, and he loved that I was forty-two; his wife was only twenty-seven. I rolled over onto my back and took his hand in mine.

"Yeah, well when you are forty-two, just remember you will still want this fifty-three-year-old old lady." I said.

"Probably, you can take out your dentures and gum Mr. Big."

"EW! You are sick, babe! That's disgusting. I plan on keeping every tooth in my mouth, so don't count on that one happening, thank you."

"Just keep your thing shaved. Gray pube hair doesn't do much for me. It's creepy." He always made me laugh, but I wasn't laughing much today. "Come here, you. Let me hold you. Are you having one of those days?" he asked as he lay next to me, holding me in his arms. I snuggled up close to him and closed my eyes. This was why I was really here, to be held close, and I felt safe in his arms, but I wasn' t thinking of Ryan as he held me tight.

He kissed me, and I never opened my eyes once as he did this as he started to take off my blouse and cup my breasts in his hands.

"Open your eyes, Teri." I must have sat there seeming rather trance like for him to notice that my eyes were closed from the time he took me into his arms. I gathered up my blouse and held it to my chest, concealing the view.

"Baby, I can't do this," I said. "I'm sorry, I just need some time."

"Why? What's going on? Are you having trouble at home?" he said with confusion in his voice.

"Yes, that's it. Just give me a few weeks, Ryan. Okay, baby?" I could not tell him about Jason. It would be months later before he would know that there was a Jason. However much I did start to feel for Jason, Ryan was my local guy, and I wasn't ready to give him up and burn that bridge, just in case things went sour with Jason. Our relationship was too new, and I would not chance losing Ryan, who for some reason would be the one that I always seemed to go back to.

"Hey, take your time. I'm not going anywhere," he said, trying not to sound disappointed

"Really? You aren't mad, are you?"

"Naw, I will just go in the shower and whack off. I'm use to that. Wanna watch?"

I did laugh this time. He was the best, I thought to myself. I needed to keep him close to me.

"Can't. I have to go. Call me tomorrow, okay?" I said as I donned my shoes and gathered up my things. I quickly kissed him goodbye and promised to see him in a few weeks. As I drove home, I called Jason to let him know that I didn' t sleep with Ryan and wondered if I just may have saved someone from getting a ticket that night.

One night later that week, I logged onto the Cheaters Club site, looking for "fishies" this time. There were several that Jason had found for us, and I had a few prospects in the works. None of the women seemed very promising. Either they weren't attractive to us or they weren't into men at all. There was one who was very promising, but she lived in Vancouver and could not travel.

Sometime soon after we had posted our profile, I had realized that I could not share him, yet it was still fun to seek them out. I knew that it would come back to bite my ass if indeed we did find a candidate. I imagined horrible scenarios of what might happen if we did go through with this. Would they wait until I fell asleep to have sex? Would he be more attracted to her and ignore me? Would he want to see her again alone and I would not know about it? Would her skin be softer than mine, or would she smell of sweeter perfume? It made me crazy to think about, so I forced these thoughts out of my mind and concentrated on hooking a fish I would never allow him to meet.

There were quite a few online that night, so I decided to browse through them and look for those who were close to where Jason lived. There was one from New York. She was twenty-six years old and pretty enough, so I thought I would say hello.

SNasties: Hi, how are you tonight sweetie?
Fishy1:   Good, so you are a couple? What is it that you want from me?

Man, this fishy was cold! If she was like this now on the first sentence, I didn't think I wanted to know what she would be like in the bedroom. I was going to move on to a new fishy but thought I'd see if she warmed up a bit.

SNasties: Yes we are a couple, is that okay? I don't want anything from you, just feeling out if we may click here or not.

I wasn't feeling the click.

Fishy1:   You are in New York? Where in New York?
SNasties: I'm actually in Provo, Utah
Fishy1:   So you lied? That's fucked up.
SNasties: Hold on, I didn't lie. My bf lives in New York and that's where we PLAY . . . .
Fishy1:   So why me?

I felt as if I were in an interview and decided I didn't want to take the job anymore, but I would finish interviewing anyways.

SNasties: You live close to him and I liked your username.

Her username was LostGirl.

Fishy1:   Why?
SNasties: Cause I'm a lost girl too. I'm married and have a boy friend, I have never even KISSED a girl and so I'm wondering wtf am I doing?!
Fishy1:   Lol

Hooray! I made cold-fish girl laugh! It was so much easier roping in the bulls.

SNasties:	So, did you read our profile? Are you okay with my bf being there?
Fishy1:	Yes, I read it. He's pretty cute but I don't do guys. I hate men. You are pretty though.
SNasties:	Thanks, you are as well. Would it be okay if he was there? You wouldn't have to do anything with him.
Fishy1:	Sure, he could wait in the other room.

It was time to cast my rod out and hook another fish. This one was never going to work. Even if she were into guys, there would be no way Jason would like her. She was a snotty thing. I told her I had to go and moved onto the next candidate. These women didn't stay online for long. Most were gone by now, but I found one that was still online. Fishy2 was from Vancouver, and she was forty-six. There was not a photo of her posted, so I didn't know what she looked like.

SNasties:	Hi
Fishy2:	Hi
SNasties:	How are you tonight?
Fishy2:	I'm good ty and you?
SNasties:	I'm good thanks, so did you check out my profile?
Fishy2:	Yes, I was just noticing it. You are very pretty. I don't have a photo posted.
SNasties:	Thanks, yeah I noticed that, it's all good.
Fishy2:	You are in New York? I really can't travel.
SNasties:	That's not a problem, my bf and I can travel.
Fishy2:	ah, a bf? I'm not really looking for a threesome either
SNasties:	He's really nice, and HOT TOO!
Fishy2:	I'm sure he is!

Jason had just logged online, so I told him I was chatting with a new fish.

MSN Chat:

Jason:	Did you tell her we are a couple? Where does she live and does she look good?
Teri:	Yes she knows we are a couple, and she said she's not looking for a threesome, but there is something about her babe, I like her Maybe because I was chatting with this girl who had a major fat stick up her bum right before, I don' t know. She's in Canada and she's forty six. What are you going to do with two older women?
Jason:	Make them both very happy and satisfied.

127

Teri: She doesn't have a photo posted so I don't know what she looks
            like. I think I will ask her if she has MSN, hold on I will see and
            if she does and I will initiate a three way conversation so you can
            chat with her too.
Jason: Okay sweetie.

    I asked her if she had MSN, and she gave me her addy. A few minutes later, we were engaged in a three-way conversation. She said her name was Marian, and when her display picture popped up, she was amazingly beautiful. She had shoulder-length dark hair and dark eyes. Her olive skin was darker than mine, and she looked as if she was from the Middle East. There was no way I would have ever guessed her to be forty—six, looking more like she was in her early thirties. She was petite and curvy, and I thought she was perfect, exactly what I was looking for, if only she were open to Jason.

    We chatted for several minutes before she had to go. Jason seemed to like her as well. She was warm and friendly, and there was something special about her. As she said goodbye, I would never have guessed that she would become someone very special to me that I would come to care for very much.

    I did something this night that I would not be proud of, but I could not help myself. As Jason was chatting with Marian, I was secretly setting up another profile on the Cheaters Club. I called myself HotChick4U, and I was thirty—one and from New Jersey. I had downloaded some sexy pictures for my profile and sent Jason an instant message on the Cheaters Club site as he was chatting with Marian and me at the same time. He had no idea that HotChick4U was me as he responded to her instant message.

Cheaters Club Site Instant Messenger:

HotChick4U: Hello sexy, care to chat?
Jason: Hello

    He had accepted her invitation to chat because I sure wasn't going to pay for it.

HotChick4U: What are you doing tonight?
Jason: Nothing much, just relaxing
HotChick4U: Do you have a key? Here is mine

    I sent him my key of the photos of the hot blond that I stole from some other Web site. I made sure that she was very attractive and that there was several of her in bikinis. He sent me his key as well.

HotChick4U: MMMMMMMMMM . . . you are yummy!
Jason: thank you, you are very pretty as well

MSN Chat:

Teri: Whatcha doin babe? I think that I found another fishy here.

I asked Jason, knowing exactly what he was doing.

Jason: Where is she from babe? How old is she?
Teri: She is from California, what are you doing?
Jason: Just watching Family Guy, chat with her, see if she likes guys.

Family Guy my ass, I thought, becoming a bit angry now.

Cheaters Club Site Instant Messenger:

HotChick4U: So have you met anyone on this site?
Jason: Yes
HotChick4U: Any luck?
Jason: Yes, but she lives in Utah
HotChick4U: That's far, too bad.
Jason: It is but she comes to see me and she is coming again soon.
HotChick4U: Well I am right here baby, do you want to meet me?
Jason: Possibly
HotChick4U: Lol, only possibly? What? You like this chick or something?
Jason: Yes I do.

I was officially an "ass" at this moment. He had passed the test. I had chosen the best-looking blond I could find, and he told her that he liked me and she was local to him. Before I wasted any more of his credits, HotChick4U logged off.

MSN Chat:

Teri: Babe, she is not interested, sorry. What are you doing? Want to play Literary?
Jason: Sure, can I see you babe? Turn on your cam

We played Literary, and as I looked at his face on cam, I felt like the biggest jerk for what I had just done. But I knew that, for now, he was mine.

———

CHAPTER THIRTEEN

September '06

We were on a deserted island, the sun was shining, and my hair danced in the soft wind as the breeze that day caught strands of it, commanding it to fly. I was in the ocean, topless and wearing bikini bottoms, splashing around as Jason sat on the beach in his swim trunks watching me

I felt warm raindrops starting to lightly sprinkle on my face. The sky turned dark almost instantly, and the sprinkles of warm rain turned into heavy cold rain, stinging my face. Jason walked into the ocean and scooped me up in his arms, carrying me away, and laid me on a bed of banana leave s under a thick family of palm trees.

He kissed my lips gently as he covered his body over mine to warm me. My shivering stopped as I felt warm blood rushed through my veins. He made his way down my body, kissing my skin in a trail until his head was between my legs. He gently kissed my inner thighs and put his mouth over my bikini bottoms. I could feel the warmth of his breath through the fabric. I reached down to grab his head in my hands, and he looked up at me. It was Ryan. Ryan moved up toward me and kissed my lips, grasping my wet hair in both of his hands. He slid himself into me as I softly moaned. I stretched my arms over my head as I arched my back. I opened my eyes, and Jason was staring at me as his fingers traced my cheekbone. Jason kissed me and held me in his arms. I closed my eyes, and I felt safe in his strong arms as he held me tightly. When I opened my eyes, I lay in my bed.

It was a dream. It was delicious but bittersweet. Jason turned into Ryan? Up until that time, I had had many dreams of Jason, but never one of Ryan, and certainly none of both of them in the same dream. I would not try to analyze this, determining that I really didn't want to understand the meaning of it.

It was a Sunday morning, and I had to do some work at my husband's club. I finished my work and received a text message from a local guy that I had been chatting with for a few weeks. He wanted to meet me later that day, and I had made a promise to Jason that I would not meet him. I told him that I could not meet him, intending to keep my promise. He would call me after receiving my text message.

"Just for fifteen minutes! Come on, what do you have to lose?"

"Um, my boyfriend? I told him I wouldn't meet you. Listen, I don't lie to him," I lied.

"He won't know unless you tell him. Meet me for fifteen minutes. Please? Don't make me beg you because I will."

"Fifteen minutes! That's all! There is a coffee shop at the corner of Harold Drive and Harrison. Meet me there in thirty minutes."

Why am I doing this? I thought to myself as I drove to the coffee shop. He was certainly young and attractive, but that wasn't it. I wasn' t looking to start anything with a new local. It was enough of a challenge to hide Ryan from Jason and all of them from my husband. I wasn't feeling nervous or excited either, so it wasn' t the exciting rush of the meeting that I used to feel. I knew he was interested in me and had been chasing my skirt tails for weeks now, so it wasn't that I was seeking a chase. I had already bagged his affection a week ago. *Why do I do the things I do?* I gave up on figuring myself out and parked my truck in the busy parking lot of the coffee shop. I recognized him instantly as I walked in. He looked exactly like his photos, except now his goatee was absent. He was very attractive and had a great smile.

"Am I late or are you early?" I said as I sat in an ugly overstuffed purple club chair across from him.

"Neither. You are right on time, and I just walked in myself. You are really pretty. Your photos don't do you justice."

"Why, thank you . . . I don't think the camera likes me too much. You, however, are very photogenic. You could be like a Calvin Klein model!"

"Didn't I tell you I was? Not a Calvin Klein model, but I modeled through college. Would you like a coffee or anything?" he said.

"No, I'm good. I don't really like coffee."

"I don't either!" he said with a laugh. "It's really busy in here, and it's hard to hear you. Would you want to take a drive?"

"Oh, the last time I did that, it was not a good thing. Not that I don't trust you, but I think we should stay here."

"Can we at least sit in your car and talk? Here, take this." He pulled out his driver's license and handed it to me.

"What's this for?" I laughed as I took it from him

"Memorize my address and driver's license number. If I kill you, then you can have me arrested."

We sat in my truck, and his cell phone beeped with an incoming text. It was his wife.

"Uh-oh, where does she think you are?" I asked.

"Here. She knows I'm with you, see?"

He handed me his phone, and the text read,

How's it goin Hun? Do you like her?

"This is too weird . . . She's okay with this?" I asked, a bit perplexed.

"She has a boy toy in San Francisco. So as long as we are open about it and stay sexually safe, we have an arrangement. She's also interested in maybe joining me and who I meet. Would you be open to that?"

"Well, I think I need to be honest with you here . . . I'm not looking to start anything with a local guy. I already see one and juggle more than I can handle as it is. I'm flattered that you want to see me, but this isn't the time for me to start something with you."

"Understandable. If you change your mind, let me know," he said as he reached over and gave me a hug before getting out of my truck. This was the *last* local I would meet, I promised myself as I drove away. I would soon learn that not only did I break promises to Jason, but also to myself. I ended up telling Jason that I had met him and would pay the price for this meeting later as he would "pay me back." After this day, he would never trust me again, and he was right not to.

The next day, I decided to have my belly button pierced in what I will refer to as an "adult only" store. I took my cleaning girl with me for moral support, but really because I was chicken and needed her to hold my hand.

"Is this going to hurt?" I asked the scary-looking guy with at least a hundred tattoos and more body piercings than I could count.

"Yes," he said, adding, "A lot."

"Great . . . You are a man . . . men are supposed to like LIE to women. You must have failed the 'E-BAM 101 Course.'"

"What's that?" he asked.

"Essentials of Being a Man. Rule number one . . . ALWAYS lie to a woman, especially when she NEEDS you to."

"Oh, okay, yeah, it's going to hurt like a mother." I hated this guy. "Whatever you do, when I count to three, don't move."

"Why? Is three gonna hurt or something?"

"Just don't move." I really, really hated this guy. Three hurt like a mother.

"Are you done?" I asked as I squeezed my friend's hand tighter. I was sure it was purple by now.

"No, don't move. Wow, you're a bleeder."

"WHAT THE FUCK DOES THAT MEAN?" I screamed as I was starting to feel faint.

"You're bleeding like a stuffed pig here . . . don't move."

"Okay, okay, okay. Have you done many of these?" I asked a bit too late as I squinted in pain

"Yeah, but never seen anyone bleed like this before."

"LIE ALREADY! For Christ sakes!"

"Okay, it's done. Make sure that you spray the sea salt solution on it starting tomorrow and limit your activities so that it can heal."

I needed to find comfort after all this pain, so we browsed the store, looking at all the naughty things.

"Steph! Lookie here!" I squealed with excitement as I pointed to a "Nurse Betty" outfit. "I have to have this!" It was a short button-down dress, complete with a stethoscope, nurse's hat, stockings, and garter belt.

"Your husband will have a heart attack if you wear that. Do you want to kill him?"

"Shush, and help me find some crotch-less panties."

It would be the next day that I would get to "play nurse." I logged online, and Marian, my new friend from mine and Jason's profile, was there.

MSN Chat:

Teri:	Morning sweetie
Marian:	Hi babes
Teri:	OMG! I went to get my belly button pierced and I bought the sweetest little nurse's outfit!
Marian:	Lol
Teri:	Jason is gonna be my first patient, I want to check his . . . Temperature, although I already know he's hot . . . .
Marian:	(inserts a smiley face) sounds like fun, I bet you do.
Teri:	How are you today? Have you heard from him?

"Him" was someone Marian had been chatting with for eighteen months now. His name was Ben, and he was twenty-nine, from British Columbia. She never met him, but they had the most sensual love affair online. They had made plans to meet several times, but they always fell through. A few months earlier, they were scheduled to meet again. She was on her way to Seattle to see her family, and they were to meet in British Columbia on her layover. He never showed.

Marian:	No Ter, I think it's over. He won't respond to my messages.
Teri:	Awww sweetie, he will give him time.

She had told Ben that she met a guy whom her family knew and she had "kissed" him. After she told him this, he disappeared from her life. She and Ben had a lengthy, perplexing relationship that I would soon learn more of and come to understand. I took refuge in knowing that I was not the only one who had found someone that I fell in love with who I met online. This would be the common ground for Marian and me.

Marian:	I don't know babes; he does this when he gets mad. He just disappears.
Teri:	Mar . . . I have a friend who lives where you do. His name is Will and he's a very nice guy, and he's SMOKIN! I think I want to introduce you to him. I met him in San Francisco in August but we are just really good friends.
Marian:	Ter, I don't think I am ready to put myself out there again.
Teri:	Well, if anything, Will is a good friend, and one can never have too many friends, especially if they look like him!
Marian:	I just love Ben so much!
Teri:	I know you do sweetie, he's young like Jason, and they don't know what they want or even recognize what they have. He will come back, they always do.
Marian:	I don't know Ter, I really hurt him.
Teri:	But you two had decided to be friends! He had no claim to you when you met that guy! And he stood you up on top of that. You didn't do anything wrong to deserve this kind of treatment from him. But I do understand why he doesn' t answer your messages, because I do that as well when I'm "done". I walk away and not look back.
Marian:	Why do you do this? I need to try to understand here.
Teri:	Because it's easier to do this. So I don't have to think about it or acknowledge that it ever existed. I have done this too many times. There is always someone else . . . . onto the next one . . . Oh man, that didn' t sound good. Sorry.

I have a way of blurting things out without thinking, and this was one of those moments. I gave Will Marian's addy, and they started to chat online. It was my hope that she would find something in Will's friendship to take her away from the pain of losing Ben. It was cruel that he didn't acknowledge her, as I realized I was cruel as well in having done this myself. Not even an "it's over e-mail" or "go fuck yourself." Just silence. Ben would come back months later, only to toy with Marian's emotions again and to disappear once more. This would be a pattern that still continues to this day. I would come to despise him, and it would be hard for me to hold my tongue as she would speak of her love for him. He was not worthy of her affections. He was not worthy of someone so kind and so gentle a soul. I decided that he was not like me. I was not like him after all. I could never be so cruel to do this over and over again to someone.

Jason was online later that day, and I told him about the sexy nurse's outfit I bought. No one was home that afternoon, so I too k my laptop upstairs to my daughter's room to show him. I called him on the phone and turned on my cam.

"Wow" he said as I leaned into the camera and held the stethoscope to my chest and then to the computer screen.

"Gotta check your heartbeat to make sure you are breathing here. Hmmm, sounds good. Now bend over, bad boy, so I can take your temperature." I said holding out a thermometer.

"How about we skip that part and you stand back so I can see you," he said.

I got up off the bed and backed away slowly so he could view Nurse Betty in all of her naughtiness. I turned around slowly and bent over to grab my ankles, trying to do this in a sexy way in my heels and stockings though I was finding it hard to balance. I was grateful I didn't fall on my butt.

"Are you wearing crotch-less panties?" he asked.

"Who, me? Let's see."

I started to unbutton the short little white dress until it was fully open and lay on the bed. I twirled my finger around the open slit of my panties.

"Yes, I do believe they are crotch-less."

We began to have our cam sex session, and then he said,

"Teri, do you want to say what I think you want to say?"

I knew exactly what he was talking about. We had not exchanged "those" words as of yet, and this wasn't the most romantic of times to say it for the first time, yet it felt so right.

"I love you, Jase," I said without hesitating.

"I love you too, Teri," he replied back.

I don't know if it was saying these words to each other for the first time, but we both had orgasms shortly after saying this. Hearing these words from him would always make my heart skip a beat, and months later, after all the deceit and lies would catch up to me, I would realize how I missed hearing him tell me, "I love you, Teri," if for only once more.

Chapter Fourteen

September '06

October was approaching quickly, and I counted the days to when I would be going to see Jason. Every day I would ask him, "How many days, babe?" and though he told me one less number each day, it still seemed like eternity. I continued to chat on the Cheaters Club site, adding more *bulls* to my Yahoo messenger list as well as meeting a new local guy for drinks. His name was Josh, and he was thirty-five and single. I was instantly attracted to him as he was my "type," more so than most I had met. He was six feet and one inch tall and had sandy blond hair and the most amazing eyes that would appear to change from an ice blue to light green consistently when the light would reflect on them. Josh didn' t spend a lot of time working out, yet he was in great shape and was muscular and toned.

I asked him why it was that he went for married women since he was single.

"A lot of married women are lonely and need attention, so I can give them this and treat them like a princess, and they know that it's not going any further. Single women want to get married, get mad if you don' t call them, plant their tampons in my bathroom . . . why do they do that?" he asked.

"Well, if they were leaving their panties or earrings lying around, I could tell you why. Never planted tampons in some guy's bathroom, so I don't know," I answered.

"They do that too! Why do they do that?"

"Sweetie, they are marking their territory if by chance some other bitch comes to your house." I said with a laugh.

"Have you done this before? Come on, you have, haven't you, Teri?"

"Hell no! Do you know how much my panties and earrings COST? I'm not leaving them for some chick to throw away! Plus, they always came to my house. Men are dirty. I'm a slob for sure, but my apartment was never dirty," I told him. "One guy I dated was a cowboy, I mean a REAL cowboy. He handled cattle all day, and he'd come over after work smelling like cow shit and plop on my waterbed with a six-pack of Coors Light with his boots and spurs on. I swear if he weren't so FINE, that cowboy would have been riding the waves of some other waterbed," I said with a wink "He was for sure dirty."

"But you like dirty boys, don't you?"

"Nope. There's a difference between dirty and naughty. I prefer naughty boys."

"Good, because I'm a naughty boy," he said with a sly grin.

After my meeting with Josh that night, I wondered why it was that I met him. I enjoyed his company and he made me laugh, but it was Jason I was thinking of all night as through my entire date with Josh, I answered not only Jason's texts but a phone call from him as well Josh didn't appear to be upset however rude it was. He knew I had a boyfriend as well as a husband. I just had to wonder why it was I still wanted to go on chatting with these guys online and especially why I met new locals. I loved Jason, and he satisfied my needs, so why was he still not enough? Was it the distance between us, perhaps? It made me crazy to think about, so I quickly dismissed it from my mind, thinking of what I would tell my husband for being over an hour late. In the years I was married, I seldom went out and only drank two or three times a year. My changed behavior over the past months was making him angry and mean.

"Why didn't you call me to tell me you were going to be late?" he asked when I got home.

"My cell phone is dead. I'm sorry if I worried you," I lied. "Are you hungry? Do you want me to fix you something?"

"Sit down. I need to talk to you," he said, and I already knew this was not going to be good. I sat on the sofa next to his chair and put on my best sober face. I didn't want him to notice I had been drinking.

"Where's my wife? Where did she go?" he asked me.

"I'm here, Honey. What do you mean?" I knew what he meant.

"What do you do all day, Ter? You aren't designing, you don't clean the house or cook, and you are drinking every night. E ven when the kids are here, you drink You are drunk now," he said, and I hated him for knowing that I was drunk and for saying these words to me, however true they were.

"Honey, we have had a cleaning lady for seven years now. I have never cleaned the house. I'm not designing because I need a break from it, I'm burned out. And I do cook, sometimes." I was grasping for excuses here that probably seemed desperate to him.

"The drinking and going out every night when the kids aren't here? If the children aren't here, then I know that my wife isn't going to be home! It's party time for Teri! Yahoo! Lets go get drunk!" He was starting to raise his voice and become mean. He was always verbally abusive, and for years I tolerated it and never responded, so as to not make it worse. He was never physically abusive, but the mental and verbal abuse was more than enough for me to reach my breaking point. A point I had reached last April when this whole thing started.

"Sit here with you and do what? Watch fucking television? That's all you do! You come home from work, I feed you, bring you your water, and get your shorts and slippers so you don' t have to go downstairs and get them yourself! God forbid you walk down the stairs if Teri can fetch them for you!" This was unlike me as I yelled these words to him. I rarely stood up to him and avoided animosity at all costs, even if it meant taking the verbal hits that would come. And a big one came next.

"You are a fucking bitch cunt! Why don't you go get a fucking job and make the donuts so I can go out and party and come home when I want to? No, because you are the queen! I have ruined another good woman. I gave you too much freedom and let you do what you wanted. It's my fault you are like this."

"Let me do what I wanted? You are so arrogant. I'm like this because I can't stand you anymore! You are a very mean man, and you are negative and controlling! I'm your WIFE, not your property!" I screamed, surprising even myself at how bold my words were.

"Then hit the door, baby! If you don't like me anymore, then LEAVE! I'm done here. It's over. I will call my attorney Monday, and we can get it on," he threatened. A threat I had heard for the first time only one month after we got married and at least a hundred times since. For the first time in my marriage, I welcomed his threat. I didn't start to shake or panic or beg for him to reconsider as I had done so many times before. I sat there and broke out a weak smile that was sad, more than anything, sad because I really didn't care anymore.

"Okay," I said as I slowly got up. "Do what you have to do."

When I went to bed that night, I couldn't remember how long it had been since I had said a prayer. I was sure that God was angry with me and wouldn' t hear it if I had said one. I decided that I would take my chances just in case he was in a good mood. This was the first prayer I had say in months:

Dear Father in Heaven, please hear my prayer, however unworthy I am right now. I know that what I do is wrong, but I will not ask forgiveness of you because I know that I will continue to see Jason and continue to sin in doing this. It doesn't feel like sin. What feels like sin is staying with someone I don't love anymore and living a lie. It hurts me to know that I am hurting my husband and children, and for this I ask forgiveness. I have cracked the vase my mother warned me of, and I cannot go back and change that. I hate that I love Jason, and I love that I love him. Give me the strength to do what is right. Please bless my babies and keep them safe. Help me to be a better mother to them. Please bless Jase as he is working tonight and what he does is so very dangerous. Keep him safe and send your best guardian angel to watch over him. Bless my husband so that he may stay healthy and regardless of what happens with our marriage he may live out the rest of his years in happiness. Help me to find my way back to myself Lord, because the person

I see right now I see through a broken mirror. Save me from myself and make me whole again. I say these things in the name of the Lord, Jesus Christ, Amen.

I had tears running down my face as I ended my prayer. I hoped that God did hear it and that I was still worthy of his love. On this night, I realized that I didn' t love myself and wondered if I ever really had.

The following week I tried my hardest to be good. My husband never did call his attorney, not that I thought he would, and Jason was still upset with me over meeting the two new local guys recently. I didn't go out, and I only drank twice that week, cutting myself off after a few drinks. My good-girl streak didn't last too long as I broke down and agreed to meet Ryan. I was going to see Jason in ten days, yet I felt compelled to see Ryan for some reason. I would not agree to meet him at a hotel, but he said that he had something for me, so I agreed to meet him in a parking lot, the parking lot that we had very first met.

I pulled up, and he got into my truck, handing me a single white rose.

"Hi, Baby, thought you may like this," he said as he handed it to me and gave me a hug.

"Oh, you remembered my favorite flower?" I asked, impressed.

"Yes, I remember everything you tell me, silly," he said as the holes of the dimples in his cheeks got bigger when he smiled. These words hit me when he said them. Jason also remembered everything that I said. I started to feel guilty for being there with Ryan now.

"Thanks, babe. You are sweet. I missed your face. Show me those dimples!" I said and then asked, "Did you miss me?"

"Of course I missed you. Why do you think I asked to see you? Duh . . ." he always had to be a smart-ass.

"Then kiss me and shut up," I said in my smart-ass way of responding to him.

He kissed me, and we talked for ten minutes as he held my hand the whole time. I missed him, and there was something almost soothing when I was with him. It was different from what I felt for Jason. I didn't love Ryan, but he was so easy to be with, funny, cute, and I knew that he cared for me a lot. With Jason, it was more intense and passionate. I may have given Ryan my body, but Jason had my heart.

"I have to go, babe. I need to get my kids here from school," I told him as I let go of his hand to give him one last hug. "Call me next week, okay? I'm going to New York on the nineteenth again, so meet me at my gate and see me off."

"You still working there? I thought it was done?" he asked.

"No, it's not done," I lied. Basically, I was done with it—the loft I designed there, that is. There were just a few minor things to be completed and photos taken, but nothing warranting a trip there. "See you later, bad boy, miss me lots"

"I always do," he said as he got out of my truck, and I wondered when I would find myself in his arms again.

CHAPTER FIFTEEN

September '06

I hired a stripper to come to my house and teach me to do a lap dance and told my husband not to come home because I was learning to do this for him. He had owned strip clubs before and wasn't impressed with the idea of me wanting to learn it but respected that I did and promised not to infringe upon my lesson. I had bought a sexy cop stripper outfit complete with gloves, glasses, stockings, boots, and handcuffs. I wanted to give Jason a lap dance too and show him how sexy this cop girl was.

Nicky, who had been stripping for ten years now, instructed me to wear something comfortable with heels. I donned a pair of short black yoga shorts and a black tank top. I had invited Jason to watch my lesson from Webcam, and he was eager to do this. As I turned on my cam for him, I regretted extending this invitation. I'm by nature a klutz, so it was probable that I would fall on my butt at least once.

MSN Cam Chat:

Teri:	Hi baby, there you are! So don't laugh if I fall okay?
Jason:	Teri, I'm just honored that you want to learn how to do this for me. No matter what happens I think you are sexy and I'm gonna love it.
Teri:	Get out your dollars then, do you have them ready?
Jason:	Oh yes I do.
Teri:	She's here, hold on okay?

I answered the door and felt instantly sick and nervous. She stood there with all of her cute blondness and stripper-perfect body, looking like a centerfold girl.

"Hi, I'm Nicky!" she said, now reminding me more of a perky cheerleader, the one that you hated in high school because she was so perfect and happy all the time.

"Hello, Nicky, I'm Teri. Come on in. Do you mind if my boyfriend watches me learn this from his cam? I told him to behave and not do any naughties."

"No! That's fine with me!" she said in almost a squeal.

"This is Jason," I told her as I showed her his cam. He smiled as he must have thought to himself, "I'm the luckiest guy on earth here." I could tell he was attracted to her, and I hated that.

MSN Cam Chat:

Teri:	Baby, this is Nicky, she is my instructor
Jason:	Hi Nicky, how are you today? Teach her good okay?
Nicky:	Hey copper, we are going to have fun here, are you ready?
Jason:	Oh, yes I am.
Teri:	Okay baby, if I fall don't laugh at me, I will try to at least fall in a sexy way . . . .
Jason:	You will be fine babe

Nicky gave me a brief talk on attitude, explaining that the most sexy strippers aren't always the most beautiful ones, rather the ones who exude confidence and attitude. She told me think of a name to call myself.

"Tawny, I feel like a Tawny, I think," I said, feeling instantly sexier.

"That's a hot name. Okay, Tawny, I'm going to show you some basic moves before we begin. Now if you ever get nervous or mess up, these are the moves you can always revert back to. Men don't care as long as you are moving."

The basic moves came naturally to me as I felt at ease and comfortable with these movements. It was all about keeping these moves slow and exaggerating the swaying of the hips. She showed me how to move my hips back and forth from side to side as well as in a circular motion, telling me to draw little "circles" with my butt. It was easy. Next she would give me a lap dance to show me what exactly a lap dance was. I repositioned the chair so that Jason could see this as well. We had his full attention as he watched intently, and before she could give me the lap dance, my phone beeped. It was a text from Adam.

Text Message:

Adam:	Hey, is the stripper there?
Teri:	Yep, she's here
Adam:	Is she hot? Are you going to do her?
Teri:	Yes she's hot, and NO!

MSN Cam Chat:

Jason:	Who' that?

Teri: It's Adam
Jason: Figures, tell him you are busy.

I cranked the music, and she started to dance. She started to dance ten feet in front of me, explaining that men are visual creatures and to "tease" them first. She moved her hips in the way she had showed me and moved closer to me with each move. She then stood before me, with her legs straddling the chair, bracing herself against the wall as she leaned into me, brushing her breasts down my chest.

"Get really close to them so they can smell you," she told me. Her scent was sweet, and her skin felt soft on mine. This was a new sensation for me as I became so enticed with what she was doing that I forgot Jason was even watching us.

Next she slid her body all the way down mine until she was kneeling on the floor with her head between my legs. This girl was naughty. She then flipped herself over with a sexy move and slowly moved her way up to my lap, straddling me. Tilting her head back, her hair was in my face, and I could smell the scent of her shampoo. I *wonder which shampoo she used*, I thought to myself, hoping I'd remember to ask her this later. She shifted herself off of my lap, balancing on her straddled legs as she ground her butt into my pelvis in circular motions. I was trying to remember each move, however distracting it was, because I was becoming a bit aroused.

Flipping herself over again she straddled my lap, now facing me. She did more grinding moves, moving her body up and down mine, with her chest literally in my face at one point. The next move frightened me. She stood and turned herself away from me, doing some sort of a backflip which resulted with her head between my legs and her crotch in my face as she was upside down.

"I think I will skip this last move," I said to her.

"Okay! So see! It's not hard! Now you try it," she said, having made this seem so easy.

I glanced at the computer and noticed that Jason was still watching intently. I needed a drink, so I poured both of us one. I waited a few minutes for the drink to kick in before I attempted my dance, and my phone beeped again. It was another text from Adam.

Text Message:

Adam: Are you guys naked now?
Teri: Lol . . . you wish

Jason was becoming upset that Adam was texting me throughout my lesson, so I stopped answering him. I was ready to try this now. I took a deep breath and cranked "Cherry Pie" by Warrant. I chose this song because Jason would sometimes call me his Teri Pie.

I started in the same position that Nicky had and moved my hips in the way she showed me to. I was certain that I was not looking as sexy as she did, feeling a bit clumsy with having to do these moves to actual music now. I tried to forget that my boyfriend was watching me do this for the first time and concentrated on Nicky.

I moved closer to her and mimicked the moves in the order that she had done it. She laughed and clapped her hands, telling me that I was doing great. I decided to throw in a few moves of my own that I had seen other strippers do. She squealed with delight, and I knew that I couldn't be doing that badly. When I bent over, she slapped my butt and tucked a dollar bill in my shorts. I got through my dance, and my legs were shaking and I was sweating.

"God, I'm out of shape!" I said, panting.

"You did great! Are you sure you are forty-two and have three kids? You are HOT!"

"I could stand to lose a few pounds here, but thanks."

"If you know that you are sexy, it shows. You aren't that overweight, and it won' t matter," she replied as to make me feel better.

"Oh, I know that I'm sexy! I just have stretch marks and a C-section scar."

"That won't show onstage. Don't worry about that," she said, reassuring me of what I already knew.

Next she showed me some floorwork moves. As she did this, she put her face so close to mine her lips brushed up against mine. I received another text in the middle of this and was agitated that Adam was still texting me. When I opened the message, I saw that it was not from Adam but from Jason.

Text Message:

Jason: Babe, lower the cam, I can't see what you are doing.

I had totally forgotten that he was still watching because I was so caught up with Nicky. After she left, I felt exhausted but excited to practice my moves now that I had grasped the basics of this art form.

MSN Cam Chat:

Teri: WOW! That was too much fun!
Jason: You really did good babe, I was impressed.
Teri: I only kinda tripped once
Jason: Yeah I saw that

Teri: You like her don't you?

Jason: She's good looking and she did a good job teaching you, she's good at what she does.

Teri: But you are attracted to her aren't you? You want her don't you?

I knew these questions were pathetic, but I was fishing for something.

Jason: Babe, wanting and needing are two different things, I need you more than I want her.

This was what I was fishing for—for him to validate his feelings for me. I knew it wasn't healthy that I tested him with questions like this, but my insecurities would drive me to continually do this in the future, until one day, he would not care anymore.

CHAPTER SIXTEEN

September '06

We were driving to the mall for a mother-daughter outing, and I had Prince cranked up on the radio.

"You don't have to be rich to be my girl, you don't have to be cool to rule my world, aint no particular sign I'm more compatible with . . . I JUST WANT YOUR EXTRA TIME AND YOUR . . . KISS!" I sang along in my best Prince imitation voice.

"Mom, don't do that. You sound like a dork," she said as she turned down the radio. "Who are you texting all the time? Is it a guy?" she asked out of the blue. It felt as if a bomb just dropped on my head.

"What are you talking about, Sis?" I asked as my heart started to race. I didn't like to lie to her, and I knew that this conversation was not going to be easy.

"Mom, I'm not stupid. I know that you are talking to someone, and I saw that site you were on the other day, so I looked it up. It's for married people who cheat. Are you having an affair?"

I was always so careful when I logged onto the Cheaters Club site, usually only doing this when my children and husband were not home or asleep. I thought back to what day that could have been that I was careless in doing this. Before I could figure this out, she added,

"Who is he, and are you and dad getting a divorce? Don't even lie to me either. You suck at it." My daughter was not very close to my husband, yet I knew she did love him, and I needed to proceed with caution as to not hurt her.

Little did she know that I had become a pro at lying, yet this was my daughter, not some random guy. I considered trying to lie to her, yet I knew that if I failed and she didn't believe me, I would never have her trust again. I tried my best to explain it without telling her more than I should.

"Well, mommy hasn't been happy for a very long time. Things aren't great between me and daddy. I have a friend who I talk to, and he listens to me. Have you ever just needed someone that you could talk to when you have a bad day?"

"Yes, but are you seeing him? Have you like . . . kissed him?" she asked, and I knew this was the question I was trying to avoid.

"I have seen him once, and yes, Sis, I kissed him." I knew that I would rather lose her respect in admitting this rather than for her to consider me a liar. Her trust meant more to me as I always told her that she could always trust me and tell me anything.

"You did? What is his name? Is he cute? How old his he? What does he do?" She was full of questions—as if I had just opened Pandora's Box here.

"Well, his name is Jason, and he's a trooper in New York"

"New York? What is a trooper?" she asked.

"Like Highway Patrol. They monitor the highways and give tickets."

"Wow, did you tell him you get tickets all the time? Does he know that you drive like a crazy person? I bet he would even give you a ticket if he stopped you."

"I don't drive like a crazy person. I just speed sometimes."

"Yeah, right. You speed more than sometimes, and yes, you do drive like a crazy person. I'm fifteen, and I fear for my life when I get in the car with you. I'd like to live to get married and have babies someday," she said, being a smarty-pants. "What else? Is he cute? Does he have kids?"

"He's cute, and no kids." I was trying to keep my answers short here and attempted to change the subject. "Are you hungry? Let's get some sushi!"

"Why doesn't he have kids? Does he like kids? Would he like us?" I was beginning to realize just how nosey my daughter was.

"He loves kids and wants them someday, and I think he would LOVE you. Who wouldn't?"

"How old is he?" I was avoiding this question more than any.

"Twenty-six," I whispered.

"What? Twenty-six! MOM! You are really just kidding me, right?" she screamed.

"No, he's twenty-six. It's not like I'm going to marry him! We are just really good friends here. I think you are jumping to conclusions and reading more into this."

"So, he's like only eleven years older than me? And . . . sixteen years younger than you?"

"He's just a friend." I was becoming exhausted with this conversation, so this time I would change the subject and make it stick. I wondered if I had just made the biggest mistake by telling this to her and knew that most mothers would never share this with their daughters. Then I remembered that I was not most mothers, and that the relationship I had with my daughter ran deep. One day she would grow up and no longer need mothering, but I hoped that she would always see a friend in me.

It was only a week before I was going to New York to see Jason and Ryan texted asking to meet me. It had been over a month since I last had sex, and I was feeling a desire to *It's only a week away!* I told myself. It wasn't Ryan I even wanted, yet I went to him anyways, feeling little guilt afterwards for doing this. Later this day I went home and was able to interact with my husband as if I had done nothing. I logged online and chatted with Jason and acted as if I had done nothing, because in my mind, I had done nothing.

Yahoo Chat Later That Night:

Teri:	Hi babe, you there?
Jason:	Hey Sweetie, how was your day?
Teri:	Awful! I missed you terribly! Thought of you all day!
Jason:	Awww, I missed you too sweetie. Can I see your cam?

We turned on our cams, and I logged onto the Cheaters Club site to look for fishies.

Teri:	Here, got one! She's twenty five and from California.
Jason:	Babe, let it go. Most of them aren't interested in having a threesome and really, lets be honest here. You wouldn't be able to do it. You would get jealous. Let's delete it.
Teri:	You are right. Okay, let's delete it. Actually, I think I will delete my other profile too.
Jason:	Then I will delete mine as well; really I don't go there much anymore since I met you.

We had been arguing a lot recently because of my excessive chatting, and I really didn't want to delete my profile, but I did this to show him that he was enough for me. He would always tell me that he thought he wasn' t enough for me because he knew I continued to log on there and add new bulls to my Yahoo list, not to mention my meetings with new locals. I decided to test it and see if, by chance, he was enough. A few days later, I knew the answer.

I made it two whole days without missing the Cheaters Club site, but on the third day, I was starting to have withdrawals. By the fourth day, I was a wreck. I knew I couldn't go back to the Cheaters Club if in case Jason might check to see if I went back and there weren't a lot of women in my area. I considered saying I was from another state, but that would defeat any purpose of meeting potential local guys. I could not go back. I got online and searched other sites and joined two of them. One was more less a "message only" site, where you would leave messages back and forth, and the men would usually have to pay to see these messages. Let me just add, there were a lot of cheap men.

The other site was free. You would go to a room, for instance the lounge, or bedroom, or living room, and chat with whoever was there. There were also *private* rooms to where, if you went, then payment was required. I never went to these private rooms even when I was invited. It seemed creepy, reminding me of live sex shows that one could view through a window in one of those dirty, nasty places that I had seen in a movie once.

There were both men and women in these rooms, and there would be a two-inch-by-two-inch green box that would pop up out of nowhere when someone wanted to chat with me. They would see who was in the room and then click by that name and the two-inch green box would appear. This is how the chat worked

Most of the time, they would just type in ASL, which meant AGE/SEX/ LOCATION. It wasn' t always easy to tell by username the sex of someone, and most weren't there to chat with the same sex

I decided to go outside to the *pool* and see who was there. I received my first green pop-up box.

Pool Chat:

Green Box 1: ASL
Teri: Um, Hi
Green Box 1: ASL please

I had no idea what this meant, and I was determining that I didn't like this site very much so far. I was really starting to miss the Cheaters Club site and contemplated going back and taking the chance that Jason would not catch me.

Teri: I'm new, what does ASL mean?
Green Box 1: Age, sex and location
Teri: Oh, okay, well I'm forty two, I'm a female and I live in Utah. What about you?
Green Box 1: 29/ F/ NY Good luck.

Then she was gone. Just as quickly as the green box appeared, it disappeared. These people were cold! Not even a hello or goodbye. I didn' t like this at all. Another green box popped up.

Green Box 2: ASL
Teri: 42/ F/ Utah

I answered quickly, as if I had done this hundreds of times before. "These people are like robots!" I said out loud to myself, amazed with how cold people seemed here on this site. I wondered if I would even want to chat with any of these icebergs.

Green Box 2: 56/ M / Colorado . . . . are you sweet little doll? Tell me what you would like me to do to you; I'm good with my tongue.

Ew. I was going to go to the lounge now. I needed a drink after this nasty bull.

Lounge Chat:

The lounge was apparently the place to be. As I crossed over to this room, there were more green boxes that popped up on my computer screen than I could count. There must have been twenty of them, distributed unevenly, some overlapping others; it was crazy I didn' t know which one to reply to first. There was no information about who these people were in the green boxes except for the username. I decided to answer the one closest to my mouse.

Teri: 42 / F / Utah

I typed this same thing in at least ten of the boxes, and then there it was . . . someone who caught my eye. I knew he was a male because his username was *Bad Boy Brett.* I liked him already, and it was not the standard "ASL" that he typed, rather:

Green Box 1: Hello! How are you tonight? It's crazy in this room isn't it? Are you keeping up okay?
Teri: Wow, you're not a robot! Hi!
Green Box 1: A what? Lol there are robots here? Where?
Teri: Look around you, we are surrounded by them! ASL please, ASL, please ASL, please . . .
Green Box 1: Lol! You are funny! Yeah, I don't like that either, but, now that you brought it up . . . .
Teri: 42 / F/ Utah
Green Box1: Really? Utah? 25 / M / Utah
Teri: That's great! We are neighbors, where are you in Utah?
Green Box 1: Orem, and you?
Teri: Provo, we really are neighbors.

I ignored all the other green boxes that popped up and popped out and chose to give Bad Boy Brett all of my attention. There were now thirty or so green boxes, and I was becoming dizzy with the "dance" that these boxes did as they came and went. I asked Brett if he had Yahoo messenger, and we met there after a few minutes and I logged off that crazy site.

Yahoo Chat:

Teri: This is better
Brett: Yes it is, thanks for asking me for my Yahoo, I was going to ask you
            but didn't want to appear too bold.

I noticed the display picture next to his name in the chat box. It was only of his midriff, showing him in jeans without a shirt, exposing the most perfect set of abs I had ever seen. He was perfect and his body defined.

Teri: Wow, please tell me this is really you—➔
Brett: Lol! Okay, it's really me!
Teri: Is it? Or are you trying to tease me?
Brett: No, it is me, here, I have some more you can see, hold on.

He invited me to photo sharing and started to send me several more photos of himself.

Teri: OMG! You have an amazing body! What do you look like bad boy?

Next he sent me one of his face. He had short dark hair and big blue eyes and dark lashes. He had the same coloring as Jason, yet he had a different look than Jason did. He was more a "pretty boy," and Jason had more "chiseled features." To me, he was as perfect as Jason was, and I had to pinch myself because he was also assessable and local. I started fishing to see what he was looking for and hoped to find.

Teri: You are cute enough I guess. So what are you looking for?

That was good, I thought to myself. *Let's not beat around the bush here, Ter.*

Brett: You. I'm looking for you.

He was good. I needed to watch out for this one.

Teri: Oh really now? You don't know what I even look like! I could be
            some cow! ☺
Brett: Your display picture shows otherwise.

I glanced at my display picture and saw what he was looking at. On my MSN, my display photo was a face shot. The only ones who even had my Yahoo were my bulls, so I displayed a photo of myself from my neck to my waist, wearing a low-cut blue silk camisole exposing the fullness of my ample breasts.

Teri: Okay then, what if my face is scary? What if I have rotten teeth and hair growing out of my nose? ☹

Brett: You don't. You're beautiful. ☺

I was enticed by him. He chatted so assuredly, without hesitation, and he said all the right things that a woman wants to hear, making you believe he wasn't full of crap but that he really meant it. That was his talent, I would soon find out, unfortunately. I sent him a few photos of me even though he had not asked.

Brett: Wow, I knew you were beautiful. Teri, you are, I was kidding earlier but you really are.

Teri: I know, JK . . . what do you do? Tell me more about yourself. Do you have children?

He told me that he was going to medical school to become a doctor and worked in a gym as a personal trainer. He also included that he was single. I assumed he was married because the site that I had met him on was another site for mainly married people. The next thing I knew, Jason had logged in and started to chat with me, so now I was chatting with both of them.

Yahoo Chat with Jason:

Jason: You there babe?

Teri: Hi sweetie, I'm here. What are you doing? Did you just get home?

Jason: Yep, went and had a few beers with my co-workers. Are you on your laptop?

Teri: Yes

He turned on his cam, and I quickly denied it.

Jason: Can I see you? Why didn't you accept my cam?

I panicked. There was no way I was turning on my cam right now, or he would notice I was chatting with Brett, who I could never tell him about. He hated it when I was with him and chatting with other guys at the same time, and if I turned on my cam, he would know this.

Teri: Babe, give me like, a few minutes okay? I'm looking for lighting here online and I'm almost done and then we can cam.

Jason: Ok, let me know when you are done sweetie.

Yahoo Chat with Brett:

Teri: Sorry, I had to pee. Where was I?
Brett: You were saying that you will let me take you to lunch this week.
Teri: I was? Don't recall you asking! But really I can't. I have a boy friend.
Brett: Aren't you married? You're married and have a boy friend too?
Teri: Yep. I'm bad
Brett: No, you are good. I'm gonna steal you away from both of them!

Yahoo Chat with Jason:

Jason: You almost done yet babe?
Teri: No, not yet, give me a few more minutes okay?
Jason: ok, take your time.

Yahoo Chat with Brett:

Teri: How are you going to steal me away from both of them?
Brett: I'm just that good. You will see you have never met anyone like me before. So, lunch?
Teri: I can't. Its hard enough you know. My boy friend lives in a different state and I'm trying to be true to him.
Brett: Why? I bet he's not being true to you. Meet me anyways and don't tell him. I bet he's out with someone right now.
Teri: I assure you he's not. He's actually online here waiting for me, so I really do have to go.
Brett: Let him wait, I'm local to you he's not. Just remember that. Stay with me here; tell him you're chatting with your new boy friend you replaced him with!
Teri: You are so bad! No really I must go
Brett: Okay, but one day . . . I'm gonna make you mine.

These words that he said should have hit me like a brick. But I wouldn't see any red flags until it was too late—almost costing me everything.

CHAPTER SEVENTEEN

October '06

The day had finally come. I could hardly contain my excitement as I got off the airplane and headed into the city. Jason would be coming to the hotel in only hours, and I needed to shower and get ready. I had brought a sexy black camisole with little pink bows on the straps with matching black lace panties that I would add stockings, a garter belt, and heels to complete. I fixed my hair and slathered my body with my favorite lotion and scent. One last check in the mirror verified that I was ready. I glanced at the time, and he would be here in twenty minutes. He was coming home from a hockey tournament that he played in Pittsburgh and was coming straight to the hotel.

The anticipation of waiting for him to show up and knowing he was on his way made me think of the excitement I would feel on Christmas morning as a child. This feeling only intensified with each visit in the future. I decided to kill time as I waited, so I logged online, hoping to catch Marian, and she was there.

MSN Chat:

Teri:	OMG! I'm so incredibly excited to see my baby!
Marian:	(inserts a smiley face) I know! Hey, Will and I spent four hours online chatting last night!
Teri:	Wow, he never chatted with me for four hours! He must like you!
Marian:	He's really nice and funny too! But I still miss Ben babes, I sent him another offline message but I think he may have blocked me.
Teri:	You are assuming that, you don't know this. Jason's going to be here any minute so I'd better go now. Ttyl ok? Kisses

My phone rang, and it was Jason, asking me which room I was in. He was in the elevator. I told him the room number and that I was more pleased with this hotel. As I started to describe the room and how it compared to the last hotel we stayed at, the there was a knock on the door. Without hanging up, I answered it, and he stood there with his cell phone to his ear.

I lunged toward him, wrapping my arms around his neck, kissing him like I hadn't seen him for a year, dropping my cell phone to the ground as I did this. Every sensation that I remembered sharing with him ran through my body and mind, and I felt that I belonged to only him with all of my being. There was nothing else that mattered to me as he held me in his arms, responding to my kiss with relentless passion.

He stepped inside the room and moved me up against the wall while he never stopped kissing me. Dropping to his knees, he moved his head in between my legs, and his mouth felt warm. I wrapped one leg over his shoulder as he held onto my waist to help balance me. It was all I could take before I begged for him in the way that I most desired for him to be—within me. What would happen in the next hour felt like a dream, and with each breath I took and each time our lips would touch, I loved him even more.

"I love you Jason," I said for the first time to him in person. The strength of these words in all of its truthfulness was powerful, and I felt as if I wanted to cry as I said this.

"I love you too, Teri," he whispered as he looked into my eyes, brushing the hair off my face as he looked down at me. There was nothing more perfect than this very moment, and I knew that it would only come once, so I relished in the moment, taking in everything around me as to memorize every detail of this special time. As I closed my eyes that night, I lay in his arms as he held me close, and I dreamt of happy dancing flowers and pink and yellow skies. The world was a happy place.

The following day was a Friday, and he had to go to work for a bit and would be back later that night. I had a surprise for him when he would come back, I had brought the cop stripper outfit with me and would give him a lap dance. I had given him a key to the room and instructed for him to come in, sit on the chair and hit the play button on the computer, and I would come out of the bathroom and give him a treat.

I decided that I would go to SoHo to shop that afternoon, and I was feeling a bit tired and bloated I started to get mild cramps, and it was then that I felt something damp in my panties.

"OH NO!" I said aloud, and I was certain that I was overheard by shoppers talking to myself. "THIS IS SO NOT HAPPENING."

I headed for the ladies room, and my fear became a reality—I had started my period. I freaked out and texted Marian.

Text Message:

Teri:	SOS! I just started my period!
Marian:	Oh no!
Teri:	I'm going to die! This so isn't happening

Marian: Give me a min and I will call you

My phone rang a few minutes later, and Marian was on the line. It was the first time that I heard her voice, and she sounded like an angel that was coming to save me.

"Hello? Marian?"

"Hi, sweetie, are you okay?"

"NO! He's coming back for the rest of the weekend tonight, and what am I going to do? I was going to give him his lap dance, and now how am I going to do that? I'm bloated and swelling up like the biggest kind of blowfish!" I said dramatically as if this were the end of the world.

"Calm down. Have you told him?" she asked in a calm angelic voice which was soothing to me.

"No, I haven't yet. How do I tell him? Hi, babe! Hey, how's it goin? I'm on the rag here. Hope that doesn' t gross you out like it does me! Love you!"

"Why don't you just tell him? I have a feeling that it will be okay."

"Have you ever like, done it when you are on it?" I asked.

"I have, and it's not that bad. It depends on how your partner feels about it."

We talked for thirty minutes or so, and she told me that Will had called her several times that day I was hoping that they would hit it off and meet; they were both very special to me. Plus I could take all the credit for this if it did work out, I joked. She was right, and when I told Jason, he didn't seem to mind, yet he did admit that it would be a new experience for him as well.

Later that night, I got into the khaki minidress that buttoned down and pinned the badge on my pocket. I put on sexy black thong panties, trying to hide my tampon string by tucking it up in front. I wore the tie around my bare neck and rolled up the black fishnet thigh—highs and almost-to-the-knee lace-up six—inch stripper boots. I put my hair in a ponytail and put on the fake Ray-Ban sunglasses and open—finger leather gloves. I was ready. I was not ready. I was a wreck. I logged online, hoping to see Marian there, and she was.

MSN Chat:

Teri: Hi! I'm so glad you are here! I feel really fat here and I only practiced my dance twice. I need a drink.

Marian: I'm sure you look great and you are not fat!

I turned on my cam, and for the first time, I saw Marian. She was more beautiful than in her photos, and I found myself staring at how graceful she looked as she sat there looking back at me. I blew her a kiss, and she blew one back my way. I modeled my "cop girl" outfit for her and she gave me thumbs up, reassuring me that I looked great and that this night would be wonderful despite my unlucky, misfortunate visit by the "rag fairy."

Teri: You sure I'm ready?

Marian: You are ready; just don't have anymore to drink. Put that drink down! You don't want to be drunk when he gets there, you want to remember this.

I knew she was right, but alcohol was something that I had no control over, so as soon as I switched off the Webcam and she could not see me, I chugged down the rest of my wine and poured myself another glass. He called me, saying that he was there, so I went into the bathroom and closed the door, giving him directions to sit in the chair by the bed and turn the music on.

"She's my cherry pie, cool drink of water such a sweet surprise, tastes so good make a grown man cry, sweet cherry pie!" This was my cue to come out dancing, Warrant's "Cherry Pie" started blasting, and I wasted no time in walking out and performing as stripper Tawny for the first time, amazed at how at ease I was when the music started and it was showtime. Then, halfway through my dance, the music stopped.

"Oh no!" I screamed, genuinely upset because I was doing very well, really. "What the hell happened?"

"I don't know, but its okay, babe, you did good You're like a slice of cherry pie." he said as he pulled me into his lap. I knew that he was ready for me before I even started my dance, so I surrendered to him, right then, right there, in the chair he was sitting in, and I forgot all about having started my period. It didn't matter after all.

The next day we decided to go out to a nice dinner and dancing. It was evident that Jason had issues with jealousy, yet I would learn the extent of it on this night. Our evening was going great until I smiled back at the waiter, and that's all it took. The night was basically over, so was the weekend. This was the second time we had met in person, and both times we fought, not great odds.

After he left Sunday, I had some time to kill before my flight, so I decided to go shopping. I was in a department store, sampling perfumes, when someone tapped me on the shoulder. I turned around, and there was this blond woman in her forties with a waiflike figure and pale skin standing before me.

"What is it that you design?" she asked. I looked around me to try to figure out how she knew I was a designer. "Do you design clothing?" she asked again.

"No. How did you know I was a designer? I design interiors and furniture," I answered, still puzzled by how she could have known this and wondering why she thought it was clothing that I designed since I was in ratty jeans with holes and a pink tube top, real fashionable.

"Be careful. There is sexuality surrounding you now, and there are very bad people out there. You don't always make the right choices. Don't trust so easily. Be careful, dear." She said this as if this was supposed to not have sounded at all strange as I stood there puzzled and dazed. She smiled at me and turned and walked away as I tried to say something, but bewilderment had my tongue. Finally, after a few seconds, I called after her.

"Wait! Why do you say that? Don't go!" I yelled in a weak shaky voice. My head was spinning as her words went through my mind again. Words of warning? Was she psychic? I don't believe in psychics even though I have my palms read occasionally out of pure amusement. *How did she know I designed?* I thought to myself. The mood to shop left me, so I decided to hale a cab and go to the airport early. As I did this, Ryan texted me.

Ryan:	Hey sexy, how's New York? Miss me?
Teri:	Ryan! OMG this weird chick just freaked me out!
Ryan:	That's not hard to do. Why what did she say? That she didn't like your shirt?
Teri:	I'm serious. She knew I was a designer
Ryan:	OH! WOW!
Teri:	Stop. How did she know this?
Ryan:	I don't know, why did that freak you out?
Teri:	That's not all. She told me to be careful. That I had sexuality surrounding me.
Ryan:	Lol, and you believe this shit?
Teri:	Well, yeah
Ryan:	You are crazy. I still want you though.
Teri:	Okay, fine. Text me tomorrow bad boy.

Ryan had no idea that I was there to see Jason, and I would not tell him. He still didn't know that there *was* a Jason, and I wasn't going to lose my best local guy just yet. A cab finally took notice of me and stopped.

"Where are you going?" the cabdriver asked me in a thick Middle Eastern accent. He was maybe my age and smiled a lot.

"JFK please," I answered, still a bit dazed and extremely tired. The night before, Jason and I had argued because of the waiter incident, and I didn't sleep well. This cabby was a chatter. In the first ten minutes of the ride, I knew that he had converted to Judaism and would seek out nice Jewish girls online to date. He was originally from Iran and had been in this country now for ten years. I must have drifted off, for how long, I don't know, but when I woke up, he was still talking to me, not having noticed I had dozed off.

"Wait, back up," I said. "I fell asleep here. What was that you were saying?"

"I say that I took her to a nice dinner. I bought her perfume she said she wanted. Then I never hear from her again," he replied.

"Oh, that's not good," I stated, actually really feeling a bit sorry for him now.

"I even buy her flowers she say she liked and some chocolate too." This story was getting more pathetic by the minute.

"Wait, this was your first date?" I asked.

"Yes."

"And you took her to dinner, bought her flowers, perfume, and chocolates, and you have called her and not heard back?"

"Yes. That's what I say. It is true."

"Wow, sweetie, that's sad. She doesn't sound like she deserves you. Move on, there are more girls out there waiting for a guy just like you," I told him as if he would maybe believe this, hoping that he would.

"You?" he asked.

"What? Me?" I asked him, not really wanting to know what he meant by that.

"Yes, when is your flight?"

"Oh, not for three hours yet. I'm early. I was shopping and this woman . . . never mind."

"I know a hotel. We can go there, yeah?" he asked. Just when I thought I was over my earlier freak-out stint, I felt it coming back, and fast.

"Oh, no, no, I'm not Jewish," I said as this was the first thing that came to my mind. "And I am married."

"But you are not happy. I see this. You need sex. You need a man. You are a very sexual woman. I can tell," he said bluntly. It was after he said this that I had to ask myself if I had *fuck me now* written on my forehead that I was not aware of.

"Well, I don't cheat on my husband," I lied. "And I am happy."

"No, you are not. It's okay though. Here is my number, if you ever come back to visit. I would take you to dinner and buy you flowers and perfume and chocolates," he said sweetly. When we got to the airport, he didn't want to charge me the cab fare, but I insisted that I pay him. He seemed very nice and a bit lost, like I was. I felt sorry for him and hoped that he would find what it was he was looking for in this world of online dating. I wondered if his "nice Jewish girl" used lonely men like him to gain things that she wanted. People like that disgusted me, then it dawned on me that I wasn't much different from her. I didn't use men for material things, rather for validation. I used them for validation to prove my self worth, yet the more validations that I received, the less my self-worth seemed.

Ryan texted me the next day, and I agreed to meet him. For the first time, I felt like the cheater I was. Not because I was cheating on only my husband, but because I was cheating on Jason too. It was not sex that I needed, yet I could not say no when he asked to see me. I wanted to see Ryan, and I hated myself for that. I drove to the hotel and put Jason's song to me on the stereo and asked myself for the hundredth time, *I love him, so why is he still not enough?*

CHAPTER EIGHTEEN

Cut to February '07

Present time: Four months have passed

They say that time flies. I say that they are right. It was only just last spring when this nightmare started, and in just a few months spring will be here again. It is now February 07, and I am no better than I was the previous April. I cannot function. I cannot eat. I have lost ten pounds in two weeks, and when I open my eyes in the morning, the reality of my world only makes me wish I were still sleeping. Binge drinking has consumed me, and I'm smoking up to two packs a day now. I try to write, knowing that I must finish this book, yet I cannot think clearly because I find that as I write about the things that I have done, the pain sometimes becomes unbearable. With every word I type, I take myself back to that place and time and pray that when this book is written, I will have healed and can once again look at myself in the mirror and maybe find myself once more. I have stopped sending Jason the chapters of the book to read as well since it would only take him back, reminding him of all the things that I did that hurt him.

When we would say goodbye there would always be that last kiss and last hug before we would see each other again. Departing would always be the most unpleasant part of my visits, and watching him walk out the door was never easy. Yet there was no kiss goodbye this time, no hug. Only one last glance was thrown in my direction, one of disgust, anger, and pity in his eyes as he cast this look upon me which haunts me still. It is a few days before Valentine's Day, and I'm here to see Jason for the sixth time now in six months. Valentine's Day will be our sixth month anniversary. Six months of both heaven and hell. I called Will, who has been my rock these past few months.

"Will, I did it again. Why do I do shit that pushes him away from me? I made him so angry last night that he left." I cried, barely able to speak as I said this.

"What happened? Why did he leave? You two have been fighting so much lately, what's the deal?" Will asked.

"I pushed him away like I always do. My counselor says it's because I am testing him, like I do my husband. I do things that make them mad to see if they love me enough to stay. I don't understand why it is I do this, Will. I want to understand why I do this."

"What happened? Why did he leave?" he asked, trying to understand.

"I told him to. As I was doing this, there was a little voice in my head screaming STOP, but I couldn't, Will. I gave him back his ring. Will, what is wrong with me? Am I a tard?"

Will tried his best to console me, and I called Marian next and she di d the same. I started to see a counselor upon Jason's request several weeks earlier. He recognized that I was not getting any better and insisted that I seek out help. I called her next.

"Celine, I'm in New York, and I'm not doing too well," I sobbed. Will and Marian had done their best with me, but I was broken-down. I was feeling for the first time of ending this pain and getting off this ride for the last time. I was in trouble.

"Teri, we talked about this before you went to see him. You weren't supposed to push him away this time. You must control the urge to do this and know that you are worthy of someone loving you back," she stated. Celine was in her fifties, with very short gray hair and glasses. She had rosy cheeks and reminded me of Mrs. Clause, with her round figure and the way she squinted her eyes as she smiled. But what I really liked about her was that I trusted her. There was one session when she actually cried with me.

"I know, but I couldn't help it. It's done, and he's not coming back. Nor is my husband," I cried, feeling sorry for myself.

"You must not think about Jason or your husband right now, you must think about Teri and her children. Are you thinking of hurting yourself?"

"Yes, but it was only a thought. I have it under control," I lied. Control was the last thing that I had. I traded in the Cheaters Club site for a MyS pace page where I was adding and chatting with many men; most were young and gorgeous. My collection of what Celine referred to as "specimens" grew daily as to validate myself with every new friend I accepted. I justified this because it was not I who would seek them out, they found me. Even though this hurt Jason, and my husband even found my page, I couldn't stop. This was my link to the chat world I could not give up.

"Teri, you are juggling too many balls here. You must give up some of them. Lay down a ball, just one," she said. "You need to confront the issues which happened to you in your childhood before you can heal. This is a lot within itself, and then you add your relationships with both your husband and Jason, the continuous need to seek out new men, and then your book, which causes you pain to write. Which ball is it going to be?"

"Jason, or my husband, or both. But not my book," I answered immediately.

"Then focus on your book, and we will work through this together," she said. I hung up the phone and took a deep breath and tried to focus. It had been a week since I was last able to write, not being able to concentrate, so I forced myself to focus. I read what I had last written and closed my eyes and took a deep breath. I took myself back to that time in October four months earlier.

October '06

"Surprise!" everyone screamed as I walked my husband into the club. It was his birthday and I had told Jason that this night was for my husband, I would not have my BGC with me. Dozens of his friends and family members were there but he wasn' t happy and he wanted to go home.

"Can we leave now?" he asked only an hour into the party. "I've had enough of this and I don't want anymore shots" His friends were sending over shots and he had decided several years ago that he was not going to drink so much anymore; this was when he decided that I wasn't going to either.

"No, we haven't had cake yet. Can you act like you're not having a rotten time at least? Please?"

He glanced at his Rolex watch and said, "I'm leaving in thirty minutes. Nine o'clock, but stay here if you want. Tear it up." I sucked down the two shots of tequila in front of me and ordered two more. I had a surprise for him and in the mood he was in it was going to be less than fun.

"No way, I'm going with you. I have a birthday surprise for you remember?" I asked the servers to help me serve the cake. I went in the kitchen, carefully lighting sixty candles. I carried the cake out, as everyone sang happy birthday to him.

"Make a wish, my husband. Wish for something grand."

"You were grand. You were so grand," he said to me, brushing my cheek with the back of his fingers. No one seemed to have heard this. I didn't shift my gaze from hearing his words as he blew out his candles and everyone clapped. I stood there frozen as his words echoed in my mind. We left the club and we were silent on the drive home.

"Now sit in this chair, I will be right back in like two minutes." I told him when we walked in the house. "You're gonna love this, promise birthday boy."

I went to change into Nurse Betty, knowing that Steph probably told him about her anyway. I cranked up my signature song and started to show him what I had. Moving my hips in a figure eight motion I lifted up one side of my dress exposing my panties. I turned around and slapped my bum, slowly bending over. I moved back up and started to walk towards him and brushed my chest up against his face throwing my hair back and then forward so that it covered the top of his head. Straddling his lap, I rocked my hips from side to side as I moved one heeled foot between his legs. This is when he pushed me away. It was not expected.

"Okay, that was great baby."

"What? The songs not over yet. I'm not done. Don't you want me to finish?"

"No, you did a great job. I loved it. Thank you."

"Okay. Well, it's your birthday. Do you want to do it or something?" I asked, leaning in to kiss him.

"Baby, don't do this. I just want to sit in my chair and relax. That's what I want to do."

"Don't you think I'm sexy? Why don't you want me anymore?" Okay, I knew that these weren't the words to ask but my ego was shattered here and I was confused to why he didn't want to see the rest of my dance.

"Fine, lets see it. Go. Finish it so I can watch TV."

"No. I don't want to now. Happy birthday." I sulked and went downstairs to change. I popped a Valium, lay on my bed and drifted off to sleep. *You were grand. You were so grand.*

Halloween was in a week, and I had already booked a ticket to go see Jason again in November. I was only able to go for one night, making up some excuse that I was going to a design showcase in North Carolina, and my husband seemed to believe me. I missed him more than I had, yet I still could not seem to tell Ryan about Jason. I made my first attempt to do so one day when I was out finding costumes for me and my children. Jason was texting me, and I started to receive texts from Ryan as well. I decided that it was time I told Ryan that I had met someone who I was in love with. I was getting fast at texting several people at the same time.

Ryan Text:

Ryan:	Hi sexy, what are you up to?
Teri:	No good.
Ryan:	That's a given.

Jason Text:

Jason:	What costume did you chose?
Teri:	My son wants me to be Snow White; I want to be a French Maid
Jason:	That will go over well. Better be Snow White

Ryan Text:

Ryan:	What are you doing now?
Teri:	Texting Jason
Ryan:	Jason Doe?

This was when I had to just tell him, but I found myself texting this instead:

———

Teri:	Yeah, how did you know? You are so smart! Do you miss me?
Ryan:	Of course I do silly.
Teri:	Good, you had better.

Jason Text:

| Teri: | I miss you baby. I miss you so much. |
| Jason: | I miss you too Teri. |

I was going to keep Ryan around. I wasn't ready to give him up or the twenty other men who had my new Bad Girl Cell number or the countless others who were on my Yahoo Messenger list. I blocked most from being able to see when I was online except for a dozen or so out of about a hundred. Will, Adam, and Brett, the twenty-five-year-old med-school student, were who I chatted with the most when Jason was not online. I wouldn't agree to meet Brett, but he was persistent in trying to do so. He was the devil, and it would be too late before I would figure that out. Brett was truly evil. I would not see that he would poison my mind against Jason just to claim me his. One night, when Jason was working, I would chat with Brett.

Yahoo Chat:

Brett:	When are you going to dump that loser and meet me?
Teri:	Hey now, don't talk about my boy friend that way. Really, it's not funny and its offensive Brett.
Brett:	You know I'm kidding baby. Have you ever thought about leaving your husband?
Teri:	Yeah, for like a minute. No, I'm not going anywhere. I am not happy and I would do anything to be with Jason, but my husband is not well. If I leave him now, and something was to happen to him I couldn't live with that. Plus I don't want to lose everything.
Brett:	All you have to say is that you are afraid of him. That he abuses you and he would have to leave.
Teri:	But he doesn't. Well, not physically that is. Well, only once he did but it was a long time ago. I could never do that Brett it would be a lie.
Brett:	So, haven't you ever lied to get what you wanted before? Don't tell me you haven't because we all have.
Teri:	Not at the expense of hurting someone, no, I haven't.
Brett:	Do you think that he wouldn't lie and hurt you if he needed too? And what about Jason? You really think he's not doing some girl there in New York and not telling you? He probably has many

	of them. He's my age baby, trust me, I know guys and how they are.
Teri:	Well, you don't know my guy. He's true to me.
Brett:	When you figure out I'm right I will be here for you. It's me that you should be with. You need to lose both your husband and boy friend.
Teri:	Never gonna happen, but thanks anyways.

It seemed as in every chat Brett would plant seeds of doubt in my head about Jason's faithfulness to me. I started to wonder if he might have been right. I became paranoid and clingy with Jason, always needing to know what he was doing every minute of the day. This was not healthy for me or our relationship. I became jealous, a trait that I always considered pathetic. I would see jealous women and would feel embarrassed for them that they were so insecure that they showed this "ugly monster." Now, with the help of Brett, I had my own ugly monster, and this monster would never leave me.

I found myself texting him through the night if he was out with his friends. I always felt sick to my stomach when he told me that he was meeting his buddies for drinks in fear that he would meet someone, or if his friends would bring their girlfriends, who would bring her friends. I was making myself crazy. On nights when he was out, I waited online for him, sneaking glances at the clock every fifteen minutes and wondering what he was doing. This was the first time that I would actually think about moving there to be with him part of the time. But how would that work? I wasn't going to leave my husband or children.

It still bothered me as well that he had not told anyone about me except for his brother and a few friends. I was the one who was married and needed to be careful as to not get caught, yet my mother, sisters, daughter, and friends knew about him. I was beginning to wonder if I meant as much to him as he did to me. This wonderment turned into anger as I added yet another new guy to my Yahoo chat list, justifying it with this newfound anger. Another reason that I added new guys to my Yahoo was because my fan club was wasting away. They all knew that I had a boyfriend and said that I had changed.

"Where's that bad girl? I miss her!" many of them would say to me. I had stopped having any type of cybersex with them, nor did I even turn on my cam for even a game of Literary. If the conversation swayed toward a sexual manner, I would say goodbye. I didn't have it in me to get these guys off online anymore, and it made me sick.

I spent most of my nights with Jason online, and our next meeting was soon. I lived for the day I would see him again. The many men on my Yahoo were still fighting for my attention, and the more that they told me how much they desired me, the more insecure I became. I needed to hear these things from Jason, and it was not in his nature to tell me that he desired me all the time or that I was beautiful or that he loved me. I decided that I needed to test his love for me, and so the games began. I would find ways to manipulate him by trying to make him jealous. This would prove to be detrimental in the long run. One day, about a few weeks before I would go see him in November, I played a dangerous game that I would soon regret.

It was a Sunday night, and we had agreed to meet online at eleven o'clock in the evening. He was leaving on a hockey tournament the next day, and it would be four days before I would get to see him on cam or chat with him online since he never took his laptop with him on these tournaments. He was going out with his friends that night and said that he would be back to spend some time with me. Eleven o' clock came and went. I was chatting with several of my guys while waiting and becoming angry. I poured myself another cocktail, adding more vodka in it this time.

As midnight approached, I was livid. He could have at least called me to tell me he was going to be late, knowing that I was waiting for him. I continued to drink, and it was after one thirty in the morning when I received a text from him saying that he was on his way home.

Jason:	On my way home now, what are you doing?
Teri:	Chatting
Jason:	Who with?
Teri:	A lot of them. Ttyl

Three minutes went by.

Jason:	What did you tonight?
Teri:	I'm busy here okay?

Knowing that he would sign onto his computer when he got home, I decided that I would turn on my cam for someone. When I did this, he would be able to see that my cam was being viewed. I decided to turn it on for Tim, who I was playing a game of Literary with. Tim was thirty-eight and from Missouri. He was a shy guy, and I only chatted with him when there was no one else online. He looked exactly like Don Knotts, and Tim was infatuated with me. I turned on my cam, and he did his as well. As intoxicated as I was, he didn't look any better on cam than he did in his photos. I squinted my eyes slightly to see if he would look a bit better when I did this, but nope, didn't work.

Yahoo Chat with Tim:

Tim:	T you are really pretty.

T was what he would call me.

Teri: Thanks Tim, you are . . . um cute too.
Tim: What are you wearing?
Teri: Down boy . . . it's your turn. Go.

Jason had signed in and noticed that I was on cam. He instantly messaged me.

Yahoo Chat with Jason:

Jason: Who are you camming with?
Teri: Alex

I knew that if I told him it was Alex he would react. He reacted exactly as I knew he would. Alex was the one who he was most jealous of out of all of my friends, remembering back to when Alex was the one that I wanted the most. In reality, I hadn't chatted with Alex for a month now, and Jason knew this.

Jason: What? Are you fucking kidding me?
Teri: Nope, I'm a bit busy here J, we are playing a game. I will buzz you when I'm done.
Jason: Whatever. Have fun T. Later

I made Jason wait for forty minutes until I was done playing my game with Tim. The whole time I tried not to notice the way Tim looked at me with his buggy eyes staring at my cleavage. If I wasn' t so angry with Jason, there would have been no way that I could have finished my game. I said a quick goodbye to Tim and turned my cam on for Jason and invited him to share his cam with me, not knowing if he would after I made him wait for so long. As he lay in his bed with a sweatshirt on, he looked tired, but there was something else about the way he looked that I could not decipher. There was no sign of anger that I made him wait for me, and he just looked at me with as if I were a stranger. He wouldn't say much that night, and as I became more desperate to gain his attention, I started to undress. He would just watch me that night, not participating in the cam sex. I then knew he must have been angry with me because this was a first. When I said goodnight to him, I felt for the first time that something was terribly wrong. My biggest fear had just come true, and I just didn't know it at the time.

CHAPTER NINETEEN

October '06

The next day I did not hear from Jason, and he always texted first thing in the morning. I knew he was driving to Toronto to his hockey tournament, and at about one o'clock that afternoon, I finally texted him. He said he was on the road and he would text me later. I never received that text. It was later that evening when he called me for five minutes, telling me that he was there and he was going out to dinner. The following day I did not hear from him either. This was not like him. I didn't want to text or call him, knowing that he was busy with his tournament and friends, but deep down inside I knew something was up.

Another day passed, and my kids and husband were out of town. I had made arrangements to take Paul to drinks for his birthday and had a gift for him. I hadn't seen him since June, and I missed his friendship. I broke down and called Jason that afternoon, thinking that it was ridiculous that we had not spoken for two days. I was going to go see him in six days, and I was a bit confused by his distant demeanor.

"Hi, baby, are you having too much fun?" I asked him, hoping he'd tell me that he was sick—at least that would be a reason for why he didn't call.

"Yep. Won the last game this morning," he said shortly.

"Good job. I miss you. Haven't heard from you, so I wanted to call and say hello." My heart was breaking here as I waited for him to say he missed me as well. He never did say it.

"Babe, I have to go. I will text you later." He said this and I heard the phone click and he was gone. I was angry, confused, and hurt by this. Only seconds after he hung up, Ryan texted me.

Ryan:	BOO!
Teri:	Hey baby
Ryan:	What's my sexy girl up to today?
Teri:	Just down, alone. Lonely.
Ryan:	Why? What's up babe?
Teri:	Nothing that matters anymore I guess. Where are you?

Ryan: I'm leaving work.
Teri: Come over I need you now . . .
Ryan: To your house? Isn't that dangerous?
Teri: No, he's out of town. I need you NOW Ryan.
Ryan: Ter, what's wrong?
Teri: Just come! Or don't, then! I don't care!
Ryan: Down girl . . . I will be there . . . tell me where you live.

I gave Ryan my address. In six months, he had never been to my house; actually no one had. I don't know why I asked him to come by, but I needed him—or thought I needed him. Thirty minutes later, he was at my door.

"Hi, you found it. I'm so glad you are here," I said sadly.

"Crazy girl, what's the matter with you?" he asked.

"Rye, I have been seeing someone. He lives in New York. I didn't want to tell you because I didn't want to lose you. I love him, Rye, but something's not right here."

"All those trips to New York were for him?" I could see the disappointment in his face. I explained to him my relationship with Jason and the things that had happened over the past few months, hoping that he would choose to stay after I told him this. "So you are telling me that you have had a boyfriend for three months now and have been seeing me? Are you still seeing him?" he asked.

"Yes," I said, looking down at the floor, expecting him to walk out the door. But instead he held me in his arms.

"Tell Jason then that today I get to do his girlfriend," he said trying to get a smile out of me without it working.

"You are staying? Really?" I asked.

"Ter, we are both married. You mean a lot to me, but I can't tell you that you can't see anyone else. I'd rather you didn't, but it seems as if you love him," he said as I looked into his big brown eyes. This was my Ryan; he was open and honest.

I took him into my bedroom and lay on the bed. This was wicked and wrong, and for some reason, I felt no guilt, nor did I think about Jason or my husband. I just spent the next few hours in his arms, and I realized that Ryan and I shared something special that Jason could not begin to understand. We were both in marriages that made us unhappy, trying to grasp bits of happiness in any form that would come our way. I had been Ryan's only affair since we had met, so I was the escape from his reality. I just wondered why it was it took more than one person for me to escape from mine. As much as I loved Jason, I needed more. I just didn't understand what it was that I needed. Ryan stayed for a bit, and we downloaded music on my computer, and I was grateful that he came over and saved me from my pity fest. I was meeting Paul for drinks in a few hours, so I said goodbye to Ryan and got dressed.

Paul texted me an hour before we were to meet, saying that his wife had invited friends over for dinner and that he could not make it. I was a bit disappointed, not because I wanted to see him. Rather, I wanted to get out of the house. It was six o'clock in the evening, and I called my girlfriends to go out, but none were free. I texted Jason again.

Teri: Hi, how are you today? Everything okay?
Jason: Yep

Minutes went by and I didn't hear back from him. I had been drinking so I knew that I was about to lose my temper here, before I could contain it I texted back.

Teri: What is your problem?
Jason: You. You are my problem.
Teri: What the fuck are you talking about?
Jason: You treat me like shit and really I'm done with it. You take me for granted, lie to me, cheat on me.
Teri: Where is this all coming from?
Jason: You. You did this. Oh and by the way, the last time you came to see me; I fucked some girl two days before.
Teri: What?
Jason: Yep. And met a girl Sunday night, that's why I was late.
Teri: You are unbelievable. Did you sleep with her J?
Jason: Nope

My head was spinning as I read what he was texting me. I was hurt and wanted to hurt him back, but I didn't tell him that Ryan was here only hours earlier. If I did tell him this, then it would validate everything that he had just said about me.

Teri: I'm not coming to see you next week. It's over.
Jason: Yeah, I figured that. Go see Alex, let him deal with you and your lies and bullshit.

That night I went out alone. I went to a club, and on the way I got pulled over for crossing over an island while making an illegal U-turn. The police officer was about fifty-five, and I rolled down my window and smiled sweetly, hoping that this would gain me some points.

"Do you know why I pulled you over, young lady?" he asked.

"I do. I crossed over that island." He asked for my license and registration and went back to his patrol car. Minutes later he came back.

"Have you been drinking?" he asked. I was wearing a low-cut blouse, and I noticed that he noticed this as well.

"Yes, I have," I confessed.

"How many have you had tonight?"

"Three. I've had three," I lied, but I knew that I had to admit to more than just a few.

"I should give you a DUI. I'm writing you a ticket for crossing the island, but you need to promise me that you will go home now," he said.

"Thank you, I promise I will go home." I watched him pull out and waited a few minutes before I headed for the club. When I got there, I ordered one more drink. I received another text from Jason.

Jason:	Tell him that you aren't worth it.
Teri:	Tell who?
Jason:	Alex. Tell him you aren't worth the trouble.

These insulting texts kept coming through the night, and my mood was dark. I switched to ice water to try to sober up before I went home, knowing that I was pushing my luck as it was. I drove home and cried, feeling sorry for myself and wondering what took him so long to do this. When I got home I cranked on Warrant's "Cherry Pie" and danced. I danced until I couldn't dance anymore and logged online. It was two o'clock in the morning, and I had stopped responding to Jason's text messages an hour ago. Brett was online.

Yahoo Messenger:

Teri:	Hi, what are you doing up so late?
Brett:	Cramming for a test tomorrow morning. Why are you up?
Teri:	Just got home from the club.
Brett:	And you didn't invite me? Bad girl.
Teri:	I almost got busted for a DUI. Jason and I broke up and he sent me nasty ass texts all night and my life is stinky dog poop
Brett:	Awww, I'm here with you now, tell me what happened baby.

I spent all night chatting with Brett and didn't sleep at all that night. He chatted with me, ignoring his studies and trying to boost my spirits. I agreed to meet him finally since it was over between Jason and me, and this didn't make me feel better. He had to go to class and said good-bye to me at eight o' clock that morning. Marian was online, so I asked if I could call her and told her the events of the night before. I was exhausted but could not sleep or eat. I had put Jason and my song on my computer and noticed that since I started chatting with Brett it was playing again for the one hundredth and fifty-sixth time now.

"Ter, turn it off, don't listen to it anymore. You are making this hard for yourself, babes," Marian said I knew that she was right, but I would listen to it another fifty times before I would turn it off.

"Guess he finally got sick of my lies. Funny, I was expecting this, but now that it has happened, I feel like dying. And guess what? Ryan came over yesterday. Everything that Jason said about me is true."

"I know it's hard, babe, but let him go. He is young, he wants children, and you can't give him that. Its better that this is happening now. Don't you want him to have what you have had? A chance for a family? For children?" she asked. These words hurt to hear. I cried as she spoke them, and I knew that there was only truth in her words.

For the next few days, I didn't eat or sleep much. I spent my time online, meeting new men as I found myself back on the Cheaters Club site. Every night, after my children went to sleep, I would pour myself a strong drink and log on. It was different this time. It didn't feel the same being back there. I had changed. It was no longer exciting or enjoyable seeking out new *bulls*; I just did it to pass the time because I still felt compelled to be online. I sifted through my conversations quickly as they would begin to bore me after a few minutes. Reading a book would have been a better option for me, yet as bored as I was, I still found myself chatting with men I probably wouldn't even speak to if I ran into them at a club. At about one in the morning, I had had enough, so I logged off and went to bed. I had my first date with Brett the next day, and I could only hope that maybe he could make me smile again.

I drove to Orem, which was a twenty minute drive. We decided to have lunch there, meeting in between his classes. He pulled up in his jeep, and he looked better than in his pictures. We had lunch and talked for hours, and he missed his next class. I had to go and agreed to meet him again soon.

"When can I see you again?" he asked as he walked me to my truck.

"Brett, I was supposed to go see him on Tuesday. That's going to be a hard day for me. Let's meet Tuesday so that I don't think about it, okay?" This had to sound pathetic, but I really didn't want to be alone that Tuesday, and my husband was going to be out of town until Thursday of that week.

"See you then, beautiful," he said as he leaned into my truck and kissed me on the cheek. I drove home and thought to myself, *If anyone can help me forget Jase, it is Brett.*

Monday night couldn't come quick enough as I couldn't wait to get online and chat after my children went to sleep. It had been five days since I had last spoken with Jason, and it was not getting easier. The more I chatted with different men, the more I missed him terribly. Adam and Will couldn't even lift my spirits. My heart was broken, and I knew that I would only be using Brett to make me forget, if only for a few hours. It was about ten o'clock that night when I received an incoming message on MSN from Jason.

MSN Chat:

Jason:	Hi Teri, how are you?
Teri:	I'm good thank you, and yourself?

The formality of our hello was strange, reminding me of the first time he said hello to me that August night which seemed so long ago.

Jason:	Are you doing okay?
Teri:	I'm great! Why would you think I wouldn't be okay?
Jason:	Just worried about you.
Teri:	Why's that? I'm fine.
Jason:	Marian told me that you were struggling.
Teri:	Don't worry about me J, really I'm fine.
Jason:	Have you gone out with anyone? Met anyone new?
Teri:	Does it really matter anymore?
Jason:	Yes, yes it does. T, I made a big mistake. I'm miserable. The new girlfriend is making me miserable.
Teri:	Sorry to hear that Jason, but that was your choice. And yes, I met Brett and I'm seeing him again tomorrow.
Jason:	Who's that? And how long have you been chatting with him for?

I began to tell him how I met Brett on another site weeks ago, realizing that it didn't matter anymore to hide that from him. I told him that Brett was his age, going to medical school, and that I had moved on. I wanted him to hurt the way he hurt me, so I made it seem as if I really like Brett. I poured another drink and felt more relaxed now; my hands were shaking the entire time I was typing I missed him so much, but there was no way I was going to let him know this. He told me that his new girlfriend was insecure and needy of him, wanting to spend every minute with him. It was not even a week since they had been seeing each other, and he was tired of her already.

We chatted for four hours that night, and I ignored everyone else online, including Brett. I knew that he was missing me as well, and I wished that I was still going to see him the next day, but I had cancelled my ticket although it was neither refundable nor transferable. I had cancelled it so that I would not be not tempted to go. I had met someone from Jersey online a few days before who wanted for me not to cancel my ticket and go to meet him. He was twenty- eight, and his name was Eric. He was extremely nice, yet I knew that I could not go see him and know that Jason was so close by. I chose to lose the ticket. When Jason said goodbye to me that night it was bittersweet. The four hours had passed by rather quickly, and for the first time in days, I felt truly happy. The moment I logged off, my heart felt heavy, and I was sad. I missed my boyfriend.

The next day Brett came to my house at ten in the morning. I glanced at the clock, and he was right on time, but then my heart sank as I realized that the flight that I would have been taking that morning was leaving in ten minutes. I forced a smile and answered the door. It was weird having him here even though Ryan was here only a week earlier. Before he got here, I had downed a half a glass of tequila at nine thirty that morning, not because I was nervous, but because I was sad. Brett was going to be my knight in shining armor who would step in and save me from my world, my miserable marriage, and from Jason.

"Hi, baby, you have a great house. Did you design it?" Brett asked.

"Yep, and did a lot of the work myself too. I have my own power tools," I bragged. "See the mantle hood? I built it, and it took me— . . . "

Before I could finish the sentence he had me in his arms and kissed me. I was surprised that I actually enjoyed this more than I thought I would.

"I want to see the cop outfit," he said. "Dance for me."

"No, that outfit was for Jason. You know that. How about Nurse Betty? She's hot."

"No, the cop one. Now please," he demanded.

"I never promised you a lap dance! Why do you want one now?" I asked.

"I want what he had and more," he said without smiling.

"Who are you talking about, Brett?"

"Who was it that you said you loved? Jason? Give me what you gave to him."

"This is no competition, I hope. Jason is not in my life anymore. You don' t have to compete with him, you know," I commented, a bit uneasy.

"Do it for me? Please?" he asked sweetly this time, and he looked like an angel as he took off his shirt and sat in a chair.

"Give me a few minutes to change. And oh, better get out your dollars—I'm not cheap."

I danced for him like I had been dancing for ten years. It struck me as odd as how I was so nervous dancing for Jason yet I exerted extreme confidence in doing this now for Brett. He was so worked up that I barely finished my dance before he scooped me up in his arms and carr ied me to the sofa. He unbuttoned my dress, and I wrapped my legs around his waist as he positioned himself on top of me. He pulled out a condom, and I sat up on the sofa.

"Brett, I don't know . . . I feel as if I still belong to him. Maybe we should not do this."

"First of all, you are married. If you belong to anyone, it's your husband, not him. And second of all, you need me. He's gone, and I am here for you now."

I did need him, or at least I needed him that day. I got up and walked into my bedroom without saying a word as he followed me. Even though I was not drunk, I don't recall much except that at one time I had my eyes closed and called out Jason's name.

"Open your eyes," he said after I had just said this.

"God, I am so sorry, Brett. I'm so sorry," I cried. This didn't feel right I felt sick to my stomach. "I can't do this."

"It's okay, baby, its okay. Just don't close your eyes when you're making love to me. I'm not Jason, and I want for you to see that it is me who is making love to you. I'm not him, but I can be more if you'll let me."

"I'll try to. I want to," I said as I was still crying. He wiped my tears away, and I could see that he was starting to feel too much for me. I wanted to tell him not to, but I was glad in a way that he did care. I needed someone who wasn't married like Ryan was to be there for me. He held me for the longest time, and I found comfort in his arms, and for a brief moment, I forgot that I was supposed to be on an airplane heading for New York, I forgot about Jason, I forgot about my husband. I forgot about my life.

CHAPTER TWENTY

October—November '06

After Brett left, I logged online. I was hoping that Marian would be there, but she wasn't. Jason was online, and I said nothing to him for the longest time. An hour went by, and I decided to say hello after I realized that he was not going to. I knew that he was upset, knowing that I was going to see Brett that day.

MSN Chat:

Teri:	Hi Jason
Jason:	Hi Teri

This was a far cry from our usual "Hi babe" greeting to each other, but he wasn't mine anymore, and I had to remember this.

Teri:	How's your day going?
Jason:	Good. So when is your date?
Teri:	He just left actually.
Jason:	Left where? You mean he went to your house? You let him come to your house?
Teri:	Yes, he was here.
Jason:	You had sex with him in your bed didn't you?
Teri:	Jase . . . .
Jason:	I have to tell you something. I had knots in my stomach all day knowing that you were going to see him today. Are you going to start seeing him?
Teri:	Yes, I think so.
Jason:	That was fast. Guess it didn't take you long to move on.
Teri:	I have to go here J; I will talk to you later okay? You have a good day.

The truth was that it was too painful to chat with him. It was time to figure out what I wanted and what was going to make me happy. I got into my truck and started to drive. I had no idea where it was I was going, but I would not go home until I had dissected my feelings and thoughts and looked within myself for some answers.

I drove for hours and thought about the hundreds of online chats with the men, trying to recall at least a quarter of them without avail. I tried to remember the names of the men that I had met in person and could only name a few. I wondered if I subconsciously wanted to be caught. This had to stop; I owed my husband the truth. I owed him his life back. I knew that I needed to leave my marriage, not for Jason or for any man, but for myself. This was the first time in my marriage that I considered ending it, yet I knew that if I stayed, the devil would own my soul, if he hadn't already. I had already shaken the devil's hand, but I wanted to keep what was left of who I used to be.

When I got home, I saw my husband's truck in the driveway. He had come home a few days early I panicked, thinking that Brett was here only hours before and wondered if there was any evidence of this. I wiped the tears from my face, as I had been crying, and went into the house.

"What are you doing back so soon?" I asked as I smiled and gave him a quick kiss.

"We are heading back to Boise in the morning. Trent had to be home today, so I'm taking Kip with me," he answered. He was purchasing restaurant equipment and hauling it back. "What have you been doing?"

"Nothing fun, for sure. I think I will go shopping for a few," I said as I knew I needed to get out of the house before he realized I was not doing too well.

"Come here," he demanded. I was sure I was caught, thinking that Brett left something or that I still smelled like him or that . . .

"What?" I asked.

"Come sit on this," he said as he unbuttoned his pants. I felt instantly sick. I could not believe that he wanted sex now. It had been almost a year now, and of all days he wanted sex today? This was his usual way of asking for sex, as I remembered. He was not the type of man who would kiss you first or was romantic in any way, and it was always "come sit on this" or "come suck my dick." It never used to bother me that he would do this when he was initiating sex, yet it repulsed me now.

"Honey, I really don't feel well," I said, and this was not a lie. "Can we do this later?" Before I knew it, he had his hands all over me, and I knew that I needed to do what he wanted. My husband was pushing four hundred pounds, and this was not at all good. I cringed when he touched me and tried to get through it quickly without showing how uneasy I was about having sex with him. I was thankful that it only lasted a few minutes.

"What's wrong, Ter?" he asked as I got dressed without saying anything or even looking at him.

"Nothing, nothing's wrong," I said under my breath so that he could not hear me.

"Then why are you crying?" he asked me. I didn't even realize that I was crying at the time. I was so exhausted from thinking for hours about what I needed to do and overwhelmed by emotions that before I knew it I confessed.

"I met someone . . . its over. I'm not seeing him anymore. I was lonely, honey, and you weren' t there for me. I needed him," I blurted out. I didn't have another "lie card" within me, and I was relieved that I told him. He asked me who it was and where I had met him. I didn' t want to lie to any further, so I made it brief. "His name is Jason, and he lives in New York. I'm sorry, and you know that I love you, but I have been so lonely. I am not happy, baby, and neither are you."

He didn't say anything as he got up, and it would be weeks before he would bring this up. It was like I never said anything to him about it. He acted no differently toward me, nor did he act as if it bothered him. I was slightly confused but at the same time relieved, knowing still that soon I would end up leaving anyways. I just wanted to get though the holidays.

My husband went to his club, and I found myself alone. I poured myself a drink and logged online. It was six o'clock in the evening, and it was eight o'clock in New York, and I fou nd myself thinking of what I would be doing right at this moment if I were in New York with Jason as I was supposed to be. Only a few minutes later, I got a text from Jason' s phone. It was a picture text of him, and when I opened it to view it, I realized how much I had missed his face.

Jason:	Babe, if my computer is working can I see you on cam tonight?
Teri:	J, I don't know. I will think about it ok? Where are you?
Jason:	At a dinner for my sergeant. I really made a mistake T. I have been miserable. I miss you.
Teri:	I have you as well.
Jason:	Babe, can you come see me tomorrow?
Teri:	You are kidding me right? Jase, I was supposed to be there today, I lost my ticket and you want me to come see you tomorrow?
Jason:	Yes, please will you?

Everything inside of me wanted to tell him no, yet I found myself searching for a ticket. I was chatting with Marian while I did this, and I asked her if I should go.

MSN Chat:

| Marian: | Ter, I can't tell you whether or not to go, that's up to you. How much money did you lose on the ticket for today? And are you willing to spend more for another one? Remember what he did to you babe. |

Teri:	Would you go if you were me?
Marian:	No. I wouldn't go. Is he still dating that girl? What is it that he wants from you, did you ask him this?
Teri:	No, but I know him Mar . . . I know that he misses me and he's just as miserable. I'm going. I know that I shouldn't but I'm going. My husband is going out of town in the morning anyways. I will be back before he even gets home; he won't even know I am gone. I'm going Mar.

I booked my ticket and packed a small overnight bag since I was only going for one night. I glanced at the time, and it was already midnight, and my flight would be leaving in less than ten hours. I spent the night wondering if I were doing the right thing already knowing the answer, yet there was nothing or nobody who could stop me from seeing him again.

New York was beautiful that day, and when the plane landed I smiled, knowing that he was so close by and that we were breathing the same air. I felt as if this was the first time I was going to see him, and I could hardly breathe as I glanced at my watch, realizing that in a few hours I would be in his arms, something that I thought would never happen again.

Seeing him again was like seeing him for the first time. He kissed me when I opened the door and didn't stop kissing me for several minutes.

"Let me see look at you," I said to him. I didn't think that I would see him again, and it felt like a dream that he was here with me.

"I have missed you, J," I said to him as he kissed me.

"I missed you too, Teri. I am so glad you came. Thank you," he whispered in my ear. We spent the next four hours in each other's arms, and the time went by too quickly. Before going to sleep that night, I logged onto my laptop to check messages. Instantly there was an MSN instant messenger pop-up from someone that I didn't recognize, yet he must have been one of the men I had befriended from the Cheaters Site. Usually I didn't give out my MSN to these guys, so I was perplexed that I didn't recognize who it was from the display photo. He was very good-looking and in a suit in his picture and appeared to be in his early thirties.

MSN CHAT:

Mystery guy: Hi baby . . . are you ready for me tonight?
Teri: Who is this? I'm sorry, but I can't remember who you are . . . met you on the Cheaters Site I suppose?
Mystery guy: Awww, I'm hurt. You really don't remember me?

Jason glanced at the screen. "Who is that?" he asked.

"Have no idea, babe."

Mystery guy: Where is your cam sexy? You told me that you would show me it this week.

Teri: I don't think I told you that . . . actually I know that I didn't.

Mystery guy: You fucking women are all alike, you are lying bitches!

Teri: You are an ass, go away and never contact me again, whoever you are.

Mystery guy: Ha! You are dead now! I'm going to bust you! I have your phone number and I'm going to tell your husband what you do. I will make it my mission to do this. I will haunt you.

"He has your phone number? Did you give him your number, T?" Jason asked me as I stared at the computer, reading what this crazy man had written, not being able to move or speak for a second.

"No, I never gave him my number. This I do know. He's bluffing."

"Are you sure? Give me the laptop. Hand it over," Jason said, and I knew he was upset with this crazy guy by now.

Jason: Hey ass wipe, go fuck yourself . . .

Mystery guy: You are a pig . . . you are a liar . . . oink, oink . . . I'm gonna tell on you piggy . . . .

I was shaking by this time, and I was thankful that Jason was dealing with this creep because this was something that I had never come across, and I had no experience with dealing with psychopaths like this guy.

"Babe, just block him now, please. Just block and delete him," I pleaded.

Mystery guy: I know your last name bitch . . . you are going to get fucked up the ass now . . . let me know how it feels . . . mmmmmmmm

"God, Jase! Block him now! I can't read any more of this! And he does have my last name! It's on my MSN. Oh my God, what did I do? What was I thinking, giving him my personal e-mail?" I said as tears were rolling down my cheeks. Jason quit playing this crazy man's game and blocked him. I was determined not to have this ruin my time with Jason, yet I could not sleep, and several hours later, at about four in the morning, I remembered who this creep was. I turned on the light and logged onto the Cheaters Club site. Jason woke up and looked at me through squinted eyes.

"Babe, what are you doing?" he asked.

"Sweetie, I think I gave him my key to my pictures on my profile, I am checking it . . . look, here he is . . . isn't that him?" I asked, a bit relieved that I had remembered who he was. Jason yawned and tried to focus on the photo.

"Yep, that looks like him. You need to turn him in. He violated the rules by not being discrete and making threats. Report him, T, so he doesn' t do this to someone else."

The Cheaters Site had a strict policy and clause for those who violate their rules or those who were threatening.

"No, babe. This man scares me, and he has my last name. He knows what state I live in, and all he has to do is Google me and he would be able to find me. I'm just letting it go. Now come here, bad boy . . . since you are up . . ."

The next morning, I forced this out of my mind. I only had seven more hours with Jason before my flight, and I didn't want to think about this crazy guy. We spent the next few hours laughing and loving each other, and I didn' t think about the incident of the night before, my husband, or Jason's girlfriend, who kept texting him. I didn't want to think about anything except for how happy I felt in his arms.

Getting on that plane to go home that day was the hardest thing, and as the wheels of the plane lifted off the ground, I closed my eyes and breathed in a last breath of the same air that he was breathing—that New York air, his air.

The following day, Jason called me early.

"Babe, I have great news. You know that I was going to end things with her, but she just called me and told me that I don't seem to have enough time for her, so it's over," he said in a pleased tone. "I was going to call her and tell her it was over, but now I don't have to do this. I am so happy. I was really miserable with her. I made the biggest mistake with her. What are you doing today, sweetie?"

"Jason, I don't know what to say, I . . . I have a date with Brett. I was supposed to see him yesterday, but I cancelled to come and see you," I told him.

"You are still going to see him? Why?"

"J, when I got on that plane yesterday you still had a girlfriend."

"Don't meet him, T."

"Jason, don't. He has been there for me, and just because you broke up with her today, you can't expect for me to just tell him that I can' t see him today. What are you trying to tell me? That you want me back?"

"Yes, I do. I have never felt the way I do about you with anyone. I love you, T."

This was when I should have told him that I would not meet Brett, something I would soon regret.

"I love you too Jason, but I don't trust you anymore," I said. These words should have burned coming out of my mouth as I was the one who was married and cheating on my husband, telling endless lies without any remorse for what I was doing. My binge drinking accelerated into something that I could no longer control, and this should have been an indication to me that hiding somewhere deep within me was the shame that I would try to drink away Drowning myself, one ounce at a time.

"T, from what you told me, this guy is dangerous. Don't meet him today," he pleaded.

"Jason, that's ridiculous. Brett is not dangerous. He's a bit spoiled, but he's young," I replied back, now becoming a bit irritated at having to defend Brett's character. It wouldn't matter who it was I was meeting that day, I knew Jason was not going to approve of anyone regardless of who they were.

"He's controlling, and you should just call him and end this now."

"I will, but I will not call him to do this. He's been a friend to me, and I won't end things with him on the phone. Give me this time with him, and I will tell him that it is over, I promise."

"You don't owe him shit. Call him and tell him you can't see him anymore. I'm serious, babe. The guy is psycho, and he's going to get you caught."

I ended up going to see Brett later that afternoon, and as I drove to his apartment, it didn't feel right. I contemplated turning around, but I didn't find myself doing this. He answered the door and he didn' t have a shirt on and he looked so good. *Stop looking! Don't look!* I thought to myself as I stared right at his perfect chest, which so closely resembled Jason's.

"Hi, sexy, look what I made you," he said as he handed me a cocktail.

"What is it?"

"Sangria, do you like sangria?"

"Love it," I said as I took the glass from his hand and gulped half of it down.

"Easy now! Come here, you look tense," he said as he led me to the sofa and started to rub my shoulders. He had strong hands, and I didn' t realize how tense I was until I felt the tension ease and I sipped the rest of my sangria. Moments later, I felt much more relaxed and calm.

"Can I have another drink, please?" I asked him, holding out my glass like a child would. "I can get it myself—"

"No, stay there and relax. I will grab it for you."

"You are too good to me. Hey, I wanted to talk to you about something," I said as he handed me another full glass of sangria. The s angria was starting to hit me. "What did you put in this? It's strong! Anyways, I went to see Jason a few days ago."

"Is that why you cancelled our date yesterday?" he asked.

"Yes. I didn't want to tell you over the phone. I just had to see him again and—"

"Shh. Let's not talk about him," Brett said as he started to kiss me. The next thing I knew, we were in his bedroom, and he was on top of me. I knew that I should have stopped him, but for some reason or another, I chose not to, allowing him to undress me.

"Brett, this can't happen. I'm getting back with—" I said without finishing the sentence as I felt him enter me. "Oh, God, we should not be doing this." It was like I was watching us through a glass window, observing every detail as if I were dreaming this. Afterwards, I got up and poured myself another drink before I spent another two hours with him in his bed. Brett got up and put on his boxer briefs.

"I have to go to work, babe, but wait for me here. I will be back at nine tonight—it's a short shift. Will you wait for me?" he asked me as he walked back to the bed to kiss my forehead. "I'm going to get into the shower here, want to join me?"

"No, I want another drink. Go, don't be late for work." When he got into the shower, I poured myself another drink and my phone beeped. It was a text from Jason, asking where I was and if I had the "talk" with Brett. I thought I had better not respond until Brett left. As luck would have it, it was ten seconds after Brett left that Jason called me.

"Where are you, Teri?" he asked. "Why didn't you answer my text? Are you still there with him?"

"I'm here, and he just left for work."

"You're still at his place? Are you kidding me? Go home. Get up now and go home! You are wasted again, unbelievable," he said, sounding disgusted.

"I can't drive, Jase, or I would, I have to stay for a bit and sober up here."

"Did you tell him it was over? Or, you fucked him didn't you? ANSWER ME, T!"

"No, but I will," I murmured, trying to almost say nothing at all. I had another text coming in from Will. "Babe, let me call you back, okay? Give me a second." I said and hung up before he could respond. I answered Will's text and gulped down what I promised myself would be my last drink. Ryan texted me next, and I answered his text as well. The Bad Girl Cell was beeping with several texts coming in as it did every day. I had an average of six guys who texted me daily. Of course, the six guys would vary depending on what day it was. This was a slow day, and I was grateful for this. I knew that I had to leave before Jason called again, so I got dressed and left Brett a note and headed for home. There was no way I was going to make it home as intoxicated as I was, so I decided check into a Hilton hotel I saw. Only moments after I got into my room, Jason called me.

"Are you on your way home?"

"No, I'm at the Hilton. I started to drive, but I need to sober up here," I said, slurring my words.

"Teri, you need to go home. You can't stay there. He will want to come see you later."

"Give me an hour to sober up, J. I won't stay here, and he doesn't know I'm here anyways."

It took three hours to get me out of that room with Jason's persistent persuasion, and he talked to me all the way home during the drive. The following night, I agreed to meet Brett again, this time at a restaurant, intending to tell him that it was over. Jason was angry that I chose not to do this over the phone and that I was to going see him again. I stayed for only an hour, and Brett was clearly upset when I explained to him that Jason and I were going to work things out.

"You're making the biggest mistake of your life if you go back to that guy, Teri," Brett said as he held my hands across the table. "He's controlling and jealous."

I laughed at this remark as it was the same thing that Jason had said about him.

"What's so funny?" he asked.

"Nothing. This is what I've decided. I don't want to hurt you, yet I want to be with him."

"What about your husband? Are you going to leave him?"

"No, at least not for now. I can't afford to leave him, I would like to though. It's getting to me—all the lies and the deception. I can't look at myself in the mirror anymore, yet I continue to do the things I do."

"Have you ever thought that's why you feel so compelled to drink all the time?" he asked.

"Of course, that's exactly why."

"Then leave your husband, be with me."

"I won't leave my husband right now. Not for you or for Jason. I would rather drink myself to death."

"I won't let you do that. It's going to be me who saves you in the end," he said.

"Brett, I will have to save myself, but for now . . . I'm going to see Jason again."

"You will regret this, but just know that I am here for you when you realize that he's not good for you."

"Okay, but he's who I love. You are so very wrong about him. I have to go now. Take care of yourself," I said as I motioned for the waiter to bring our check. "I got this one," I said with a wink.

I left him with one last hug, and he stood there watching me as I drove away. There was something creepy in the way he was watching me drive away, but I shrugged it off and called Jason.

"Hi, baby. I told him it's over. He won't be coming around again." Little did I know as I said these words what was in store for me next.

CHAPTER TWENTY-ONE

November '06

Thanksgiving was around the corner, and my family was coming into town to spend it with us. Life had become bearable, and my binge drinking became a once-a—week thing at the most. My status was usually set to "invisible" when I was online because I was getting weary of denying those who wanted to have cybersex or see my cam. I ended up creating a new Yahoo address and only invited those who knew I had a boyfriend and would respect that. My messenger list went from approximately two hundred men to thirty, something more manageable.

It was the Monday before Thanksgiving, and my cleaning lady was just finishing her work as I was finishing a design that I was working on my computer.

"I'm craving sushi, Steph. What about you?" I asked her as she was folding the last load of laundry.

"That sounds really good, actually," she answered.

"How much more do you have to do before you are finished?"

"I'm about done. Why?"

"Finish up, and I will treat you to sushi, and hurry! I'm starving!" Before I could finish saying this, Brett popped up on yahoo.

Yahoo Chat:

Brett:	Hi gorgeous, how is my beautiful friend today?
Teri:	Hello Brett, I'm well thanks. Just finishing up some things and going to take my friend to sushi. What are you doing?
Brett:	Studying right now, I have to take a test in an hour so just cramming. How are things with Josh?
Teri:	Jason and I are fine thank you, and you? Are you dating anyone new?
Brett:	No, I'm waiting for you to come back to me . . .
Teri:	Good luck on your test today, and it was good talking to you.
Brett:	Thanks sexy . . . say hello to Josh for me.
Teri:	Real funny Brett . . . Bye . . .

I logged offline and took Steph for the best sushi in town. We ordered a spicy tuna roll as well as a few teriyaki salmon bento boxes and a large sake to share. Our meal had just arrived when I received a phone call from my husband.

"Hello?" I answered as if I wasn't aware it was my husband on the phone.

"I just got a call from your boyfriend in New York. He told me everything. Your game is up." He said to me in the calmest of voices. Ten seconds must have gone by without a response from me or even a breath taken when he added, "You told me that it was over, and now I have your boyfriend calling my bar and rubbing it in my face."

"I don't know what you are talking about. I don't understand . . ." saying this as my words trailed off to almost a whisper. I was numb and in shock as I glanced over at Steph, who stared at me through her thick glasses, trying to figure out what the conversation was all about. Steph was fifty-five, and she could clean a mean toilet, but she was nosey as well as a close friend to my husband.

"Tell your boyfriend not to call me anymore. I don't need him calling me at my club when I'm working."

"What exactly did this person say to you?"

"He said, 'I'm your wife's boyfriend from New York. Where do you think she's going when she comes to New York? I met her online, and she is in love with me. She wants a divorce. She doesn't love you or want to stay in this marriage anymore. Do us all a favor and give her a divorce.'" my husband said and then added, "I don't have time for this bullshit, Ter. Figure out what you want to do, and let's get it done. I'm tired of your drinking and your secret life. What do you do on the computer all night?"

"I have to call you back . . . I don't understand this," I stated as I hung up the phone.

Steph raised an eyebrow and stuffed a piece of sushi in her mouth and started to say something, and I could see the food churning in her mouth as she spoke.

"You knew this was gonna happen," she said as she swallowed what was left in her mouth. "It was a matter of time before he found out."

"What are you talking about, Steph?" I asked her while I was shaking out of control.

"I know what you are doing, I see you online when I'm there. I'm not stupid, Teri. Don't think it's not obvious to everyone. I have been married five times, remember? I know what you are going through. Your husband don't pay any attention to you."

"I'm in trouble, Steph. I'm in so much trouble," I repeated as my mind was racing with these thoughts: *Why would Jason call my husband and tell him this? I'm going to go see him in less than two weeks. This doesn't make sense.* "I have to make a call. I will be back. Finish eating, I just lost my appetite," I said as I walked out of the restaurant and dialed Jason's number.

"Hello?" he answered.

"Jason, did you just call my husband and tell him about us?" I asked without even saying hello.

"What?" he asked, sounding confused.

"Did you or did you not just call my husband and tell him that you are my boyfriend and that I want to divorce him because I am in love with you?" I asked again with a hint of irritation in my voice. I was shaking uncontrollably by now and pacing up and down the parking lot. I lit a cigarette and felt as if I was going to get sick as I inhaled the first drag.

"Babe, why would I call your husband and tell him that? What's going on?" he asked, confused.

"Someone called him and said that he was you," I managed to mutter as I exhaled the last of my cigarette. "I'm sorry I had to ask you this. I really knew that you weren't the one who made that call. But who did it?"

"Teri, remember that guy who flipped out when you came to see me the last time and you wouldn't show him your cam? He said he was going to tell on you. It's gotta be that guy."

"No way. Impossible. First of all, he doesn't have that kind of knowledge. Even if he did know my last name, we are not listed, and besides, he didn't call my house, he called the club and asked for my husband by his first name. That crazy ass doesn' t know that much about me. I'm certain it's not him," I stated with assurance that what I was saying was true.

"Then it has to be one of the locals who know which club it is and your husband's name. I know who it is, and so do you, babe"

"No, I don't know who it is, Jason. None of my locals would do this," I replied as I started to go through the list of contacts that I had on the BGC. I browsed through the names, and there wasn't anyone that I believed that would have done this. They all had something to lose. Most of them were married, and the majority of them on my phone were my friends, people who I knew, who I trusted. "No, babe, I checked my phone list. If it's a local guy, there is no one on here that I could see making that call."

"Brett. Brett made that call, T, and you know it," he said so surely. I considered this for exactly ten seconds but then remembered that less than an hour ago, I had chatted with Brett online, and he seemed fine and happy.

"No, it's not Brett," I said without offering a reason to why I believed it wasn't.

"Call your husband back. Ask him to check the caller ID."

"Whoever made that call isn't that stupid! I am sure they blocked the number."

"Humor me and do it anyway, okay?"

"Fine. I will call you back," I said and hung up. I dialed the club, and my husband answered.

"Hello?" he said.

"Honey, check the caller ID. Is there a number from the person who made that call?" I asked.

"It's a local number . . . so your boyfriend must be in town."

"Jason is not in town, and it was not he who called you, and don't call him my boyfriend. I told you that he is only a friend, and I don' t even talk to him anymore," I lied.

My husband gave me the number, and I recognized it immediately. I dropped my phone to the ground in disbelief, and I felt faint as I picked it up and held it back to my ear.

"Thank you. I know who that is, and it is not Jason."

"Enlighten me then. I'd like to know who he is, and I told him already that if he had anything to say to me, he obviously knows who I am and where I am, so to get his ass over and tell me about my wife," my husband said, and I could feel the anger he felt coming through the phone.

"Just a guy I met at the club. He knew I had a friend in New York, and he kept asking me out. I told him I was married and that I couldn't see him. That's how he knows you and where you are. I don't know him very well, and he's crazy. He is telling you a lie, and you believe it," I said as I made this whole story up so quickly I prayed I sounded believable.

"Tell me who he is. I want to know who's coming in my club and asking my wife out."

"I can't remember his last name; I don't even know him that well."

"You knew him well enough to tell him you had a boyfriend in New York, obviously," he shot back at me.

"I told him I had a FRIEND there, and I don't even know why I told him that. I was drunk, and we were talking," I lied again.

"So now he could come in and laugh at me because I don't know who this son of a bitch is."

I felt horrible for my husband and angry with this person who rubbed it in his face. I wanted to tell my husband that this person never had been in the club, and that he wouldn't dare go in, especially now.

"Honey, I'm sorry that he called you. But I am certain he's not a member, and I will personally go through all of the memberships, and if he is, you will be the first to know. I have to get back to Steph. I will see you at home, okay?" I said through tears of anger and disbelief and sadness for what this person just put my husband through. I dialed Jason back, and I didn't want to tell him who it was, yet I knew that I had to.

"Hi, babe. I got the number. You were right . . . it was Brett," I told him as I was still trying to understand why Brett would do this.

"That fucking son of a bitch! Give me his number now! I knew it was him, T, and I have something to say to him. Give me his number," he demanded, and I had only heard him this angry once before. I gave him Brett's number, and I knew that this was only going to be nothing but ugly. "I will call you back. Give me a few minutes with your boyfriend," he said sarcastically.

"Um, he's not my boyfriend, J. Why would you say that?"

"Because, T, this is your fault! We are broke up for one day, and you go running to this ass wipe, and now look at the mess he caused. He had no right to disrespect your husband in the manner that he did, and he just fucked this all up. There is no way now you can come in two weeks. It's over. He just ruined it for us," he said while I didn't want to believe that it was over or that I would never be seeing him again. I refused to believe this, and I didn't argue the boyfriend comment to anger him any further.

"Okay. Call me back," I only said in hopes that Jason would not be angry with me.

I went back into the restaurant, and Steph was finished with her meal.

"You don't look so great. I saved some of this for you," she said, and I could tell that she was feeling pretty good from the tall vial of sake she finished all by herself.

"Not hungry, thank you. I'm okay," I told her as my phone rang. It was Jason.

"I called him, and the pussy wouldn't answer the phone. I left him a message and then I sent him a text. He's a coward and doesn't have the balls to even respond," he explained, and he was almost halfway yelling.

"What did you say to him?" I asked, not really wanting to know the answer.

"I called him and told him that we knew it was him who made the call to your husband and that he was a jerk for doing that. Then I sent him a text, asking him to pick up his phone and talk to me like a man. He then texted me back, saying that he only did this for us, to help us out because he thought that we should be together." As I listened to what Jason had said to Brett, it finally made sense to me as to why Brett did this.

"I know why he did this," I said.

"'Cause he's a psycho freak?"

"No. Think about it for a minute. Instead of calling my husband and just saying that I had a boyfriend in New York and that I wanted a divorce so I could be with him, he chooses to pretend that he is you. It was his hopes that I *would* believe that it was you who made the call, causing me to be angry with you, and then my husband divorces me, and he was thinking that I would go running to him, as I did when we broke up. I truly believe that that was his intention, yet because this was a bar that when he called, he didn't count on it having a caller ID option, and really, up until a few months ago, we didn't," I explained my theory as Jason listened.

"Well regardless, T, your husband is not going to allow for you to travel. There is no way now that you can come see me in December now."

"Leave that to me. Yes, I am coming in December. He thinks I'm going to see my sister in San Francisco. I will work it out."

"Did you tell Brett you were coming to see me?"

"I believe I did mention it to him, yes. Why?" I asked.

"He will call your husband and tell him. Let's face it, sweetie, you aren't going to be able to pull this off."

"So now what? Is it over now? Do we just walk away from this?" I asked as I started to cry as these words I just spoke pierced a hole in my heart. The thought of never seeing Jason again was too painful to think of.

"I love you, T. But I don't want for you to lose everything because of our relationship."

I knew that what he was saying was true. I didn't want to believe or accept it. "You breaking up with me, Jase?"

"Babe, let's do this. Come in December only if you think that it is safe. I want to see you, I just don' t want for this to ruin your life. I know that you are going to leave him eventually, but you have to get yourself established here first."

"Trust me, baby. It will be okay, I promise," I told him while I doubted secretly that it would be okay.

Later that evening, I made my husband his favorite meal, and I didn't bring up the events t hat had taken place earlier that afternoon. It wasn't until later that night that my husband asked to talk to me. I put the kids to bed and didn't log online.

"How many drinks have you had tonight, Ter?" My husband asked me.

"None," I lied. I had been a wreck, and I had already drunken four cape cods.

"You are lying. I can't even trust you to tell me when you are drinking. What else do you lie to me about? I' m guessing everything. You and your secret life. You would make a great spy. I believe nothing that comes out of your mouth. Are you really going to see your sister in December?" T hat was the question that I was hoping that he wouldn't ask.

"Yes, if you don't believe me, then why don't you come with me?" I said, knowing that there was no way for him to do this because he had just purchased the new bar, which I had designed, and had several contractors who would be working on remodeling it. He could not leave town, and I knew it.

"Baby, I love you. I do. But I can't live with someone I can't trust anymore. You have taken my pride away and brought me to my knees. Congratulations,

Teri, no woman has ever been able to do this before. I want out of this marriage. It's done, baby," he said, and I knew that this time he was serious. All of the hundred threats of divorce never sounded like this. This one had a different ring to it, the ring of truth and determination. I didn't know what to say to him, so I said nothing. Then he added, "I will tell you this, though—you are the last bitch I will have for a wife. Be proud, you are the last Mrs. Brooks."

"I don't want to do this now . . . Can we get through the holidays at least?" I pleaded. This was the dreaded conversation I knew would eventually come up, and I found myself torn. Part of me wanted save my marriage, and then I realized that if I *did* stay, I could never be faithful to him. I panicked at the thought of losing the security I had established in my marriage. I had a good life, with cleaning ladies and spa days and working only when I chose to do this. Thoughts of having to find a job and not being able to control my work schedule and possibly losing my home frightened me beyond belief. I pushed these thoughts out of my mind and looked at him, hoping to read something in his face to make me think he was only threatening this once again without really meaning it.

"I won't file for divorce until after the holidays. I will wait to do this, and it's not for you, but for the children," he said with a straight face. And as I studied his face, what I saw was a man who was almost broken. My husband had been the strongest, most confident man I had ever known, and who I was looking at now was someone who had no fight left within him. For the first time, I saw him as old and weary. I wasn' t looking at my husband, rather an old man so beaten down that I cried for him. I cried for us.

CHAPTER TWENTY-TWO

November–December '06

We gathered around the table and held hands. I had a full house; most of my family was visiting on this Thanksgiving Day.

"Thank you all for sharing this day with us," I said we grasped hands in a circle. "Before we pray, may I ask each of you to share what you are most thankful for?"

As the children shared their comments first, the circle was closing in, and I silently struggled to think of what to say as I would be the last to comment.

"I'm thankful for my wife, who made this great meal today. I am a lucky man, and I couldn't ask for a wife more beautiful," my husband said as he looked at me, and I knew that he did mean every word he spoke. I wondered how he could pay such tribute to me, knowing what he did. Then I realized it was because he loved me, after all I had done, and he loved me still. I had tears in my eyes after hearing his words, and I lowered my head to hide my shame. I held his hand to my lips and kissed it, never looking up. It was my turn to speak. I cleared my thoughts of guilt and spoke.

"There are so many things I am grateful for, most of which stand before me. I love all of you so very much. The rest of what I am grateful for doesn't compare to the love I have from my family and friends. Thank you for making this Thanksgiving special," I said to them.

It was a special Thanksgiving, and in the back of my mind, I knew it would be the last one I would share with my husband. I pushed this thought out of my head as it was too disturbing to contemplate. Jason would text me all through this day, and I would hide in the "man-box" the sunroom that we recently had constructed to text him back until I stopped trying to hide the fact that I was receiving text messages. I think back now to how I didn't care if anyone knew and feel ashamed at the disrespect I must have shown my family. I was in Utah, yet on this Thanksgiving Day, my mind and heart was in New York. Later that night, my nephew decided to have a "roll" fight with the dinner rolls that no one ate because I had burned them. They were as hard as hockey pucks and hurt when one was thrown at you. Rolls were flying everywhere as I tried to dodge several coming from different directions. I regretted making four dozen of them by now.

"Stop this now!" my husband yelled. "Enough!" He was the only one not participating in this war of rolls.

"Settle down, honey," I said as no one even paid attention to him. "They are just having some fun. No one is hurting anybody."

"Why don't you just go back to texting your boyfriend and let everyone trash the house?"

"Can we please just not do this?" I asked him, not denying anything.

"Sure, just pretend this isn't my house and I don't live here. Tear it up, I don't give a shit." My husband didn't see the humor in many things lately. A house full of children was starting to wear on his nerves, so I ended the roll party and settled everyone down. This was the end to any Thanksgiving spirit in our home. The festivities were over; the king had spoken.

It was late that night when the children were asleep that I found my nephew on my computer.

"Whatcha doin there?" I asked him. He was a year younger than Jason and Kirstin's youngest son. He was an educated, handsome young man, and I was proud of him. He was an engineer and had already developed a device named after him. I watched him as he typed away, remembering that I had changed his diapers when he was a baby.

"Checking my MySpace page," he said.

"What's a MySpace page?" I asked.

"Are you kidding? It's like a personal Web page, see?" he said as I viewed his page.

"Cool. I want one. Can you help me set one up?" I asked. He showed me how to set up my page, and then added me as his friend. I added photos of my children and my husband and even Jason, which later proved to be a wrong move. I would become obsessed with this new site; it would soon become a substitute for the Cheaters Club site.

"What's this Aunt Teri?" my nephew asked me as I loaded a picture of Jason and me on my new page.

"He's a friend of mine," I told him. He threw me a look that I recognized. A *yeah right* look. "Cool, so it's done. I have a Myspace page! WooHoo!" I looked back at my nephew who was not amused. He was looking at the photo of Jason and me. He looked at me for an explanation without ever asking for one. "Okay. I've been seeing him. I'm really unhappy and have been for a long time."

"He looks like he's my age."

"He is."

"God Aunt Teri," he said shaking his head. "I'm not going to tell you what to do, but maybe you need to just go somewhere alone for awhile and think. Go to Italy, you always wanted to do that. Go there and think about what you need to do to be happy. Be alone with yourself. Away from my uncle and whoever this guy is."

"Maybe you're right, but I hate being alone. I scare me." I didn't know how to be alone with myself. And I didn't know how to fight despair and welcome the company of my grief in so many empty moments.

My family left town several days later, and my house became quiet once more. When my children weren't there, it was tense between my husband and me. We hardly spoke, and when we did, we were polite yet distant towards one another. December was now here, and I would be going to New York. I wondered if my husband believed that I was going to see my sister, but he never questioned me. It was the beginning of the second week in December that I went to see Jason.

I checked myself into the same hotel that I usually stayed at in Manhattan. He would be here in less than two hours. I showered and put on the Santa Clause sexy lingerie that I had brought with me. It was a red velvet camisole with white fur trim and matching thong panties, stockings, hat, and gloves. I glanced at the clock, and my heart started to race. He would be here any minute. I had opened the door and clicked the deadbolt lock over so that when the door would shut, the deadbolt would stop it from closing. I wanted to be ready for him when he walked through the door, not having to open it. I sat on the bed and put pillows behind my back so as to prop me up. As he walked in the door, I had a fruit-flavored candy cane between my legs. He entered the room and stopped at the foot of the bed, dropping his bag to the floor as he noticed what I was doing with the candy cane.

"Have you been naughty or nice?" I asked him as I could hardly stand to sit still. I wanted to jump up and wrap my arms around him He crawled up onto the bed and kissed me.

"Naughty. I have been naughty," he said as I wrapped my arms around his neck, kissing his delicious lips. I missed his smell, his taste. I rolled him onto his back and pulled out the soft black blindfold that I had tucked under my camisole. After covering his eyes with the blindfold, I reached over the side of the bed to a tray which was on the floor. I had ordered several deserts from room service earlier. I took a chocolate—covered strawberry and dipped it in whipping cream and rested it on his lips. With the feel of this, he opened his mouth to take a bite, but I pulled it away and put my lips on his instead. As I kissed him, I put the strawberry between both our mouths, and we consumed it together. I then took my fingers and scooped up some ice cream and traced his lips with it. I let him suck the ice cream from my fingers and licked around his mouth where the ice cream had settled. There was an éclair that I used to trace circles onto his stomach, dipping it in warm caramel, and I never tasted such sweet caramel before. I could hardly contain myself as he entered me. As the hours passed, it seemed as minutes as we made love over and over again.

"I have something for you," I said to him. "Open it." I handed him a perfectly wrapped gold present with a generous gold ribbon tied around it. He unwrapped the gift and sat there, staring at it.

"Babe, I don't know what to say," he said as he looked at the Movado watch which had his initials and the date we met engraved on the back of it. "Thank you."

"You're welcome. Will actually helped me pick it out. I really didn' t know what to get you," I said. He went over to his bag and took out a small box. He opened it and pulled out a small silver band with tiny diamonds on the front of what resembled two waves in opposite directions joining together at the front of the ring. He put the ring on the ring finger of my right hand.

"If you take this off, I will know that it's over," he said as he slid it onto my finger. It was not an expensive or even a grand ring, with its tiny dull diamonds, and it paled compared to my six carat wedding ring that I wore on my left hand, yet I could not take my eyes off of it.

"Jason, I love it. Thank you," I said as I kissed him. It was the meaning behind the ring that touched me. I knew that this was huge for us, yet there was something sad within me. I shrugged off the sad feeling, not knowing where it was coming from, and kissed him once more. "I will never take it off. Ever."

The next night, we went to see the Christmas tree at Rockefeller Center. It was cold and crowded. The tree stood tall with thousands of red lights, and I was in awe of it. For the first time it felt like Christmas. I had no holiday spirit within me, and this was what I needed. We walked around New York and decided to go back to the hotel to have dinner. The restaurant at the hotel was nice, and I ordered sea bass in a basil sauce. After having my second cocktail, that sense of sadness hit me once more. I was perplexed by why I was feeling this.

"What's wrong, babe?" Jason asked, sensing my feelings.

"How would you feel about dating others?" It came out of my mouth before I realized what I had said. *What did I just say?* I thought to myself. I went with it like I knew what I was saying.

"What? What are you trying to say, T?" he asked. "I had a feeling before you came here that something was up," he added. I didn't even know that something was up.

"It is the distance. It's hard. I don't want to feel as if I am cheating on you, yet there are times that I need someone local." I had not a clue to what I was saying. These words just escaped my lips as if someone else were speaking them. "Don't tell me that you haven't thought about meeting women local to you."

"Actually, I am supposed to be set up with this girl from my MySpace page," he said. These words hit me like a brick. When was he going to tell me this if I hadn't brought it up? Or was he going to tell me?

"Oh, I just set up a page. You never mentioned that you were going to meet anyone," I said calmly as if it didn't bother me.

"I don't know if I am or not. Maybe its better that you do see other people. But really, you should start to date guys that are at least thirty-five to forty," he said to me. I was angry that it was so easy for him to say and angry that he said it at all. Did he really mean it? My head was spinning as I tried to digest this conversation. I realized then that in the back of my mind I was trying to end things on a slow-kill method—that wa s why I felt so sad. I was too weak to just tell him it was over, so I was introducing to him what I knew would sooner or later end the relationship. I had had enough of the long-distance-relationship thing, and I was tired of wondering if he was being faithful, knowing that I was not. I tried to keep a cheerful face throughout the rest of dinner, but something inside of me was dying. I didn't expect him to agree with me. I wanted him to fight for our relationship as it stood. I pushed it out of my mind, not wanting it to ruin the rest of the evening; I had something naughty planned for later.

The thought came to me several weeks earlier. What could I do that would be so very naughty that even Jason, as uninhibited as he was, would be shocked? Then it came to me. I knew that it was sinful and blasphemous, but that wa s what made it so delicious. I was certain that God would strike down my plane if I did this and was thankful that there were babies onboard my flight home and he would spare them and me because of them. When we went to the room that night, I told him to wait on the bed for me

"Put this on, and lie here. Wait for me, I have to change," I said to him as I handed him a candy thong to get into.

"What in the hell is this?" he asked, holding up the candy underwear. It had dozens of little round tarts, similar to those candy necklaces, that made up the front V-shaped patch and string thong. "You want me to what?"

"Put it on, and like it! I don't eat this much sugar, but if you are a bad boy, I just may have to take a few bites," I said with a devilish grin. I went into the bathroom and changed into a short plaid pleated miniskirt and white shirt that only covered my breast as it tied in front. I put on white thigh-high stockings and six-inch black Mary Jane-style buckle shoes. My hair was in ponytails and ribbons, and I painted my lips an innocent shade of baby pink. A pair of matching candy panties went on last, and I was ready. I opened the door and walked toward the bed holding a Bible in my hand. The look on his face was more than what I expected as I threw the Bible down on the bed and lay on it. I spread myself out like a wooden cross.

"Fuck me and save me now," I whispered and looked up at him innocently. There was nothing innocent about me, or this. I took the crucifix from my neck and put it on my candy panties. Thoughts of hell flashed through my mind as I wondered if this was worth losing my salvation over. The devil claimed my soul a long time ago, I reasoned, as this should have been unsettling in some slight way, yet it was not. I was perfectly comfortable with what I was doing. I was on my way to hell.

The next morning, I was hung over and thirsty. I reached for the bottled water on the nightstand, which was sitting on the Bible. *Holy shit, I am so going to hell.* I thought as I put the Bible back in the drawer of the stand. I didn't realize how much I had to drink the night before, but I remembered most of what had happened. I went to the bathroom and washed my face to freshen up.

"Babe, why don't you go back today?" Jason said as I walked out of the bathroom, feeling a bit fresher now. He had a hockey game to play that night but was supposed to come back to the hotel afterward.

"What? Why?" I asked, a bit confused.

"My game won't end until ten or so, and I have to work tomorrow. I don't know if I will be able to make it back here tonight, and I don't want you to be alone," he said.

"J, you knew you had a game, so why didn't you just tell me this before I booked another night here?" I asked, very annoyed with him.

"I wanted to come back, but I think that maybe you should try to get on a flight today."

"Unbelievable. Fine. Okay," I said, not trying to hide my annoyance toward him. He left me there at the hotel four hours before the flight that I was able to get on departed. He didn't bother staying to take me to the airport as he usually did, and his game was seven hours away. I was upset and hurt. My phone beeped as a text message came through. I thought it was Jason, saying that he had changed his mind, but it was Eric. Eric was from New Jersey, and I met him online and he had wanted me to come when Jason and I had broken up back in October. I had forgotten that I told him that I would be in New York this weekend. I texted him back, telling him that Jason left and that I was going home. He wanted me to stay, but I had already changed my flight and wanted to go home. For the first time, I actually wanted to go home. I agreed to meet him at the hotel restaurant before I had to catch the shuttle to the airport. He was twenty-eight and had dark hair, with dark eyes. I waited for him in the restaurant and was on my second glass of wine when he walked in. I was not at all attracted to him, I realized when I saw him for the first time, and felt even sorrier for myself now.

"Hi, Teri. Wow, you look great," he said as he took a seat across from me. I had dark circles under my eyes, and I was still hung over and tired. I don't know where the tears came from, and I tried to hold them back but failed. I could tell my tears came as a surprise to him, and he was noticeably uneasy.

"I'm sorry, Eric. This has been a bad day. Maybe this wasn't a good idea," I said to him, knowing that I must have seemed crazy. I told him about my conversation with Jason the night before at dinner. He listened as I drank more wine and confided in a stranger that I knew so little of.

"He doesn't deserve you. You said that you felt sad, before you talked to him about this. Have you considered that maybe you've known that there is no real future with him, and you are conditioning yourself to end things?" Eric said as I watched his mouth. His teeth were large, almost too large for his mouth. He had kind brown eyes that drooped at the outer corners, reminding me of a puppy dog. His ears were large, and his hair was cut short and stuck up straight from his head about a half an inch, forming a flat surface. I considered what he said before I spoke.

"I can't let him go. You may be right though, maybe I am just weaning myself from him. I need to slowly just wean myself . . ." I said in a whisper, looking at the last sip of wine left in my glass. "I have to catch my shuttle. Thanks so much for listening," I said, breaking the solemn trance I was in moments earlier.

"Let me drive you, I would be glad to. I did drive an hour here to see you, you know."

"No, really, I can just take the shuttle. You should go before the traffic gets bad," I said to him as I got up and gathered my bags. He walked me to the front door, and the shuttle was waiting. I gave him a hug and promised that I would text him when I got home safely.

It was on this flight home, from this trip, that I opened my laptop on the plane and started to write down my thoughts. I didn't know what it was that I was writing, I just knew that I had something to say. The nosey plump older woman sitting next to me was stealing glances toward my laptop.

"Are you writing a book?" she asked me during a moment when I looked up to think.

"No," I answered her

"It looks as if you are writing a book," she said again. I read what I had just written.

"I'm not writing a book," I said to her, rather annoyed now. What I was writing was personal.

"Reads like a book to me," she said, adjusting her glasses to get a better glimpse of what I was writing. I shifted my laptop away from her view.

When I got home that night, I read what I had written, and it did read like a book. So I called it chapter one.

CHAPTER TWENTY-THREE

December '06

"Tis the season to be jolly, Fa-la-la-la-la, la-la-la-la," I sang, chomping on a mouthful of roasted cinnamon almonds. "Deck the halls with boughs of holly, Fa-la-la-la-la, la-la-la-la."

"Mom, don't sing with your mouth full, that's disgusting. And you got the words backwards," my daughter said to me as I browsed through a rack of jeans. I didn't know how she would notice this because she was faithfully texting messages to someone on her phone. It amazed me how she could walk and text, never running into anything as I would if I were doing that.

"Help me find a size six, Sis," I said with my mouth still full of the heavenly almonds, and a small piece of almond flew out of my mouth, hitting her in the face. She looked up from her phone and brushed the spewed almond off her cheek. My mother always would talk with her mouth full of food, and it drove me crazy growing up. It seemed as if she would actually wait until she had a mouthful of food to speak sometimes. I was turning into my mother.

"I thought we were shopping for the boys? You have enough jeans," she said after removing the food particle from her face while still texting.

"I need a new pair. I'm going back to New York after Christmas." These words got her attention because she stopped texting and tucked her phone in the pocket of her jacket.

"You were just there. Why do you have to go back after Christmas?" she asked me with an inquisitive look on her face. My daughter was beautiful. She was a good mixture of her father and me. She had my olive skin and hazel eyes, with long light brown hair that she colored darker. She had a small frame and stood two inches taller than me, at five feet, five inches. I remembered back to when I was fifteen years old and I was more athletically built than she, with defined, muscular thighs and calve s compared to her long lean legs. Inheriting her father's large yet perfectly shaped teeth, she had my full lips and slightly upturned small nose.

"It's just for a few days. I just need to take some pictures of the job that I designed there." This was something that I did plan on doing when I was there.

"I doubt it. You are going to go see him, aren't you? You could hire someone to take those pictures for you, and it would be cheaper than you flying there," she said to me slyly. I hated lying to my daughter, but I couldn' t admit that she was right so I changed the subject. I felt ashamed that she knew about Jason and I was not the example that a mother should be to her children.

"You are right, I have enough jeans. Let's go eat, I am starving." The mall was filled with people on this late Sunday afternoon. I gazed around and wondered how many Mormons there were here shopping, breaking the oath of keeping Sunday holy. It seemed as if they had a "hall pass" during Christmastime when during the rest of the year they frowned upon those who would wash their cars or allow their children to play outside on Sundays. This was my favorite time of year, and I felt annoyed with the crowds and the concept of Christmas altogether this year. Family traditions such as baking sugar cookies to ice and hiring a Santa Clause to come to the house on Christmas Eve were things that I elected to not do this year. It didn't feel like Christmas, and it was a struggle for me to even decorate my home with the thousands of dollars worth of holiday décor I had collected throughout the years.

There was a tension between Jason and me that I could not understand. We never discussed our conversation about seeing others, yet it loomed over us, like a dark cloud. I had accumulated over sixty friends on the new MySpace page that I created and had already met several men for lunch or over drinks. I never told Jason that I was going on these meetings. I could not seem to fight the temptation to meet them. I deleted the comments they would leave on my page before Jason could see them so as not to tip him off. One afternoon, a week before Christmas, Ryan had texted me. He wanted to see me, and I had a lunch date with someone on my page I logged onto my MySpace to leave a message for the person I was going to meet. My husband was out of town for the day, and Ryan came over.

I answered the door in Christmas boxer briefs and a tank top; I noticed it was snowing outside.

"It's zero degrees out here, and you are wearing that?" he said to me as he walked into the house, giving me a hug. I had the fireplace burning and heat up so that my house was warm. I was a big fan of sweat pants that I would wear around the house most of the winter, but there was something nonsexy about them.

"Well now, if you'd rather I not wear this, I can take it off," I said to him as I started to slide off my boxer shorts.

"No, down, girl. I didn't come for that," he said as he pulled my boxers back on. "I can't stay. I just wanted to say hello."

"What? Okay then," I said to him, a bit confused.

"I don't want your boyfriend to get mad. How is Jason?"

"He's fine, Rye. I'm going to see him on the twenty-seventh," I told him, regretting that I had because I expected the next comment he would make.

"Oh, well how long has it been? A week? Can't go too long without a Jason fix."

"Rye, I left on the terms that we are going to see other people. So hop on me now, bad boy," I said as I wrapped my arms around his neck and placed his hand on my chest.

"No, Teri. I won't play second to him anymore. We can be friends, but I am done being number two," he said as he sat down on the sofa. I sat at the end of the sofa and put my legs over his lap.

"Ryan, don't be like that."

"I don't trust him. He's the type that would go crazy, and the scary thing is that he's in law enforcement. I know guys like him, Ter, and what if he found out my name? I have to be careful—I have a wife."

"And I have a husband. Jason would never call your wife, Rye. He's not like that."

"Regardless, I don't think he's stable. Do the math—let's see, he still lives at home at age twenty-six, and you are his longest relationship, and you don' t even live near him. Do you honestly believe you would have made it this far if you two saw each other every day? He's controlling and verbally abusive, just like your husband is, and for some reason you don't seem to see that!" he said to me. I didn't respond. I knew that what he said was true. I just looked at him sadly and hoped that he could not see the pain that had stricken my face at the sound of his words. "I don't mean to hurt you, but how do you know he's not sleeping around? You don't know that he isn' t for sure, and you aren't using condoms with him. I don't need to be catching anything."

"Okay, okay! Calm down now. You' re getting all worked up here," I said to him as I grabbed one of his hands and gave it a tight squeeze.

"I'm just sayin that you don't think of these things." Rubbing my legs with both of his hands, he lifted his hand nearest me and jammed his index finger on my forehead as he said the word "things," overpronouncing "things" as well "Give me a kiss. I have to go."

"You only just got here," I said, sounding more like a whine.

"Have to do some Christmas shopping for my wife. Give me a kiss and be good."

"I'll give you a kiss, but I'm never good."

"Yeah, I know that," he said as I kissed him at the door. He walked out and took a few steps before he turned around to look at me.

"Merry Christmas, Teri, and give Jason my love."

"Merry Christmas, and I won't do that, thank you." He laughed at this and winked at me. I watched him walk away until he turned the corner and I could no longer see him. It had stopped snowing but was chilly out, and I could see my breath in the air even though I was standing in the threshold. I rubbed my hands over the top of my arms as to warm them and closed the door with my foot. *Wonder what he's getting his wife for Christmas?* I thought. *Wonder what my husband will give me this year?* Was the next thought, and then came the answer to that one. *Probably nothing.*

It was Christmas Eve, and the house was quiet. My ex husband had the children until Christmas afternoon. I had spent most of the evening with Jason online, chatting on my laptop in the dining room, where I would always chat when I was on my laptop. It was far away from the living room, where my husband practically lived. Midnight was minutes away when I went into the living room where my husband was asleep in his chair. I sat on the sofa and picked up a magazine. Minutes later, he awoke.

"Merry Christmas" I said to him. The clock chime was ringing at the stroke of midnight.

"Merry Christmas. I hope you didn't get me anything, because I didn't buy you anything," was what came out of his mouth.

"Yeah, you told me that last week, so I didn't. But I did get you this card," I said as I reached into a drawer next to me and handed him the card. It was a card filled with tender words, filled with hope and promise that I knew would never be. I wrote a passage to him which read:

> *Merry Christmas my love, I don't know what's going to happen, and things aren' t looking good. I only want for you to know that no matter what, it wasn't a waste of years. I loved you then, I love you today, I will love you always.*
>
> *With all my love your Wife.*

He didn't say anything as he folded the card and stuck it back in the envelope. There was no glance my way, no words spoken, nothing. I tried to break the ice, talking about what we would do on this Christmas day.

"Do you mind? I am watching television," he said to me. This remark made me angry.

"It's Christmas. Can you find it in your heart to be kind? Just for twenty-four hours?" I asked him as I tried not to raise my voice.

"Take my picture off your MySpace page. It's weird when I see myself there. You are advertising your life to the world, and there are weirdos out there. Take me off your page," he said to me, and this threw me off guard. I had no idea that he knew I had a MySpace page, and then I remembered there was a photo of Jason and me on there as well.

"What are you talking about?" was all I could manage to say. I was in a silent panic, trying to remember what was on my page and who was on it. I remembered that Jason was my first friend, then the nephew who helped me create my page, his friend, as well as one of my sisters and two nieces. There were tons of young guys there as well, most not wearing shirts, and all of them great looking. They didn't make my page if they were over thirty-two or not sexy.

"I found your page. You have tons of young guys on it, and I don't know what you are doing. What are you doing, Ter?"

"Did you notice that under your picture, the caption reads: all of my favorite guys?" I asked as to proclaim some kind of innocence for this page. The photo that I had posted of him was a picture taken in Cabo San Lucas; he was standing with my two sons. "And my sister, nieces, and nephew are my friends. My profile states that I am married, don't trip out." I presented this defense.

"Yes, and I also noticed who your first friend is, and the picture of you and him. Must you rub this in my face?" he asked. I didn't ever think that he would find my page or had any idea he knew I had one. This was a man who didn't know how to turn a computer on. He must have had one of his friends look for me, and I knew which friend that was. I became angry and felt violated that he would search me out, although he had every right to do so—I was still his wife.

"I check it every day, Teri. Last week you changed your marital status to 'divorced?'" he asked.

"Yeah, that was the day you gave me the divorce papers!" I snapped back at him. He had handed me papers that had not legally been filed, something that he had drawn up in hopes that I would sign them and not contest it. I read them and threw them in the garbage, insulted by what he had offered me, which was basically nothing "So, Mr. Detective, did you also notice then that the following day I changed the status back to 'married'?" I asked. "It doesn't matter . . . I am deleting my MySpace, and I think I will do this now!" I screamed, walking to my desktop to delete my account. Before doing so, I read through comments left by my friends, sighing in relief that there was only a few Christmas wishes. I was careful to erase those comments that were "sexual" in nature from my many guy friends because of my nieces and Jason. I deleted my account that night.

"You'd better talk to your son too. He has a page, and it's not good for kids to have shit like this. There are perverts out there, Teri . . . what are you thinking?" he asked me as I was deleting my page.

"My kids DO NOT have a page!" I screamed to him from the other room where my desktop computer was. I would learn that he was right. My eldest son, who was thirteen, did have a page. How could I not know this? On his page, he stated that he was thirty years old and lived in Uganda. I texted Jason immediately after reading my son's page.

Teri:	J . . . where the hell is Uganda?
Jason:	Africa, why? What's up?
Teri:	WTH? (What the hell)
Jason:	Why babe?
Teri:	My son has a myspace page; he is thirty and is from Uganda.
Jason:	HAHAHA!
Teri:	So not funny J . . . I have a black kid who is thirty.
Jason:	It is funny T. Just tell him he needs to delete it.

This is exactly what I did. That Christmas night, I had him delete his profile. Christmas was a sad day. We watched my children open their gifts in silence They were so excited that they did not feel the tension between my husband and me. My parents and my husband's children joined us for dinner that night, and I don' t remember much that happened that day, except that it was one of the saddest days of my year. It was almost over, this Christmas night. I tucked my eleven year old son into bed while singing to him.

"*Oh, holy night, the stars are brightly shining . . . ,*" I sang softly while covering him with a blanket.

"Mom, is tonight holy?"

"Yes baby, tonight is holy. It was the night baby Jesus was born. *Long lay the world in sin and error pining . . . ,*" I would sing, brushing back his sandy blond hair that had grown out too long.

"What's sin and error pining?"

"Well, sin is when you do something bad. Like lie or steal. Error is a name for what we might call sins of our imagination. Beliefs and judgments we hold even though we should know better. Pining in this case probably means wasting away. This has always been mommy' s favorite Christmas carol. So sad it makes me though."

"Don't worry mom, I won't let sin and error pine you," he said sweetly taking me by my hand.

"You won't?"

"Nope. I will protect you. It won't get you. So now you can be happy when you sing it, okay?" The innocence of his words and of this child lying before me brought me hope for the first time. Hope that sin would leave me.

"Thank you, my little protector from all things bad. Shall we sing it together then?"

"*Fall on your knees, oh hear the angel voices. Oh night divine, oh night when Christ was born . . . ,*" we sang together. And for the first time, I was joyful and not sad when I sang it.

It was late on Christmas night, after my children went to bed, that I logged onto my laptop in the dining room and met Jason online. We turned on our

Webcams and blew a Merry Christmas kiss to each other and counted the minutes to when we would see each other again. It seemed like forever since I had last kissed him.

I woke up early on the morning several days after Christmas. This was the day I was going to see Jason. My husband thought that I was going to see my sister in San Francisco, and I begged her to cover for me. She didn't want to do this, but she did anyways when I explained to her that this would be the *last* favor I would ever ask of her and that I was going anyways, with or without her help. I wondered if my husband really believed my story, and though he never would ask to speak to her when I did really go visit her, I cringed at the thought that this time he would want to. Lies I would tell to him if he asked started to become jumbled in my mind, so I decided not to worry about it for now. Tonight I would be in Jason's arms. That was all that mattered.

What could I wear for Jason this time? I came up with another wicked plan several days ago—this was just as wicked, if not more so than the Catholic schoolgirl I role-played last time.

As I unpacked my belongings when I checked into the room at the hotel I always stayed at, I dialed housekeeping.

"I need some assistance in room 1101 please. Can you send someone up in thirty minutes? Oh, and it must be a woman," I demanded.

"What can we bring you, Mrs. Brooks?" a woman with a heavy Hispanic accent asked me.

"Nothing, my room is fine. I need help lacing up a dress that I will be wearing It must be a woman that comes to assist me please."

"We are short-staffed, Mrs. Brooks. If there is anything we can bring to you, let us know."

"Okay, bring me two pillows and an extra blanket, please."

"There are extra pillows and blankets in the closet. Is there anything else?" she asked. I was tired from the long flight and needed to get into the shower. Jason would be here in less than two hours, and I needed extra time tonight to get ready.

"Yes, please bring me a toothbrush, and have a woman bring it to me please," I said with my teeth clenched.

"Very well, Mrs. Brooks. Is there anything else that I may assist you with?" the woman asked me in a deliberate, almost rehearsed, manner.

"No, that will be all. Thank you. Oh, and I will be getting into the shower now, so please have her here in thirty minutes."

"Very well. Have a good evening, Mrs. Brooks," she said as I hung up the receiver and got into the shower. I was careful to shave my legs as to not cut myself. I was in a hurry and knew that it would take me extra time to get prepared tonight. Thirty minutes later there was a knock on the door.

"Housekeeping. Here is the toothbrush that you requested, Mrs. Brooks," an older Hispanic woman said to me as she handed me the toothbrush. She was tall—at least five feet eight inches to my five foot three inches—and very thin. I could tell by the lines on her face that life had not been easy for her. She looked as if she was in her late forties, yet I had to wonder if she were really closer to my age of forty-two.

"Please come in. I understand that you are short-staffed tonight, but I need a favor to ask of you," I said as I grabbed her gently by her arm and pulled her into the room. "This won't take but a few minutes. Please help me?"

My wedding dress was lying out on the bed. It resembled something that a ballerina would wear, tea length, with a full organza skirt and a fitted bodice which laced up the back. I had designed it six years ago and had it made to be married in. The simplicity of it was what made it so beautiful as I was careful to keep the pearl beading which traced the front deep V-neck sparse.

"It is my wedding anniversary tonight. I am surprising my husband by wearing my wedding dress. Could you please help me to lace it up?" I pleaded with this wicked lie.

"Oh! Absolutely! I would be happy to do this!" she said, and I felt no guilt but much relief.

"Thank you! I want to make this so special!" I added, only now feeling a bit guilty for expanding on my original lie. I went into the bathroom and put the dress on. She laced the back up for me as I sucked in my gut, so that it was almost like donning a corset.

"You are muy bonita, senorita," she said, admiring the dress

"Muchos gracias. Here, please take this for helping me," I said, handing her a ten-dollar bill.

"No! I cannot take! Please, it is my pleasure," she said to me, holding out both of her hands, palms facing me.

"Please, this means so much to me that you have helped me. Please do take this," I insisted, taking one of her hands and placing the money in it.

"Gracias, your husband will be pleased, you look beautiful," she said as she walked out of the room. I locked the door behind her and thought about the words she just said. *My husband would be pleased.* I wondered when the last time my husband was pleased.

I spent an hour curling my hair in tiny ringlets and pinning them up in a diamond clip. I rolled white thigh—high stockings up my legs and put on my satin white sandals. The final touch was my favorite perfume and a white garter that I sprayed with my favorite scent. I looked into the mirror only minutes before Jason would be here, and I looked like the bride I was six years ago. I hadn't aged, looking closely into the mirror, studying the curve of my face. There were no wrinkles on my forehead or around my eyes. I silently thanked my mother for passing on her good genes. My fingers trailed through the locks of long curls as I sought for any gray hairs as I was certain one would pop up any day now. I gave myself a final glance, and when I did this, my image became distorted and grotesque. I closed my eyes and opened them, still seeing the monster who was staring back at me through the cracks of the mirror. Many deep, long cracks, that seemed to mate on top of each other. Seconds ago I felt beautiful, and now I was looking at something that I didn't recognize. I couldn't seem to look away from what I was looking at, and I knew that I must put myself into a positive frame of mind. *You are beautiful, you are sexy, and this is not what you look like,* I thought to myself. I couldn' t seem to look away from my image as it did not change, so I reached up and felt for the light switch and flipped it off. I stood there in the dark for a few seconds and took a deep breath. It would be any minute that he would be here.

I opened the deadbolt to the door and locked it so that the door would shut but not lock; the same thing that I did the last time. I positioned myself ten feet away from the door and bent my knees and squatted. I gathered my dress around my legs, and I looked like a cupcake. He walked into the room only seconds later and stopped for a brief second to look at me.

I rose and walked over to a wall and leaned up against it as he followed me and kissed me passionately. His kisses tasted sweeter than I had remembered, and I drew him in closer to me until he could be no closer unless he was inside of me. I pushed him away from me so I could catch my breath. He looked at me with his beautiful navy blue eyes and long dark lashes. I loved him with everything that I was, and with every kiss, I loved him even more.

I put my hands on top of his shoulders and pushed him down to his knees. Lifting my dress, I buried his head underneath the full skirt of my wedding dress and I threw one leg over his shoulder. His lips felt warm and wet as he kissed my inner thighs. The only things that I wore under this dress were thigh—high stockings and a garter, the kind that the groom would toss to bachelors. His teeth found the garter and he gently bit it and it snapped lightly against my leg. He put his mouth between my legs and his tongue found my wet spot. I had to have him inside of me, so I pulled him up to me in an urgent manner, kissing him and tasting his sweet lips.

He lifted me and carried me to the bed as a groom would his bride on their wedding night. I moaned as he entered me. F eeling him inside me made me crazy with desire. As he lay on top of me, I moved my hips in a slow circular motion, controlling the gentle rhythm of his hips moving with mine. Then a wicked thought crossed my mind.

"Suck on my wedding ring, Jason, suck it!" I screamed. He followed my order and sucked on my ring. I could tell that this had turned him on as I could hear him panting more heavily. Another wicked thought struck me.

"Cum on my dress," I whispered this time. With hearing this, he came almost instantly and released himself all over the front of my wedding dress. I collapsed in his arms and my dress was wet, wrinkled, and smelled of him. Did I have this much disrespect for my husband? I must have, for me to do this. It never crossed my mind until that moment, but I realized that I had some hidden anger toward my husband, a faint feeling of hatred even.

"I hate him, J. I don't want to hate him, but I think I do." These words came out of my mouth so easily.

"Who?" Jason asked.

"My husband. Why do I feel as if I am starting to hate him?" I asked, not really expecting for Jason to know the answer.

"I don't know, babe," he answered while I already knew what his response would be. "That's something that you need to figure out," he said, and he pressed his lips together and raised his eyebrows. "I don' t know what to tell you, babe, but I know that you aren't happy. He has ignored you for too long."

I had shared stories of things that happened in my marriage with Jason, telling him things that I never told anyone. Jason never said much, but he always listened contently and never forgot one detail that I ever shared with him. It was remarkable how he remembered everything about my husband or children or me. I fell in love with him not only because of how he made me feel when I was with him, but for how he made me feel about myself. I felt important; as if my thoughts mattered—he wanted to know what I thought and what I was feeling, and he remembered every detail of it. Never once did he tire of my thoughts or feelings. He had a certain kind of "patience" for me that no one else ever had. If I tried to share my thoughts with my husband, it would more than likely turn into a fight as he would disagree with something I would say, and his opinion was always right. Yes, I had resentment toward my husband, and I didn't like who he had become any more than he probably liked who I had become.

I had ordered room service to be delivered as I changed out of my dress into fleece shorts and a tee shirt. I brushed through my tangled curls and put my long hair up in a clip. Room service brought p orterhouse steaks, asparagus, salads, as well as several bottles of champagne and strawberries. I had ordered this several hours ago to surprise him.

"Babe, what's all this?" he asked, looking at the two tables required to fit all that I had ordered.

"It's a special dinner. It will be next year that I see you again," I said with a wink. He was actually coming to Utah in the middle of January, which was just over two weeks away. "We must celebrate the New Year."

I poured us both a glass of champagne that cost a hundred dollars a bottle. I added a shot of crème de cassis and dropped a fat strawberry into each flute glass.

"What is that?" he asked.

"It's called a kir royal. It is a shot of crème de cassis, which is blackcurrant liquor. It makes it a bit sweet. Champagne tends to be dry and tart, so I prefer this," I said, handing him over a flute. "Do you like it?" He tasted it and made a sour face.

"It's okay."

"Good, there are three bottles, and we are drinking all of them. Okay, a toast," I said, holding up my glass.

"Here is to the New Year, and to all the good things it may bring to us, much happiness, and hope. May the New Year find us healthy, happy, and together," I said as he touched his glass to mine and we both took a sip of the champagne. He made yet another sour face, and I laughed.

"It gets better, babe. Drink up, and I promise that after the third glass, you will be thinking that you are drinking some really bad kinda expensive beer." We talked and laughed and shared our thoughts throughout dinner. This was a special moment, and I felt closer to him now than I ever had before. I fed him bites of my food and kissed him in between bites.

After dinner, we made love once more, this time more slowly and deliberate, taking our time to examine each other's bodies. His skin was smooth, and his muscles tight. I could spend hours just touching and kissing him. He was everything that I desired in a man, and he was my man. I gave him a massage, and then he turned on the television I brought my laptop to the bed and logged online. I had deleted my MySpace account, so there wasn' t much for me to check, so I checked my e-mails. I thought that my status was set to "invisible" on my Yahoo. I was mistaken. Within seconds of me logging on, Eric, the guy from New Jersey that I had met during my last "not so happy" visit, messaged me. I forgot that I had told him that I was going to visit Jason again. I turned the laptop away so Jason could not see the screen, or so I thought.

Yahoo Chat:

Eric: Are you here in New York?
Teri: Um yeah, but I can't chat, I'm with my boyfriend.
Eric: Does he know that you met me?

"WHAT! What the fuck did he just say? LET ME SEE THAT NOW!" Jason screamed, pulling the laptop away from me. I struggled to take it from him and closed the lid, but he was too quick and stronger than I was. He read the words again, and typed something back to Eric.

Yahoo Chat:

Jason: So you been messaging my girlfriend?

"Jason, don't!" I yelled as I managed to shut the computer off.

"You are unbelievable, Teri! So when did this meeting occur?" he demanded to know as his nostrils where flaring and his face flushed with anger. "T! When did you meet him? Is this that MySpace guy from Jersey?"

"I met him when you LEFT ME! The last time I was here and you told me to go home a day early!" I screamed back at him, and then I took a deep breath. "Jase, please calm down. It is not what you think. I met him for an hour, and I was upset about our conversation of seeing other people, and I was upset that I was leaving a day early. I only talked about you, about us."

Jason got up and started to get dressed.

"Don't leave me. Please don't leave me again," I said these words softly and very slowly. I think I may have been holding my breath at the time. He threw his shirt down on the bed and was clearly still very angry. He turned off the television. I usually get a room with either a king or queen bed, but the only smoking room available this time was one with two double beds. He opted to sleep in the bed that I was not in.

"I'm pissed. This is so 'typical' Teri here. I leave for not even *one* hour, and you have someone lined up to meet. I'm going to bed, T, and you just stay in that bed. I don't want to sleep with you tonight," he said with his teeth clenched. I knew better than to argue with him, so I just said nothing and turned off the light. I struggled to sleep and wondered how this perfect night had turned into such a nightmare. I remembered the last visit and how it ended in the worst kind of anxiety attack for me, and I started to cry. I thought about when I got on the plane and I started to write to release the pain, this pain. I thought about my book and the ugly details of things that I had done to Jason and my husband. All of the many lies and the deceit. My tears soon turned into sobs.

"What is it? T, stop crying," Jason said to me.

"I can't, J. I'm sad, and I need for you to hold me." I heard him sigh loudly as I finished my sentence.

"Fine, you can come and lie next to me, but T, don't expect me to hold you. I'm mad. It is so typical of you to pull this shit. You meet some guy as soon as I leave. Were you planning to meet him?"

"NO! I was planning for my boyfriend to stay with me, to come back after his hockey game and not to tell me to go home early or that he wants to date others!"

"Um, pretty sure that you were the one to bring up the dating of others." I had been the one to present that, and even though I had met a few guys on my MyS pace page, I was certain that Jason had not met anyone. We didn't speak anymore after this, and it wasn't until the middle of the night that I woke up and reached over to him.

His back was facing me, and I reached over and put my arms around his stomach and my hand touched his inner thigh. I started to rub his thigh, and he became hard. He turned around to face me and kissed me gently. I pulled myself up and sat on his lap as he lay there. I kissed his stomach and made little circles with my tongue down his chest, to the soft spot below his belly button. I kissed his inner thighs and ran my hands up his stomach and rested them on his firm chest as I did this. I could not stand to wait to feel him inside of me for one more minute, so I pulled my body up and forward on top of him and slid him inside of me. I rocked gently back and forth in a slow rhythm while gradually increasing it. As I arched my back and leaned on both of my hands, bracing them behind me, he felt like heaven, and I only realized that this was as close to heaven as I would ever get.

In the morning, Jason seemed to have calmed down. He was still angry, but I knew that he loved me enough to let this slide, at least for now. We made love several more times before he took me to the airport. I kissed him goodbye, telling him I loved him, and I tried not to cry. It was only weeks before I would see him again, but saying goodbye to him was never easy.

My flight was cancelled. Denver was having terrible snowstorms, and flights all over the country had been either delayed or cancelled. The only way that I was getting home was via San Francisco. My husband thought I was in San Francisco, so maybe this wasn't a bad thing I would just have to tell him that I decided to stay another day. I called my sister, asking her if I could stay the night, and flew to see her. Before that night was over, she spoke with my husband, and I felt better about my alibi. Before that night was over, I spoke with Jason, who was still angry with me.

"I love you, babe," I said to him on the phone late that night before I went to sleep. "I love you, J," I repeated. We sat in silence for several awkward seconds before he said anything.

"Goodnight, T. Have a safe flight home."

I had lost him. For the first time, I felt this. All of my lies which were chasing me had caught me. I had lost the man I loved, and I would miss the words which still haunts me to this day, words that I had taken for granted. I can still hear his voice saying these words that I would never hear from him again, "I love you, Teri."

Chapter Twenty-Four

January '07

It was the last day of the year. I lay in bed on this morning, replaying the events of this past year in my mind. How could a year which began with such promise and hope end with such pain and despair? I felt my world slipping from under me, and I could not find my balance. I said a silent prayer that the next year would offer happier blessings, even if I didn't deserve it.

Of course you deserve it Teri, just because you are a wicked, horrible person doesn't mean that you don't deserve to be happy. Even horrible people who shoot cats just for the hell of it or people who trip old ladies deserve to be happy, a voice in my head told me.

Don't listen to that garbage; you are not a bad person. Get over the bad people in your life, and you will be fine. It was not your fault that you became so incredibly lonely that you strayed in your marriage. Two people are responsible for a failed marriage, another voice in my head said.

Bullshit! You are wicked and evil, and you KNOW it! Not only did you cheat on your husband, but you cheated on your boyfriend! And may I remind you that you did this on several occasions? You have no regard for anyone but yourself. You are selfish and heartless, the other voice said.

"Stop it! Shut up now! I don't want to hear this!" I screamed aloud to myself. I was losing it, speaking to the voices in my head that I heard very clearly. Maybe it was time to call the doc for some funny meds that they give out when people start to lose it?

I spent my New Year's Eve working as a hostess at the club. My children were with their father this year, and I didn't want to be home with my husband. His idea of spending New Year's Eve was sitting in front of the television and watching the Big Apple drop in Times Square. I needed to visit the land of the "living" and surround myself with people who thought this night was worthy of celebrating. I texted Jason a message at midnight, wishing him a Happy New Year as it turned midnight in New York. I missed him already, and it had only been a few days since I last saw him. Right before midnight, I snuck out the back door and left. It was too much for me to bear, watching lovers embrace in kisses and hugs. I was driving home when it officially became 2007. I pulled over to the side of the road and cried, feeling sorry for myself. I felt so alone. The man I loved was two thousand miles away, and I knew that it was only a matter of time before I would lose both him and my husband. The thought of losing my husband was something that I had already accepted, but I could not imaging not having Jason in my life. Besides my children, he was my world.

Ironically, for some ungodly reason, I was speeding the process of chasing Jason away. I was writing my book a few days earlier, shortly after I returned from seeing him, and he had asked me which chapter I was on. I told him that I was working on October and November.

"Is there anything that I should know before you send me this chapter to read?" he asked me.

"Maybe you shouldn't read this one," I told him.

"Tell me, T. What is in it that I should know?"

"Ryan. I was with Ryan in October and once in November when we broke up—well, the day we broke up, that is." I said quickly and quietly. I didn't want to tell him, yet I knew he'd find out either now or when my book was done.

"I didn't hear you. What did you say?" he asked.

"Ryan. I was with Ryan in October and in November, the day we broke up," I said more clearly this time and then held my breath.

"You are kidding me, right? Wait. When did you sleep with Ryan in November? Before we broke up?" he asked me, clearly upset. "Did he come to your house?"

"Yeah he did, that afternoon. Then you sent me those texts that night, admitting that you met your 'new girlfriend,' and we broke up," I said as to shift the blame, yet we both knew that I was the one who was in the wrong. We hadn't broken up yet when Ryan came to my house that day. There was not one excuse or valid reason I could possibly come up with to get out of this one.

"And you made me feel like I was the ASS for breaking up with you that night. The reason I did was because I finally had enough of your shit! What else should I know about? Who else did you meet?" he demanded to know in his scary "cop" voice. It intimidated the hell out of me when he used this voice as he would distinctly pronounce every syllable of each word forcefully and slowly.

"No one! AND I HAVE BEEN TRUE TO YOU SINCE WE HAVE BEEN BACK TOGETHER!" I promised. Then I had to wonder if I had, so many lies and meetings were clouding my memory. Yes, I decided, I had been faithful to him.

"Fuck you, Teri! Forget me coming to Utah this month! I can't trust you. You are not worth the trip!" he yelled and hung up on me. I called him back, crying.

"Jase, please don't hang up! I'm sorry, baby. This book is tearing us apart," I cried.

"Don't send me any more chapters to read. I don' t want to read them. The book isn't tearing us apart, the THINGS you did are tearing us apart. I'm done, T. I don't trust you because you are a liar and a cheat," he said. "I'm not coming to see you." And he hung up on me once more. For several days, he would hardly speak to me and still insisted that he was not coming to see me. I had no one but myself to blame.

On New Year's Day, I became angry over the fact that Jason was angry with me. *Why is he punishing me for things that happened so long ago? I have been true to him since we got back together.* Because of my anger, I had agreed to a spur-of-the-moment meeting with a guy I had met on MySpace before I deleted my profile. I agreed to meet him for coffee, and only ten minutes into our meeting, Marian called me. She only called if something was wrong, so I excused myself and took her call.

"Teri! Jason was just online, and he is livid! You told him about Ryan? Babe, he's not coming to see you this month. He told me he's done with your lies," she said in her sweet soft voice, which was filled with concern.

"I know. He told me this. Great way to start the new year," I replied. I didn't want to tell Marian that I was on date; she didn't understand why I continued to do this, really, nor did I. We talked for a few more minutes, and I made up a reason to go, thanking her for calling me. I went back to the table to where my date was.

"Is everything okay?" he asked. He was a tall fellow, twenty-nine years old and fairly good-looking.

"No, I have to go. I'm sorry," I said, sobbing by now.

"Okay, is there anything that I can do for you? When can I see you again?" he asked.

"You can't. Listen, I just realized something. You know that I am married. You also know that I have a boyfriend I can't do this to him anymore. I don't WANT to do this to him anymore."

"Who? Your husband?" he asked, clearly confused.

"No. My marriage is essentially over. It's only a matter of time before we get divorced, and my husband and I both know this. I was referring to my boyfriend. I love him, and really, I met you today because I am angry with him. He can't seem to let go of the past crap I did," I told him. "I'm sorry if I wasted your time, but he has my heart. I' m so close to really losing him—that is, if I haven't already—and it scares me to death."

"I see. Well, if you change your mind, let me know. I'd like to get to know you, but it seems as if you have too much drama going on right now and need to sort things out. If he loves you, things will work out. Forgiveness is obtainable," he said to me as I wondered if my last "forgive me" card had already been used.

He walked me to my truck, and I gave him a hug. I drove away knowing that I would never see him again and that there would be no future meetings with any more new guys. What mattered now was that I held on to the man I loved.

It took days of pleading and literally "begging" Jason to change his mind and come to Utah. I had already reserved the hotels in Salt Lake, Jackson, Wyoming, as well as Ogden and Park City. With much beseeching on my part, he finally did agree to come, and for the next two weeks, I behaved myself, careful as not to do anything which might have led for him not to visit. My game was up, and I had to make a choice—Jason or life without Jason. I chose Jason. My desire to meet new guys had left me. I didn't chat online with anyone besides Will. I felt "free" of my *alter ego*. I blocked and deleted the dozens of men on my Yahoo, only keeping Will, Tony (my Italian friend who took the photo of me on my truck last summer), Adam, and Marian.

I told my husband that I was going to Jackson, Wyoming, for a week with my friend Madeline, and I don't know if he believed me, so I had her call the house phone, leaving a message about our trip, knowing that he was the one who checked all messages. My sister Kirstin would later tell me that he believed that I was going with Maddy, but he had a suspicion that Jason would be there as well. The day had finally arrived—he was coming to Utah.

I checked into a hotel in downtown Salt Lake. We were going to stay one night in Salt Lake before heading to Jackson for three days. Before going to the hotel, I met Tony, my Italian friend, to lend him a projector that he needed to borrow. We met in a parking lot downtown, and I was rushed to get to the hotel and shower before I would pick Jason up from the airport.

"Hi, Tone, here is the projector. It's easy to use, and keep it for as long as you need it for," I said as he settled in the passenger seat of my truck. "What's wrong, Pop Tart? Something bothering you?" I asked him, reading the distress on his face.

"I'm in trouble, Ter. I fucked up," he said to me.

"What happened? What's wrong?"

"I went to Cedar City and met a woman. I didn't wear a condom, and now my wife has some sort of infection, and she's suspicious," he told me.

"What kind of infection? Has she gone to the doctor?" I asked.

"Not yet. She goes tomorrow. I'm freaking out here! I feel fine and don't have any symptoms, but every time I get an itch 'down there,' I drop my pants to see if I can see anything."

"HAHA! Sorry, it's not funny, but it kinda is. ARE YOU CRAZY ANTHONY? Why didn't you use a condom, babe?"

"I had one out, but it was too small. It was tight, and I couldn't get it on, and I was really horny . . ."

"Oh my God! Okay, I had no idea you were that, um . . . that big. Use *Magnums*. They are bigger. Just don't admit to anything for now, unless she does have an STD. If so, babe, you have to tell her. This is a dangerous game we play."

"I called the woman and told her about my wife, but she insists she is clean."

"Tone, how long have you known this woman for?"

"About a week online before I met her. I know, I know," he said, knowing how I would respond.

"Okay, don't panic until you know for sure what it is that your wife has. But then if it's bad and she has the *gooey stuff* you have to tell her the truth. Give me a hug. I have to go. There is a certain cop boy I have to molest," I said, giving him a hug.

"Yeah, cradle robber, have fun with the baby, and please let him drive to Jackson so that you both get there alive," he said. He had driven with me on several occasions, holding onto the door handle with some kind of death grip when I scared him while making sharp turns or while speeding.

"Shut up, I is a good driver!" I laughed.

I checked into the hotel downtown and showered. It was chilly out, so I opted to wear a long-sleeved low-cut black minidress and high-heel boots. His flight was delayed by twenty minutes, and I sat there, anxiously waiting, for what seemed like hours. When he walked out of the terminal, I saw him and jumped out of my truck to kiss him.

"HI! You look so good, babe!" I said to him, smothering his face with baby kisses. He looked a bit tired, but other than that, he was perfect to me.

"Hi, babe, thank you. You look beautiful," he said to me.

I drove us to the airport short-term parking lot and parked on the upper level.

"Get in the backseat," I told him as I unbuckled my seat belt and crawled in the back of my truck. He opened the passenger door and joined me in the backseat.

I reached over and kissed him passionately while loosening his belt and unzipping his pants. I threw my leg over his lap as I straddled him. I slowed the kisses down and kissed his mouth gently, feeling his breath on my wet lips as my tongue brushed across his bottom lip.

I could feel that he was hard, so I reached behind the back of his jeans, sliding them down to his knees. As I slid inside of him, I moaned gently as I always did with him. I arched my back, reaching both of my arms behind me, bracing them on the front seat headrests so as to take him as deeply as he could possibly go. I threw myself forward once more to kiss him.

"You aren't wearing any panties, bad girl," he whispered in a sexy voice, pulling away from my kiss. I grabbed him by the back of the neck with both hands and moved up slightly so that his head was between my breasts. Slipping one side of my dress over, he sucked on one breast as I lowered myself down again, taking him deep within me as his hands grasped my buttocks, assisting me.

"God, J!" I screamed uncontrollably.

"Ter," he said softly as he pulled me in even closer yet.

We came together, and I collapsed on his chest, putting my head on his shoulder while he was still inside of me. I inhaled the scent of him, a mixture of sweet cologne and sweat. I didn't want to move, I didn't want to speak, and I only wanted to stay like this forever.

CHAPTER TWENTY-FIVE

January '07

We went from the airport parking lot to a club for drinks, the same club where Paul and I would meet. Ironically the booth that was available was the one that Paul and I would sit at, yet I didn't think of Paul. Sometime before midnight, we drove back to the hotel, which was only a few blocks away. Both Jason and I had a lot to drink, so the sex only lasted thirty minutes before we passed out.

The following morning, we woke up, and I opened the curtains in the room. It was a beautiful day, and the view of the mountains clear.

"Wow, this is beautiful," he said, having never seen mountains like ours. This was the farthest west he had traveled, up until now Pennsylvania had been the farthest west he had been. This seemed bizarre to me, as by the time I was his age, I had not only traveled the country but other countries as well when I was a flight attendant. I was cultured and well traveled, and I wanted to share this with him. I wanted to take him places and introduce him to new foods, the arts, things that he didn't know.

"That's nothing, wait until you see the Wasatch Mountains to the east of us," I told him as he was looking westward toward the Great Salt Lake. "See that over there? That is the copper mine. That dude that flew to the moon not only saw the Great Salt Lake, but the copper mine as well," I told him, probably sounding not as cultured as I couldn't remember the name of the "dude."

Jackson, Wyoming, was a five-hour drive, so I decided to drive the first half of it. He wasn't too pleased because my driving frightened him and he would yell for me to slow down every thirty minutes or so, criticizing the way I made turns and ran yellow lights. I had to remember that I was driving with a state trooper, so I excused his comments and did my best to drive well. Somewhere near the border of Utah/Wyoming, the radio was cranked as I sang badly to Prince. I was smoking a cigarette and driving too fast. I'm one of those bad people that you see on the road who tosses cigarettes out the window as to not ash in my car, so I did this.

"Jeez, do I have my heater on my seat? It's hot in here," I asked him.

"Doesn't look like it," he said. A minute went by, and I felt a burning sensation on my upper back, and then I smelled smoke. I realized then that the cigarette didn't make it out the window but to the back of the sweatshirt jacket I was wearing.

"Um, babe, don't freak out, but I think I'm on fire," I said calmly as I reduced my speed.

"Fuck!" he yelled, reaching into my hood, trying to retrieve the smoldering cigarette. "You burned a hole in your jacket!" he yelled, obviously upset.

"Good thing I clipped my hair up!" I laughed, trying to lighten up the situation. He was not amused. He sat fuming for a few minutes and said nothing.

"Are you angry with me, Jase?"

"Yes! You drive like a maniac, don't pay attention to the road, and text while you drive. You chain smoke. You are a danger to the road, T," he said to me in that dreaded "cop" voice.

"Okay, I will try to do better." I didn' t want to fight with him on our first day together, so I promised to pay attention. It only lasted a few hours before trouble found me.

In a small town in Wyoming, population 200, I had to use the restroom and refuel the truck. I pulled into the only gas station in town and proceeded to get out of the truck while Jason went to pump the gas.

"Fuck. Great, Teri. You just got pulled over. Stay in the truck, get back in here," he said as I was getting out.

"What? Why?" I asked as not one but two police officers approached the driver's side.

"Did you know that the speed limit is forty miles per hour?" the heavier-set officer asked me.

"No, I didn't see any speed limit sign."

"You passed it several miles back. Didn't you see me turn on my lights?" he asked.

"No, actually I didn't see the sign or the lights. I was in a hurry—I have to pee!" I told him.

"You were going seventy-two miles per hour in a forty zone."

"I was? Wow." I played dumb.

"License and registration please," I handed him my driver's license, car registration, and proof of insurance card.

"This is going to take a few minutes. You can go pee now," he said, granting me permission to do so like I was a schoolkid raising my hand to go "potty."

Jason fueled the truck as I relieved my full bladder and grabbed drinks and snacks. Twenty minutes went by, and the two officers were still in their truck, laughing and talking. I was becoming irritated.

"It takes TWO officers thirty minutes to write a speeding ticket in Mayberry?" I asked.

"Teri, you were over the limit by thirty miles, you didn't stop when they flashed their lights . . ." Jason said, taking the stance of defending the two lazy officers sitting in their truck.

"I didn't see them, and does that give them a right to sit here and take their time? What are they doing? Lunching? In this town, they probably only write one ticket a week! This is ridiculous. I'm going to ask them why it's taking so long."

"No you're not. Stay right here," Jason demanded. I could tell that he was angry with me again. Twice so far in just two hours. This was going well. "And I'm driving the rest of the way."

"Fine, do it then," I said, sulking. The lazy cops finally got around to getting out of their truck to give me a ticket. I just took it without saying a word and got into the passenger side so that Jason could drive. We didn't speak for thirty minutes or so. I decided to let him calm down, and then I reached over and unzipped his pants and reached inside his briefs.

"You're a bad girl," he said, not resisting

"Yes I am, and you like it. Do you like it, baby? Do you like this? And this?" I asked him as I touched him. I unbuckled my seatbelt and moved over to him, burying my head in between his legs. It amazed me how his driving didn't falter as I did this. We didn't appear to either slow down or speed up.

"Babe, there is a semi coming up next to us," he said to me. I sat up and positioned myself back into my seat, buckling my seat belt.

"That's too bad. I didn't get to finish last time either," I said to him, remembering the night back in December when we drove around New York. A stop at a toll bridge interrupted us that time.

As we approached Jackson, it was a clear day, the terrain was amazing, and I could see Jason was in awe of this part of the country as it was very new to him.

"See that over there? Those are the Grand Tetons. In French, it means *big titties*," I proudly told him. I loved sharing what I knew with him; plus it made me seem smart.

"It does?"

"Yep, when I was a flight attendant, I used to fly here. One of the first officers who liked to hear himself talk on the intercom would proudly announce this fact."

"Ladies and gentleman, we are now approaching Jackson Hole, Wyoming. If you look to the left, you will see the Grand Tetons. In French, this means big Titties. Enjoy your time here in Jackson and thank you for choosing to fly with us" He would say this as if he was announcing the local time or weather. Every time I had to fly a leg with him to Jackson, I would mentally prepare for what I would say to the offended passengers when he would say this. It went on until a certain captain who was a bishop in the Mormon Church put an end to him sharing this educational fact.

The Swedish bed-and-breakfast that we were staying at was located two blocks from the center of town. Each room had a gas fireplace, and each was painted in either baby blue, yellow, sage green, or pink. Our room was blue, with white moldings framing the walls. Thick, fluffy white down comforters layered the bed, and the room was filled with Swedish hand-painted furniture. It was unlike the hotel rooms we stayed at in New York, having more of a "homelike" feel to it. Jason unloaded our things from my truck, and I collapsed on the bed. Long drives always wore me out as I preferred to fly rather drive. When he brought in the last of the suitcases, he stood next to the bed, and I reached up to take his hands in mine, pulling him down to the bed with me.

"Thanks for driving. You may have saved our lives, you know," I said with a kiss and a giggle.

"Yeah, I know. You're welcome. You didn't get to finish what you were doing earlier," he said, unzipping his pants. A n hour later, we lay there totally exhausted. I got up and fixed us both a cocktail and decided to give him a pedicure as he checked his e-mail messages on my laptop.

"You have nice feet, babe," I said as I took the "Credo" knife, a device to shave off calluses and proceeded to scrape his heels with it. He never looked up when I did this—he was fixated with the laptop.

"Does this tickle? Wow, you are brave. I only cut like eight people before," I joked. Still silent, he didn' t stir. Minutes later, he finally said something.

"What happened to the rest of chapter seven?" he asked.

"Are you reading the chapters? I thought that we agreed that you shouldn't read them anymore."

"What are you hiding?" he asked.

"Nothing, baby. I don't know why it didn't transfer. Can we get ready for dinner? I'm starving."

"What happened with you and Will in San Francisco? Why isn't it in here?" he asked.

Jason knew that Will was my best friend, and there was nothing that I didn't tell him about Will. He had chatted with Will on several occasions, and I knew that Jason wasn't jealous of Will.

"Babe, I told you everything that happened. I don't know where it is. Can we go eat though? J, I don't want you to read any more chapters. If it's hard for me to write, then it is going to be hard for you to read."

"What else are you hiding from me, T?"

"Let's just not do this tonight, okay?"

He closed the laptop finally, and we got ready for dinner.

I had spent my honeymoon with my husband in Jackson, and Jason and I went to the same restaurant that my husband and I had the first night of our honeymoon. It was ironic that we were even seated in the same table and I felt no shame or guilt. I was only happy to be there with Jason, and the thought of my husband left my mind and didn't return again that night. After dinner, we went to my favorite cowboy bar for a few drinks, but we had a big day of skiing the next day, so we didn't stay out too late. I showed him how to do the two-step, and although he wasn't a fan of country music, he was a sport about it and stayed for a few hours as I sang along to the band playing loudly.

It was freezing the next morning as we drove to the ski lodge. We decided to take ski lessons because Jason had never skied, and it had been years since I had. I was never really a great skier, and I always seemed to hurt people when I skied, running into them as if they were cushions to brace my fall. Jason played hockey, so he caught on quickly, and it came back to me as well, yet for some reason, I have always preferred to ski "straight" down the mountain, making me one of those dangerous skiers that people are afraid of. We argued most of the day, starting from me misplacing the ski—lesson tickets not once but twice (I always lose things) to the way I would not make my "S" curves and plow straight down the mountain. He accused me of being reckless, and he was probably right.

Toward the end of the day, our instructor thought we were ready to take the more advanced run, and although I was exhausted, I went anyways. It took me an hour to get down the mountain as my legs were weak and shaking as Jason effortlessly skied down the mountain. I would ski fifteen yards and fall, having trouble getting up because my legs were so weak and I was so cold. I was becoming frustrated and agitated with myself for attempting this. I hated that he waited for me, watching me fall every twenty or so feet, wondering why he didn't just finish the run without me. By the time I made it down the mountain, I was exhausted and angry, and if I didn' t ski again for five more years that would be okay with me.

"Why didn't you just go down without me, babe?" I asked him.

"I was thinking about it, but I wanted to wait for you," he said.

"You should have gone down without me. You would have had time for one more run. I'm sorry—I had no strength in my legs," I apologized.

"It's okay," he said. "It was fun."

We went back to the room and rested before dinner. I felt like getting dressed up, so I put on my little dress and cowboy hat.

"You are the only one wearing a cowboy hat" he said.

"So?"

"So you look silly."

"Um, babe, this is Jackson, its cowboy country. I don't look silly."

"Then why isn't anyone wearing a cowboy hat but you?" he asked.

"Because they are tourists. And who cares? I like my hat."

"It's four degrees outside, and you have a short dress on and a cowboy hat and boots. You look crazy. Everyone else is wearing jeans, Teri."

"Jason, I don't care what everyone else is wearing, and I don't look crazy, I look sexy. And I don' t want to argue with you anymore, okay?" I wanted to stay out and dance, but he wanted to go back to the room, so we did. We were leaving to go to Ogden the next day, and I knew he was tired.

The drive to Ogden was a long stretch of highway, not a lot to see, and Jason was quiet as he was driving.

"Did you have fun in Jackson, babe?" I asked.

"Yes. It was beautiful. And skiing was fun. I was surprised how well I picked it up."

"I wasn't. You're a hockey player. I knew you would do well," I told him. He didn't say anything for a long time.

"So is your middle name Johnathan?" I asked, already knowing that it wasn't. His middle name was John. I was just trying to find something to talk about. For the first time I was grasping for conversation. It had never been so hard to talk to him.

"NO! Why do you always ask me that? You know my name is not Johnathan! Do you do that to piss me off?" he screamed.

"Babe, calm down, sheesh . . . I was just kidding. What's wrong with you?" I asked him.

"I want to go home tomorrow, Teri," he said

"What? You're kidding me, right? It took me a week to get that room in Park City because of the film festival, Jase. Why do you want to go home?" I asked, hurt and confused. I had paid for the hotels, gas, ski lessons as well as ski gear since he didn't have any, and since the film festival was in town, it took extra efforts to book the room in Park City. It really wasn't about the money, but I found it very selfish that he had no consideration for all of the time and planning that went into our trip, and then it occurred to me that it was his idea to even stay an extra day to go to Park City.

"I just do. I want to go home. We can go to Ogden today, but I don't want to go to Park City tomorrow. I want to go home."

"But it's just one more day, babe. I don't understand. Is there something that you want to do at home? Did you make plans or something?"

"No, I'm just homesick. I want to go home." I could not even believe what I was hearing. It took me a week to get the room in Park City, and he was homesick? I was so angry with him that I didn't speak to him until we got to Ogden. Meanwhile I texted Ryan.

Teri:	Jason is homesick and is leaving in the morning. I have a room in Park City tomorrow. Can you come up?
Ryan:	You're kidding me right?
Teri:	No
Ryan:	Ha-ha!
Teri:	It's not funny Rye

"Who are you texting?" Jason asked.

"Will, I told him that I would let him know when we were leaving Jackson," I lied.

Ryan Text:

Teri:	So?
Ryan:	I will be there
Teri:	Thank you babe

I didn't feel one ounce of guilt for asking Ryan to meet me in Park City. I was so angry with Jason for leaving me a day early, especially after he knew what I went through to get the room.

We went to my friend's strip club in Ogden that night. When we walked in, I panicked. There was the manager of my club, who was filling in cocktailing for our friend, and I was paranoid that she would say something to my husband. She reassured me that she wouldn't, but I never did trust her much.

"Oh my God, he's hot!" she said to me.

"I know, please don't tell my husband."

"Teri, I won't, don't worry. I promise." I wanted to believe her, but it was too late for me to worry about this for now. Minutes later, a dancer came over and sat with us.

"Are you the new dancer?" she asked. Her name was Kitty, and she was the top dancer.

"NO! I just told them I would do it for one night, but I am not going to work here!" I replied. I had always wanted to dance, and my friends who owned it had been asking me to do this for years. All night long, dancers sat with us, and Jason and I were having a great time drinking and tipping the dancers. I made several requests for the DJ to play songs, and at one point, Jason came up to the DJ booth with me. I was puzzled to why he left so quickly until I got back to our table.

"I can't fucking believe you just kissed the DJ right in front of me, T," he said.

"What the fuck are you talking about? I so did not just do that?" There was no way that I kissed that DJ, I was drunk, but I think that I would have remembered doing that. Plus, the guy wasn't at all cute.

"T, I just saw it with my own eyes!" he said, trying not to yell.

"Baby, I don't know what you thought you saw, but I didn't just kiss that guy!" I really didn't believe that I kissed him, and I have to admit that I was very drunk. If I did, then I have no recollection of it. To this day, it is still something that I do not believe, but I know that Jason does believe that he saw it. He now used this as his excuse to why he was leaving early. The next morning, he was hungover and sick. He made me "fetch" the truck this time and help load our things. I estimated that it would take about forty-five minutes to get to the airport, but I didn't count on the traffic being so heavy heading south, which was a mistake.

"FUCK!" he yelled and then sat back and sighed. I could tell he was pouting and very angry. He stressed very easily, and I knew he was concerned with missing his flight and honestly I shared in his concern though I pretended to act as if he were overreacting. I didn't give him a response, only turning on the radio and putting on music that I knew annoyed him. I kept glancing at the clock in my car, wondering if I would make it on time since he had no idea how far the airport actually was, he seemed a bit calmer now, sensing that I didn't seem concerned about the traffic. A bead of sweat started to form on my eyebrow, and I surreptitiously wiped it away. I was relieved to see that the exit to the airport was a half a mile away and there was no traffic in that direction. I had hope that we would now make it on time. I didn't want him to think that I was intentionally going to make him miss his flight, and really, I had had enough of fighting with him. I really was looking forward to seeing Ryan today. For the first time, I wanted Jason to leave. I was seeing the "little" boy that he really was, yet I still loved him regardless. Even after all of the fights, all of the pain, I still loved him.

"See, your flight leaves in fifty minutes. Go to skycap. Here is two dollars. Give it to them with your flight information, and then they will issue you your boarding pass so that you may go directly to security. Then to your gate," I told him. He hadn't flown very much, only a few times, so I knew that he needed to know this.

I gave him a quick kiss goodbye with my best fake happy smile and watched him make his way over to skycap. When I was certain that he was given his boarding pass, I drove off and texted Ryan.

Text:

Teri: Just dropped him off, why don't say hello

Ryan worked security at the airport.

Ryan: I'll pass
Teri: Are you still coming?

Ryan:	Hell Yeah, I will be there when I get off work, but I can't stay too late.
Teri:	I understand, thanks for coming Rye. I just don't want to go home.
Ryan:	Ter, maybe you should go home later tonight, you don't want to be there all by yourself after I leave. I don't think that's a good idea.
Teri:	Don't worry about me love, just come and make me feel better.

Jason texted me when he was on the plane, and I was already in Park City by then and in my room. I was hungover and needed to take a nap before Ryan showed up. I lay down, and my phoned beeped with another texted coming in. It was from Josh, the single guy I had the "why do women leave their tampons in my bathroom?" conversation with. Josh and I had met on several occasions for lunch, dinner, or drinks, but I never told this to Jason. We had "messed around" a bit, but I had never had sex with him.

Josh Text:

Josh:	Hi baby, what you are up to?
Teri:	In Park City, Jason left me a day early
Josh:	You are kidding me?
Teri:	Nope
Josh:	He's crazy. I would never leave you.
Teri:	Then come up and stay the night with me. Will you? I don't want to be alone.
Josh:	I can't be there until eight tonight and I have to be up at six in the morning, is that okay?
Teri:	Yes, so will you?
Josh:	I would love too. See you at eight sweetie

I should have felt like the biggest tramp, but I didn't. I needed, or thought I needed, both of them. I lay down on the bed to take a nap before Ryan came and hugged the pillow next to me. *Jason should be laying here next to me, I don't care. I don't care. I don' t care* . . . I thought as I drifted off to sleep.

When I answered the door, it surprised me as to how much I had missed Ryan as my face lit up when I saw him. I jumped in his arms, wrapping my legs around his waist. He caught me and carried me into the room, kicking the door shut behind him, and sat me on the bed while I kissed his neck the entire way.

"Miss me a little?" he laughed. "Too bad Jason boy had to leave."

"I missed you bunches! And I am glad he's gone!" I lied. I wasn't glad Jason was gone, even though we did argue much of the time. It was Jason that I wanted there with me in Park City, however much I did miss Ryan, because it was Jason who I loved. I dismissed him from my thoughts as I started to become angry thinking of him leaving me and kissed Ryan.

"Thank you for coming, baby. I didn' t want to be alone," I told him.

"Well, I don't know why you keep going back to him, Mrs. Brooks. All he ever does is hurt you."

"The same reason why I always come back to you, Rye—because I care about him. It's hard to let go. Why do you always come back to me, knowing that I love him?"

"I care about what happens to you, Teri, I really do. I came today because I knew that you were upset that he left you and you asked for me to be here," he said to me as he pushed away a strand of hair from my face, lifting my chin that I had let fall to my chest. I knew that he didn't come for the sex, and that if we didn't have sex it wouldn't have mattered to him. It was I who initiated it. I needed to be close to him and to have him. When Ryan left several hours later, Jason' s plane was still in the air, and I felt no remorse, but I did feel sad that he was not here with me still. E ven though Josh was coming over, it was Jason that I wanted here even more now.

Josh arrived at eight o'clock, as he said, with flowers and chocolates.

"What is this?" I asked?

"I knew that you were upset, Teri, because he left you, so I wanted to cheer you up."

"How did you know that white roses were my favorite?"

"I didn't," he answered. He poured us both a drink and started to rub my back. I received a text from Jason saying that he had landed but didn' t respond. It seemed as if every time I was with Josh, Jason would text all night, and I would always respond, but not tonight. I turned off my phone. I did something on this night that I never had before: I had sex with two men in one day, and I had just now officially become a "certified" (what my Italian friend Tony would call) *Cum-Slut*.

It was early the next morning when Josh left, and he kissed me and pulled up the covers to my neck, making sure that I was warm. I was too tired and hungover to open my eyes or say anything, and I only rolled over to my side as I felt his hand stoking my hair to the side. When I finally woke up hours later, I found that he had left me another gift—it was a pink Harley Davidson cap he had left in the bathroom.

As I showered and packed to leave, it felt bittersweet to go home, yet I was ready. I called Jason and made up an excuse as to why I didn't text him back with mixed feelings of anger and sadness, wondering what our time would have been like if he had stayed. Ryan and Josh did not fail me, and this would not be the last time that they would come to my rescue.

CHAPTER TWENTY-SIX

February '07

It would appear as a hauntingly familiar image of a place and time long past, pushed back in the depths of my mind that would resurface every few years like a bad rash. It had been years since I had remembered it, yet the night in Park City I had dreamt it.

The week before my sixth birthday there was an exceptionally hot June day as we ran through the sprinklers in our backyard. The water had been running all day, so the long uncut grass was soaked as we skid into each other, screaming and ignoring the heat. Hours of playing in the water wore on my younger brother and sister as well as the neighborhood kids, but I was a water lover, so I decided to stay outside and take advantage of having the sprinkler all to myself.

I turned up the sprinkler as high as it could go, so it sprayed in a fanlike motion spanning twenty feet in the air back and forth.

"Woo!" I screamed to myself. I loved the water and wished for a pool for my birthday. My parents didn't have much money, but I had a good idea that they had purchased one of those small pools that was not more than three feet deep, and that was perfect. I would have been happy with a "baby" wading pool, really. As I ran and slid through the grass, the sprinkler shut off. I turned around to find that my father's best friend was sitting on the edge of the deck.

"Why did you turn the water off, Mr. Buck?" I asked. "Is it time for dinner?"

"No, I have an early birthday present for you. Come here," he asked me. I walked over to him with my hair dripping, wondering what he had for me. Mr. and Mrs. Buck always gave good presents, so I was excited to see what it was that he had for me.

"Now you can't tell anyone. This is our secret, okay?"

"Okay! I promise!" I screamed.

"Shh" he said, looking around. "You need to be quiet. Your present is in my pocket, so if you want it, then you need to reach into my pocket and get it," he said to me

I reached into the pocket that he told me to, and at first all I felt was a hole in the pocket, and then skin. Then I felt something hard. I had taken baths with my younger brother years ago to know what my Chinese mother referred to as what a "choo-choo-chow-chow" was, and I knew that I was touching Mr. Bucks "choo-choo-chow-chow," but it was much bigger than my brother's. I tried to pull my hand away, but he was stronger than I as he held my arm in place. Suddenly I became cold in this heat and started to shiver.

"This is my *key*. Do you like it?" he asked me.

"No!" I said, struggling to pull my hand out from his pocket. He held my arm steady and would not let go.

"Grab my key tighter, Teri."

"NO! LET ME GO NOW!" I screamed.

"Shh . . ." he said, holding his free finger to his lips as he looked behind us. "Do you think Dara would like to do this for me instead? Huh? Should I go get your little sister?" he asked me. Tears were streaming down my face as I struggled to stay still and hold his "key." My sister was only four years old. I could not let him harm her, so I did not say anything, and I tightened my grip as he asked me to. Moments later, I felt something moist on my hands and he let out a moan and released my hand. I didn't know what was on my hand, but it felt sticky and slimy. He got up and started to walk over to the sprinklers and turned them on for me.

"Now run through the sprinklers, and don't tell anyone about this, Teri. This is our secret. This is our game now. If you tell anyone, then I will have to play this game with Dara. Do you understand?"

I could not answer as I looked at the *goo* on my hand, wondering what it was. I nodded not looking at him. I walked over to the grass, never getting near the water and wiped my hand on the already wet grass to clean it. This was the last time that I ever ran through a sprinkler, and I never got into the pool that I received for my birthday. I am terrified of water to this day, and on that day, a week before my sixth birthday, a sexual abuse would begin that would last for eight years.

I tried to push this out of my mind, wondering as to why it would resurface now. I finally broke down and told Jason about it, and he insisted that I seek therapy, something I had never done. Only a few people had known about it. It wasn't until I was twenty—one before I finally told Kirstin and my parents, and both of my husbands knew, but there had to be a reason that it was resurfacing again now. My therapist was named Celine, and I would find that I would trust her almost instantly.

It was not the molestation that she wanted to hear about at first but my *alter ego* and the things that were happening *now*. After several sessions, she determined that I wasn't bipolar, something that she thought I may have had yet I did not display the *manic* side to this disorder. What she determined that I did have is called *Attachment Disorder*, something usually found in children. She explained to me that because of what had happened to me as a child along with being separated from my mother after birth for so long, I never felt safe.

As I explained to her my past and present relationships with men and the many *bulls*, she told me that I have trust issues. I want to *attach*, but I don't trust that they will stay, so I test them. I push them away by testing them until ultimately they leave because no one will ever pass the test. I make sure of it by doing things to hurt them. The sessions helped me to better understand myself, and I was glad that Jason insisted that I seek help. He even spoke with her, but I couldn't get my husband to go with me. I really wanted for him to understand what was going on with me as well, but he showed little interest. I spent the rest of January and the beginning of February in therapy, trying to figure out who I was and which direction I needed to take.

I was going to see Jason again right before Valentine's Day and made up some excuse to go see my sister. It wasn' t like I would be spending Valentine's with my husband, who had already handed me divorce papers, now officially filed. Something inside of me felt as if this would be my last trip to New York, yet I wasn't strong enough to plan a breakup. I knew that my divorce was going to be hard enough, but I couldn't fathom the thought of losing Jason, whom I really did love, however miserable he did make me sometimes.

The more I learned about attachment disorder, the more I realized how he played on it. One day he would tell me how worthless I was, and the next he would let me know that he would be there for me throughout my divorce to support me, that I needed him. He had me in a constant state of emotional ups and downs, and between Jason and my husband, I found myself planning some kind of fairy-tale future without either of them. I was grateful that my husband didn't seem to care that I was leaving town that day to see my "sister" and I insisted that I drive myself to the airport.

Usually I get trapped sitting between two heavier people, or at least one, so I was please to see that I was sitting in the middle of two thin women on the flight that day. The girl sitting to my right was nice, and she laughed a lot and shared her fruit tray with me. The girl sitting to my left was quiet. It was about an hour into the flight when I heard a sniffle coming from the quiet girl' s direction. I glanced over at her and noticed that she was young, in her middle twenties maybe. She was very beautiful, with dark hair pulled back in a ponytail, and she wore glasses. Her sniffles turned into sobs until she was crying uncontrollably.

Not knowing exactly what to do, I did nothing. What do you say to a stranger who is so sad? I was at a loss for words, which is so unlike me since I always seem to have something to say. Ten minutes later, she was still very upset, and I reached over and took her hand into mine without realizing that I had done this, and she looked over at me and squeezed my hand tightly.

I don't know where my tears came from, but I cried with her without ever saying a word to her. Minutes later, she stopped crying, and I had to wonder what made her so sad and took some comfort in knowing that maybe I had helped her in some way. Then I wondered what made me so sad and realized that for some reason I need to cry just as badly.

When the plane landed and I watched her walk away, I hoped that her day would get better and wondered if my life would as well. Here I was in New York, and I was probably the saddest I had ever been. Something was not right

I checked into a room in the all-too-familiar hotel, and Jason would be there in an hour. I had brought a special Valentine's outfit that Marian had helped me pick out from the Fredrick's of Hollywood catalog. It was a low-cut one-piece crotchless panty with a red teddy that was cut to the belly button and had a heart-shaped rhinestone pendant attaching the crotchless panty to the teddy. I wore white thigh-high stockings and white six-inch stilettos. Wrapping a thin red ribbon around a small strand of hair from each side of my head, I tied it in a bow, giving me that "little girl" look.

I cleared the desk and opened eight boxes of heart candies and spread them on the desk, then I ordered three bottles of wine and hors d'oeuvres. Before he arrived, I opened the door, leaving it cracked open, and I got on top of the desk and unwrapped a round red lollipop. I leaned back and put my heels to the edge of the desk and slid the lollipop into the slit of my crotchless panties as he walked into the room.

He stood there, watching what I was doing for a few seconds before he went to take me in his arms. I pushed him gently away with one of my heels and pulled the lollipop from my panties.

"Wanna lick my lolli, little boy?" I asked him, now seductively rolling myself forward to the edge of the desk. I put the lollipop in his mouth, and he sucked it for a few seconds before taking it out and kissing me passionately. I pushed him away gently again and took a heart-shaped candy from the desk that read "kiss me" and put it between my teeth. He kissed me, taking the candy into his mouth, and I could hear it crunch as he chewed it. He then carried me to the bed while I wrapped my legs around his waist and one of my stilettos fell to the floor.

He laid me on the bed, and my legs were sitting on his shoulders as he slowly rolled down my stockings. He kissed my legs, working his way up to my stomach, and I pulled myself up to a sitting position.

"Let me see you. I have missed you so much, babe," I said to him, kissing his face with "baby" kisses.

I pulled away for only a few seconds to look into the navy blue eyes that I had missed so much. He was everything that I had physically desired in a man, and I wanted him inside of me. I unzipped his pants while in a kneeling stance on the bed as he slid his shirt over his head, exposing his perfect chest. As he entered me, it felt as if it were the first time we were together, and I realized why I had cried on the plane earlier that day. The love that I felt for him was more than what he felt for me. I had lost control, and he had gained it all. He could have just called checkmate right then and there. We made love for two more hours, and then we ate and drank our wine. I showed him my ex-cheerleader moves, he showed me how to throw a ball (joking that I throw like a girl), we talked, and we laughed. Things were going perfect, too perfect, and then I had to do it. It was two o'clock in the morning, and we were almost asleep.

"I want for you to leave," I whispered "Just go now," I said under the bravery of the wine.

"What? You are kidding me, right?" he asked.

"No, go. It's over. I can't do this anymore," I said to him, getting up from the bed now.

What are you doing Teri? Have you gone mad? Do you have any idea what you have just done? The good voice in my head was asking me.

It's about time Tell him to take a hike! How many times has he left you? Take back control here! He treats you like dog shit! Get some balls girl, and while you are up, put that cheap-ass ring in his pocket! The bad voice in my head told me. Before the good voice could come back, I acted on what the bad voice said, and I took off the ring that Jason had given me at Christmas, putting it in the pocket of his jeans. I knew the moment I took it off that it was a mistake, but it was too late. He was already behind me.

"What? You are always pushing me away, T. Why do you push me away? We have been together for six months, and I always come back to you when you pull this shit. How many times are you going to do this?" he said as he gathered up his things. "You want me to leave? Fine, I'm gone. I'm done trying to figure you out. I'm tired of not being enough for you. Bye T."

I fought to understand why I asked for him to leave. I fought to understand why I had given him back his ring. I found none of the relief I thought I might have in doing any of this. I struggled to say something, yet nothing came out of my mouth. I must have opened my mouth a dozen times as to say something while he was dressing, yet I was mute. It was as if there was a force from keeping me from saying anything or from moving. I could only watch him walk out of the room and hear the door slam behind him. It would be five minutes before I could move or speak. I grabbed my phone and called him.

"Jase, please come back. I don't know what came over me. I'm sorry. I don't know why I keep pushing you away. Celine and I are really working on it, baby, I swear. Please come back. I love you," I begged.

"I found it, Teri. The ring. What did I tell you? I told you that I would know that if you ever took it off that it would be over," he said to me as I recalled him saying these words to me as he placed the ring on my finger back in December. "I'm not coming back to you this time, T. You just made your choice when you took my ring off your finger." He hung up the phone and I sat there, numb and drunk. I already knew that this was going to happen. I knew it earlier on the plane. I knew it yesterday. I knew it last week. I knew it last month. I just didn't want to know it. I cried myself to sleep that night and dreamed about a little girl running through sprinklers.

The next morning, I woke up with swollen eyes and a hangover. The first thing that I did was call Will.

"Will, I did it again. Why do I do shit that pushes him away from me? I made him so angry last night that he left," I cried, barely able to speak as I said this.

"What happened? Why did he leave? You two have been fighting so much lately. What's the deal?" Will asked.

"I pushed him away like I always do. My counselor says it's because I am testing him, like I do my husband. I do things that make them mad to see if they love me enough to stay. I don't understand why it is I do this, Will. I want to understand why I do this."

"What happened? Why did he leave?" he asked, trying to understand.

"I told him to. As I was doing this, there was a little voice in my head screaming STOP, but I couldn't, Will. I gave him back his ring. Will, what is wrong with me? Am I a tard?"

Will tried his best to console me, and I called Marian next, and she did the same. I wanted so much to call Celine, my therapist, for guidance as I felt so lost and out of control. I wasn't sure if Jason would answer his phone, but I called him anyways.

"Hi," I said to him, surprised that he did answer.

"Hi, T."

"Whatcha doin?" I asked him.

He didn't reply.

"I know that you are really angry with me, and I don't blame you. I am really trying to get better, Jason, and not push you away here."

"You have done it too many times. You know that I love you. I gave you a ring. I don't know what else you want from me. I'm sick of your lies, your MySpace guys. You don't have ONE girl on your page. They are all guys that just want to fuck you, and you have a boyfriend. How do you think that makes me feel? You just traded in the Cheaters Club Site for MySpace. That's all you did. Let's face it, T, I'm not enough for you," he said to me, and the last sentence burned in my ears. *I'm not enough for you.*

"Okay, babe, I'm not going to beg for you back, but you are wrong. You are enough for me. If this is what you want, then I'm moving on. Good-bye, Jase, and just know that I really do and always will love you."

I hung up the phone and cried for about ten minutes before I logged online. I had three hours before my flight was leaving, so I signed on to my new MyS pace page. I don't know how I managed to do this, but the next day would be Valentine's Day, and I set up a date for not only Valentine's Day but for the next three days after as well. I had made four dates in an hour with four guys from my MySpace page.

Valentine's Day was sad, and I missed Jason terribly. I had forgotten that I sent him a dozen roses, and he had texted me to thank me as I formally told him that he was welcome. When he asked me what I was doing, I told him I had a date, and I could tell that he was crushed by that. He sent this e-mail:

T,

Guess when you say you are moving on you are moving on, didn't take you long but did you have to do it on Valentines Day which happens to be our sixth month anniversary? You say that you love me but you have a funny way of showing it. Wouldn't surprise me if you had more dates lined up this week either, that would be a typical Teri move.

When I read this, I wanted to throw up because he knew me so well. I didn't respond to the e-mail because there was nothing more to say.

If I hadn't lost him then, I had now. But I had a plan to get him back. He would come back to me, he always did.

CHAPTER TWENTY-SEVEN

April '07

I spilled my coffee down my crisp white button—down shirt as I was trying to apply a soft smoky liner under my eyes. I was running late and was frustrated that I had to now find something new to wear to pair with the soft pink skirt I had on. I had to be at my client's home in less than thirty minutes, and I was still half asleep. Why did I schedule morning appointments? I always ran late and could never think clearly before noon as it was. I applied a shade of pink lipstick after taking another quick sip of the very hot coffee that I managed to spill again, this time on my skirt.

"Dammit!" I said to myself as I grabbed a blazer to put on to cover the coffee spot, realizing that I had no time to change. I put on my pearls and checked my hair once more and headed upstairs. The BGC beeped, and it was a text message from Jason.

Jason: What the fuck is your problem?
Teri: J, I'm running late here, what are you talking about?

Before I received a text back, he called me. Not knowing what this was about but knowing that it was not going to be good, I contemplated not answering it because I was running late. I decided to answer it anyways.

"Hey, what's this about now, Jason? I'm late for a client meeting," I said when I answered the phone without even saying hello.

"What was that bullshit about your new boyfriend answering your phone last night?" I had gone out the night before with one of the guys on my MyS pace page and remembered that he did answer my phone when I was in the bathroom, telling Jason that I was his "girlfriend now" and to stop calling me.

"Listen, I don't know what that was about and Ken is not my boyfriend and I'm very sorry he did that. I will talk to him about that," I promised. "But I don't know when I will see him again."

"Bullshit. You have a date with him tonight."

"No, I am meeting Daniel tonight. Remember Maddy's friend? We are going to sushi and to karaoke."

"Unbelievable. You are a MySpace whore," he said in is abusive way which I was getting used to, and in a disturbing way, it didn't seem to even faze me anymore

"It's been two months, J. I have BEGGED you back for two months now. Since that night right before Valentine's Day when we broke up, and you won' t take me back. What do you expect me to do? I call you every day, I ask you to forgive me, I have gone to therapy, slowed my drinking down, started to take on more clients, and you won't take me back. So what do you want me to do? Sit home and wait until you forgive me while you are on that new nasty porn site, looking to fuck married women in front of their husbands?"

I few weeks ago, I found out that Jason had joined this pornographic dating site which made the Cheaters Club Site look almost G-rated. This site featured most people with only their private parts showing with descriptive things that they were looking for. I found Jason's profile, and I almost dropped out of my chair as I read what he was looking for it read something like this:

> "No sleeping tonight. I am a sexual person and looking to find a married woman whose husband may want to watch his wife being pleasured. I am serious about meeting."

I was sickened and angry. He had made a comment about looking to do this, so I had checked every site that I could think of until I found him on this one. I don't know what came over me, but I created a fake profile in his area to see if he would bite. Every word I typed to create this made me sick, yet I found that I could not stop myself having to know just how far Jason would go.

I searched the Web and found the most ugly, fat buttocks of some woman with huge cellulite dimples, and the user name I chose for her was as foul as her bum. I made her profile nasty and made sure that I misspelled every other word on purpose. I wanted to see if he would wink back at this nasty girl but found that when I sent him a message, he did not respond. I wasn't sure if I was relieved or not, yet I deleted this profile and never said anything about it. I did however know that he was still on it. This site was unlike any other site I had seen. I felt as if I was a rookie again when I browsed it one night out of boredom. I was searching and browsing and came across something that said "Live—Video Cams." I wondered if it meant what I thought it did, and so I pulled one up.

Not knowing exactly what to expect, I sat there in amazement. I clicked on the first one that I saw without reading the profile, and before me was a woman who appeared to be in her late fifties and weighed at least two hundred and fifty pounds. She had her fingers inside of herself, and the camera was very close to view what she was doing that it was almost as if you were in front of her. I noticed the stats next to her profile, and there were over three hundred people viewing this ugly act. I felt as if I was going to vomit, and it was then that I decided to delete my "Ms. Huge Dimpled Bum" profile, knowing that I could not stay on a site so incredibly disgusting. I think the thing that hurt me the most was the profile picture Jason had posted. It was the one that he took for me and sent to me that night back in November to persuade me to come see him when we had broken up. I was getting angry thinking of this, so I dismissed it from my mind and got back to the conversation at hand.

"You are on that nasty site looking to basically get laid, and you have no right to interrogate me on who I may be seeing right now, Mr. Cop."

"The biggest mistake I made was coming back that first time I met you in September. You are a liar and a cheat, and you manipulated me into coming back that Saturday night, making me feel I was inadequate. You wanted me to come back for your own reasons, and you manipulated me to come see you again," he said the same thing that he had said a hundred times before. I could almost finish the sentence for him because I had heard this so many times.

"When are you going to stop living in the past? All you ever do is bring up shit that I did. This is NOW, and I can't change what I have done Jason, nor can I rewrite what has already been written. I just want to move on here. I have tried everything I know to get you back, and I don't know what it's going to take anymore. I do however know that I'm incredibly late for my appointment, and I won't have this discussion with you right now. I'm sorry Ken was an ass to you last night, but I must go."

"Fine, have fun on your date tonight. What does this one make? Number ten?" he said sarcastically. Without answering or even saying goodbye, I hung up the phone. Months had gone by, and I had begged him to take me back, and yet it seemed as if every day we fought about things that happened in the past. He could not forgive me and yet he could not seem to let me go. I ran out of the house, forgetting my paint schedule as well as other necessary documents, not realizing this until I got to my client's house. I made some excuse to why I could not stay and went home.

Living with my husband through this divorce was hell. When he walked into the house, the temperature would drop twenty degrees. I hated being there. I decided that I would go to the sushi bar early and have a few drinks before Daniel got there, just so I could get out of the house. An hour later, he walked in and I was glad to see his handsome face. His hair was dark, and he had the most amazing green eyes, which reminded me of a glass marble. Daniel wasn't much of a drinker, but he loved to sing karaoke—the worst kind of "ham boy" on the microphone who sang Elvis songs as I cheered him on as if he were really "The King."

The club we were at was across the street from my husband's club, and we decided to go to my husband's bar for a bit to meet up with Maddy. It sounded like a good idea at the time yet ended up being the beginning to what would become a nightmare.

"I'm starving again!" I screamed over the sounds of the loud music of some guy singing what I think was supposed to be Frank Sinatra.

"We just ate sushi. You can't be hungry," Daniel said.

"That was an hour ago, and you know what they say about Chinese food—you are always hungry again afterwards," I replied.

"Um, sweetie, sushi is Japanese, not Chinese," he said with a wink. He was a heavy stocky guy who reminded me of a teddy bear, and I was amazed he wasn't at all hungry like I was.

"Chinese, Japanese, Siamese, it's all the same . . . I'm gonna go make us a burger. The kitchen is closed, but I can make the bestest burgers in the world!" I said.

"You allowed to do that? Go in and make us food?"

"Pretty sure I have only done it a hundred and one times . . . it's my bar! I always cook when the kitchen is closed. It's all good," I said, slurring my words a bit.

I went into the kitchen and laid two hamburger patties on the grill that I had turned on. I buttered the buns and laid them next to the hamburger patties that I oversalted. Five minutes went by, and they were ready, just as the bartender came into the kitchen.

"You have to go, Teri," he said to me as I laughed, thinking he was kidding.

"Yeah, okay, hey, hand me the spatula next to you. These are done."

"No, I mean you have to go NOW," he insisted again, and this time I knew he was serious.

"Are you kidding me? This kitchen runs under my license, and this is my bar. The burgers are done, so move over. I will get the spatula myself," I demanded, not too happy with him. He grabbed my arm and led me to the back door of the kitchen.

"Let go of me! Are you nuts? What the fuck is your problem? Don't make me call my husband, asshole."

"I've already called him. You have to go," he said as he opened the door and threw me outside into a dark alley. He closed the door and locked it, and I stood there in the dark cold alley, unable to move in disbelief at what had just taken place. I didn't have my coat or purse, and I needed a cigarette in the worse kind of way. Minutes later, Daniel pulled up to get me.

"They just fucking kicked me out of my own bar!" I screamed through tears of anger. I grabbed my cell phone out of my purse and dialed home, and my husband answered.

"I just got kicked out . . . Your bartender physically manhandled me and threw me out into the alley!" I screamed, explaining what I already knew he knew.

"You shouldn't have been in the kitchen, Teri. You are drunk, and then you bring in your boyfriend? Classy wife I have."

"He's a friend of Maddy's, and I didn't do anything that I haven't done before, and you know that. I cook all the time after the kitchen is closed, and I'm not drunk! What is this really all about?"

"Oh well, I guess now you know not to do it again, don't you?" he said snidely. "Maybe it's a good idea that you just don't go into my bar again at all."

"Your bar? Are you kidding me? YOUR bar would be shit if it wasn't for me. Everything in that place and how it is run was under my influence. You are a real ass."

"Yeah, I am, and you are a drunken slut."

"How are we to live civilly through this divorce when you are verbally abusive?" I asked, trying to hold my temper. Before he could answer, the question he hung up the phone, and I put my face into my hands and sobbed. Daniel took me in his arms and held me for several minutes before he kissed me.

"If I let you do this, then I make him right, I am a slut," I told Daniel.

"You're not a slut, Teri, and what happened to you tonight is all about control. Between your husband and Jason, you have no self-confidence left. Don't let them tell you who you are or who you aren't." I forgot about my sorrow as I wrapped my arms around his waist. Daniel was the tall dark and handsome type. Even though I never considered him to be my type, it felt good to be in his arms.

It may have been a combination of anger and the alcohol that led me to be intimate with him that night. But it felt good to be in his arms. Daniel would become someone very important to me and a special friendship was born on this night.

When I went home, I didn't want to go into the house, so I parked down the street and sat in my truck. I'm not sure how much time went by when I heard a knocking at my window. It was a young police officer.

"What are you doing?" he asked me.

"Listening to music," I said.

"Have you been drinking tonight?"

"Yep, lots, really. I don't want to go home," I said, not realizing that I had just incriminated myself.

"Where do you live? And why don't you want to go home?"

"I live right there," I said, pointing two houses down. "And my husband, whom I am divorcing, is mean. I just don't want to go home, you know?"

"I can't let you sit here all night. Get out of the truck, and I will walk you to your house. Is he abusive?"

"Not physically, no—or he hasn't been for years, that is. Why can't I just stay here?"

"Because you are drunk, and you need to go home. Come on, I will walk you to your house." He said, and I knew not to push the issue with him, knowing that he could have taken me to jail. He walked me to my house and helped me open the garage as I gave him the code. That's when I noticed how incredibly cute he was.

"You're kinda cute too, by the way. Thanks for not taking me to jail," I blurted out, sounding like the drunk I was.

"Should I walk you in to make sure you will be okay? Do I need to speak to your husband?" he asked, ignoring my compliment.

"No, that will only make him angrier. I will be fine. Good night, officer," I said. I walked into the house, hoping that he would be in our bedroom, asleep, but he was in his chair, with the television on. I was headed to the bedroom, hoping not to have a conversation with him, when he said something.

"There are amended divorce papers by your computer. I suggest you read them because I can't deal with being married to you anymore," he said.

"Not tonight. I am tired and angry."

"And you are drunk! My wife is a fucking DRUNK! You are an embarrassment to me. Congratulations, baby, you have done what no woman before you has done, you have taken away my pride and brought me to my knees," he said with the undertone of anger in his voice.

"I'm sorry, baby. I never wanted this for us, but I read the first papers, and if you think I am leaving with nothing from this marriage, you are mistaken. Those papers are a joke. You are going to give me my truck and ten grand? Don't offend me with offers like that. You had nothing when we were married, and everything you have today is because we built it together," I said, trying to stay civil.

"If you go after my businesses and bars and I lose everything, then I won' t be responsible for what I do. I won't have anything to lose. Remember that, and don't take it lightly," he threatened.

"What do you mean you won't have anything to lose?" My husband ran with a tough crowd and he was known to his friends as "the godfather," yet it never scared me before.

"Just what I said. Don't fuck with me, Teri. I walk on the evil side, and you know this about me. Your body will never be found. One bullet is all it takes, baby. Don't forget that." Now he was scaring me. He tapped on the small gun safe next to the chair he was sitting in, trying to intimidate me, and it worked. Something in his eyes looked dead, as if all life was gone from his soul, and life didn' t matter to him—his life or mine. I contemplated calling the police, but I realized that I was still very drunk, and they would not likely believe a drunk over a sober person, regardless of the truth. I opted to lock myself in my daughter's room since she was not home and her room had a lock on it.

It was a long night, and I was aware of every noise in the house. The heater would kick on, and I would flinch. I never did sleep that night, knowing that he didn't go to our bedroom and sat in his chair all night. I opened the window regardless of the cold, just in case he did try to come in. It would give me a chance to jump out and get away.

Early the next morning, the phone rang, and I cracked the bedroom door to listen to what he was saying.

"If I put a bullet in her head at my age, I would only get five to six years. It would be worth it just to get rid of the bitch and save me thousands on a divorce," he said to one of his friends, and I had a good indication of who it was he was talking to. I closed the door, not wanting to hear any more, and waited for him to leave the house before I came out of the room. I called Maddy.

"He's gonna kill me, Mad. I got to get out of here," I said to her and explained the events of the previous night and what I had heard that morning. "I'm packing a bag and going to my mom's house NOW."

"If you leave the house, Teri, you won't get it. You need to call your lawyer and go get a protective order now!" she said. "I have done this before. You can't leave if you want to keep your house."

I took the advice of Maddy and my attorney and filed a protective order through the court against my husband It was also advised to me that I withdraw any monies in joint accounts that we may have shared because he would for sure cut me off financially after this. After filing the order, I went to the bank and withdrew six thousand dollars from the business account that I was still on. He had already closed our personal accounts and credit cards we shared together a month earlier. It was now four o'clock, and I thought I was going to faint from lack of any food or liquids that day, so I grabbed a diet Coke and sat in the parking lot of 7-eleven. Today would be the darkest day of my year, and it was not over yet.

CHAPTER TWENTY-EIGHT

April '07

"It's done, Maddy, I have the order in my hand, and I took some money out of the bank," I said as I called Madeline from my car.

"Call the police and have them serve him now," she said.

"No, I can't do that. He's at the club, and I won't have him served in front of his friends and employees. I will wait until he gets home tonight," I said stubbornly.

"Call your lawyer, Teri. I don't think you should wait on this, but it's up to you." Instead of calling my attorney, I called Jason. He didn't answer his phone. Where was he when I needed him? I called my attorney next.

"I have the money and the order, Mr. Smith," I said. My attorney was in his late forties to early fifties, and he was tall and handsome, with dark hair. He reminded me of a James Bond type, and I found him in the phone book. I remember our first meeting when I was distraught and didn't have makeup on and I wore a baseball cap. Upon meeting him wished I had looked a bit more presentable. He was straight to the point and offered no promises, and that was what I liked about him, besides his rugged good looks.

"Call the sheriff and have him served, then," he said as if I didn' t already know that he would say this.

"Mr. Smith, I would rather wait until he gets home. I don't want to have him served at the bar—he will be so mad."

"So, what? What did we discuss, Teri? We don't care if he' s mad or what he thinks. Call the sheriff now. Go home and gather anything that you don't want him taking because they may allow him to go get his belongings."

"Okay, I will call you tomorrow then," I said as I hung up the phone, knowing that I was not going to follow his advice. I would not have him served at his club. I was feeling badly enough. I sat in the parking lot for another hour, calling my sister and texting my "guys" for moral support. Jason was not to be found. My husband always got home between seven and eight at night, so at seven-thirty I decided to drive by the house to see if he was home. He wasn't.

I parked down the street and waited and watched for his truck to pull around the corner, taking careful attention not to be noticed by him. Hours went by, and he still was not home. I called the club finally, and they told me that he had just left. It was not like him to get home so late, and by now I was going out of my mind. I had second thoughts of having him served, yet I didn't want to chance another fight nor spend another night locked up in my daughter's room The hardest phone call I made was at that minute to the police to have them meet me. I made that call when I saw his truck pull up to the driveway.

The police showed up several minutes later, and I handed them over the legal document of the protective order. They asked me to wait for them, and I watched them go to the front door and walk into the house. It seemed like hours went by, yet they were back in twenty minutes. My husband didn't take anything—no clothing, no meds, nothing. They told me that he didn't seem that upset, yet I knew that he must have been furious. I drove to the house and locked the doors as Maddy instructed me to do before calling my sister Kirstin.

She tried to calm me, but I was too upset, and when she made the comment that I started this whole thing, I hung up on her.

I called Jason next, praying that he would answer this time. He did.

"He was just escorted out of the house, J. I feel so alone, and I feel so hurt for him." I sobbed. "Did I do the right thing? Please tell me that I did the right thing."

"Teri, I can't tell you that," he said coldly.

"I didn't want to have to do this. Did I do the right thing?" I repeated.

"T . . . I DON'T KNOW!" he said in only one octave less than a yell.

"Then don't answer it as an ex-boyfriend, Jason, answer it as a cop would," I pleaded, hoping that now he would reassure me that I had done the right thing.

"I don't know if you did the right thing. How many times do I have to tell you that?" he said again in a monotone voice this time. I heard him laugh at something on the television and knew he was watching his favorite show, *Family Guy*. I needed him now, more than I ever had before, and in my darkest hour I realized that he was not going to be there for me as he had promised me he would. I couldn't deal with Jason right now as thoughts of my husband leaving behind his medicines kept going through my mind. I had to get them to him.

"I have to go. I need you right now, babe, and your head is somewhere else. I will let you get back to watching *Family Guy*," I said, and I hung up the phone. I realized then that I was going to have to walk through this without him, yet I was too concerned for my husband to care. I called my husband, knowing that this was not the smartest thing to do, but he didn't answer his cell. I then called his best friend and asked him to come get his meds and some clothes. No one came that night, and no one called me back. I knew that he was hurting, and I cried myself to sleep.

———

The next few days were lonely, and I received no word from my husband's friends as I continued to call to make sure that he was okay. Finally, on the third day, his friends came over to get his motorcycles, meds, and clothes that I packed for him. They said nothing to me and didn't even make eye contact. I was grateful my children were in Hawaii with their father through this, yet I missed them terribly though I was to pick them up the following day. I was alone and I had no support from anyone. I made my bed and I was lying in it.

Early the next morning, I received a call from the police stating that my husband reported his gun stolen. I checked the safe and assured them that it was there. I wondered why he would report it stolen, and the police advised me to change the alarm code in the house, which I did as soon as I hung up the phone. I was excited to see my children and couldn't wait to hold them. I felt so alone, and although I had support from Will and several other male friends, it did little to console me. I needed my children. I called my ex husband to find out when they would be landing.

"Hi, how was Hawaii? Are the kids around? God I have missed them so much." I said excitedly. My ex husband was a pilot for an airline, and we had worked hard to establish a civil relationship over the years for the sake of the children. I even threw his new wife her baby shower and befriended her and invited her into my home and my life. I was also friends with my husband's first two wives as well. I remembered a party I had once at my house, and as they went around the room introducing themselves as the ex wife and the wife of the ex husband, I received strange looks, yet I didn't believe in the "ex" thing—as long as they were good people, I welcomed them into my life.

"Well, we never made it to Hawaii. We got bumped. We were in San Diego and San Francisco," he said. "How's your husband?" he asked, and I thought that to be strange.

"What? You mean I could have called them this week? Why didn't you guys call me and tell me that?" I asked, a bit peeved.

"Well, you could have called," he said to me as I tried to hold my temper back.

"My husband is gone. Please don't tell the kids. I want to tell them and explain. I understand that this will be very difficult for them," I said sadly.

"Well, he called me and told me a few days ago, and I already told the kids. I gave you two days to call them and tell them. When you didn't, we decided that they needed to know."

"What? You told them? My husband called you, and you told them without calling me? That was not your place to do!" I screamed this time.

"We were thinking of the children, Teri, calm down. They have a right to know."

"And you robbed me of MY right to tell them! Why would you think that I should have called them when they were on vacation to tell them something like this when I am to see them a few days later? I don' t get you. What did you tell them then?" I demanded to know.

"Just that their stepdad isn't going to be home when they get there," he said.

"Fine, but you were wrong to do that. When can I come and get them?"

"Well, we aren't getting in until midnight, so it will have to be tomorrow," he said. By this time, I was livid. I knew better than to talk to them now on the phone and decided to wait until the following day. I hated my ex husband at that very minute and I hated Jason for not being there for me and I hated my husband for calling my ex. At this moment, I hated all of them.

Chapter Twenty-Nine

April '07

The following day couldn't come fast enough. I went to pick up my children and was expecting hugs and kisses but instead received a cold welcome from them. My eldest son, who was thirteen, didn't want to come for the weekend, but I insisted that he come to lunch at least so I could explain to them what was happening. They didn't want to go to a restaurant, so we opted for a drive-up burger place. After ordering the food through a microphone that was way too loud, my daughter spoke first.

"How could you kick dad out of the house and steal his money and mess up his motorcycle?" she asked me with anger in her voice.

"What? Who told you that? Your father?"

"Yes, dad called our dad, and he told him that," my youngest son said this time in answer to my question.

"Baby, listen, listen to me okay?" I pleaded, not knowing what to say to this. I had rehearsed what I was going to say, but this threw me off. I was angry that my ex husband would tell them this, oh, and in their best interest of course. "It's not like that. I was afraid, so I had daddy removed from the house, and I did not steal any money. I think if I did I would be in jail right now. Mommy doesn't steal."

"But mommy had an affair, and mommy is a liar," my daughter said bitterly. I wanted to smack her right then, but I held back my anger at hearing her harsh words and the manner of which she was speaking to me. I couldn't deny this since she knew about Jason, yet I didn' t know how to respond. I took a deep breath, and calmly tried to finish my explanation.

"Like I was saying, I was afraid. That is why daddy is not home. This is hard, I know, babies. It's hard for me too. I do love your stepdad, and I didn't want for it to be this way."

"You are a liar, mom. Dad would never hurt you!" my daughter snapped back. This time she went too far.

"Do not talk to me that way. You may not believe me, and I hope that you do, but I am your mother. W atch your mouth." I took a deep breath and tried to go on. "Listen, I made some wrong choices, and I will admit to that. I don't want to hurt daddy. I love him still, I do. But you have to trust me now. I need you by my side. You three are all who matters and I need to know that you are going to be by my side," I said as I tried not to cry but did anyways. I hated this conversation, and I knew that I had lost the respect of my children. Both of my sons went to hug me, and they were crying. They told me that they loved me and they were by my side, and I instantly felt better. My daughter sat in the backseat, texting someone, ignoring everything that was going on.

"Put your phone away, Sis. I need for you to understand something. I know that you are angry, and I know that you are hurt. But if you continue to talk to your father about my divorce then it may be detrimental."

"What do you mean?" she said, squinting her eyes at me.

"First of all, it's obvious that your stepdad has called your dad and your dad's sister. This is a divorce, Sis, and it's going to be getting ugly. If you tell them anything about me, it will hurt US. I don't want to be living in an apartment, do you? I need to know that you won' t talk about this divorce to anyone but me. If you have any questions then ask me, babe. This has nothing to do with your father or his sister. I know that you don't want to believe this, but your stepdad has drawn a line in the sand, and people are taking sides," I tried to explain as best I could.

"Who do you have on your side, mom?" my youngest son asked.

"No one, but I only need you three. That's it. Just you three, but that's all I need."

"I'm on your side, mom, but I don' t agree with what you did. I think Jason is a nice guy and all, but I don't think you were right," my daughter said. I instantly regretted letting her talk to him that one day in December. She was asking about some song lyrics, and I was on the phone with Jason that night.

"Ask him if he knows what this means," she asked me.

"Ask who what, Sis?" I said, trying to pretend that I didn't know what she was talking about.

"I know you are talking to Jason. Let me ask him something then, okay?" she said as she reached out for the phone. I knew better than to hand it over to her and let her speak to him, yet I did it anyways. This would be one of many mistakes that I made.

We finished our lunch and talk and went home. I was livid at my ex husband for telling them what he did, in what he referred to as doing so "in the best interest of our children." I decided to call my ex husband later that night and confront him on what he told them. It was not a good conversation. I asked him why he told them that I scratched up my husband's motorcycle.

"Well, did you?" he asked.

"Actually, it's not your business if I did or didn't. I'm just wondering why you would tell the kids this. How is telling them I scratched up his bike in their best interest? Oh, and by the way, I have told them not to talk to you about the issues of my divorce. If they want to know anything, then I told them to ask me. This has nothing to do with you, so you need not bother trying to nose your way into my business," I said bluntly, hoping that he would get the picture and stop asking the kids about my life and my divorce. I knew as I hung up the phone with him that this was not over and that he would make sure that he had the final word one way or another. I would learn how he would do this only too soon.

When the children were home with me, I was now careful not to go online or chat. I spent time with them and didn' t even answer text messages from anyone. We spent time shopping and going to movies and playing Scrabble and Monopoly. This was a good thing for all of us, yet when they left to go back to their father's house, I found myself online again, seeking out more bulls to make me feel better about myself and setting up more meetings to meet new ones. I was drinking heavily when my children were away, and I could feel myself spiraling into something or somewhere I didn't need to visit.

Every day I texted Jason asking him to take me back, and every day he denied me. I was alone, and it didn't matter how many new guys I met or chatted with, I felt empty inside. There was a guy that I had met from my MySpace page, and we would occasionally go to Wendover, a town in Nevada where we went to gamble. We had made several trips there already, and it was a Thursday night, the night before Jason's twenty-seventh birthday, that we decided to go again. I had sent Jason flowers and candy for his birthday, knowing that I shouldn't have but did it nonetheless. It was not busy that Thursday, and we visited several casinos as I lost money that I really didn' t have to lose and I drank enough tequila that they had to actually wheel me out to my truck in a wheelchair. My friend drove us home that night, and he dropped me off at my house.

"Are you going to be okay, Ter? Do you need any help getting inside?' he asked me.

"No, I am fine, sweetie. Thank you for driving me home. I just need some sleep," I said. I hated being alone, and I missed my husband these days for some reason. I walked into the house and locked it up and set the alarm. I went over to the sink and poured a glass of water and opened up the cabinets, searching for two small brown bottles. I had just had them filled and I forgot where I had left them. It took me several minutes, but then I found them. I opened the first plastic brown bottle of prescription pills, called Seroquel, that helped me to sleep. There were forty of them in the bottle. Tiny white pills, I managed to swallow all forty in just two mouthfuls. I opened the next bottle, which was Xanax, a prescription drug to help for anxiety. There were twenty of them in that bottle, so I swallowed all of them in one mouthful. There wasn't really a reason to why I decided to swallow these pills. I just had enough. I had enough.

I went to my bathroom and washed my face and flossed and brushed my teeth. I checked my eyebrows and thought that I should have maybe plucked them earlier. I crawled into bed, thinking that I probably wouldn't wake up, but I didn't really care. I closed my eyes and didn't say a prayer. I knew that it didn't matter anymore, and I wouldn't get to heaven even if God did hear it.

It was nine—thirty in the morning when the phone rang. I went to answer it and felt as if a truck ran me over. I was stiff and so very tired. *Wow, I'm alive,* I thought to myself as I reached to grab the phone.

"Hello?" I said as I answered it. It was my older sister, Kirsten, and she sounded angry.

"Where have you been? I have been so worried about you!" she screamed as I squinted from hearing her yell, feeling hungover and tired.

"I went to Wendover last night. I just talked to you yesterday. What's the problem?" I asked her, now annoyed.

"Teri, you talked to me on Thursday. Where have you been these past two days? Jason and Maddy have been calling me worried about you," she said.

"Oh, it's Jason's birthday today. I hope he got his flowers. I sent him flowers for his birthday," I said to her.

"Teri, his birthday was Friday. Today is Sunday. Where have you been?" she demanded to know. "Jason called me, saying that he couldn't get ahold of you. Maddy called me, saying the same thing."

"It's Sunday? Are you sure?" I asked. Then I understood. I had taken enough pills to put me in a minicoma. I was amazed that I survived with all the alcohol I had in my system at the time I took the pills. I couldn't tell her what I had done.

"What's going on, Teri?" Kirsten asked again.

"I'm depressed. Jason's birthday, this divorce, so I just stayed in bed and didn't answer my phones. I just took it easy. I didn't mean to alarm anyone, I just didn't want to talk to anyone," I lied. She must have believed me because she didn't challenge my story. After hanging up with her, I called Jason. I didn't know what I was going to tell him.

"Hi," I said as he answered his phone.

"Where have you been? Your sister and Maddy are worried, so are your parents and kids, probably," he said.

"Oh, well, I just slept all weekend. I was depressed," I told him, sticking to the same story as I told my sister.

"Bullshit! You were probably with your new boyfriend somewhere. You should have at least answered your phone. You are so selfish, Teri, and you don't give a shit about people. You only care about yourself."

"It wasn't like that, J. I promise. I don't want to make anyone worry. I really just didn't have my phones on."

"You are a liar. Since when do you turn off your BGC? Like NEVER!" he yelled. I knew he was the only one that I couldn't lie to about this because he was the one who knew me the best.

"Fine, okay. I went to Wendover Thursday like I told you; I went home and popped what I thought were enough pills to not wake up. Then I get a call today and woke up," I said matter-of-factly like as if what I did was no big deal.

"You fucking did what? What did you just say?" he asked.

"Don't tell my sister, please. I just had enough. Please don't tell her or Maddy, okay?" I asked him.

"Are you crazy? I should call them both right now and tell them what you did!" he screamed again. I pleaded with him not to tell.

"If you pull something this stupid again, T, I will tell them. You have to get sober and your life together. You want me to come back to you? Why should I come back to this? Tell me? After the shit that you have pulled these past few months with your serial dating and now a suicide attempt? Get sober, T. Do it for your kids, at least." His words stung, and I wasn't feeling too well. I didn't want to argue with him, so I just promised that I would get sober even though we both knew it was a lie.

I managed to get dressed, and Maddy came by. She insisted that we go shopping to get my mind off of things, and she bought the story that I told my sister. I was driving when I got the phone call from my youngest son.

"Mom?" he said through tears.

"Hi baby, I'm sorry mommy hasn't called you these past few days. What's wrong? Don't cry, baby," I said to him, thinking that he was upset that I had not called him. It dawned on me then what it would have done to my kids had I not woken up. Jason was right—I was selfish.

"Haven't you heard, mom? What happened?" he said through heavier sobs now.

"What happened, baby?" I asked, now very concerned.

"Papa . . . he died. Didn't you know?" he asked. I pulled over to the side of the road. My heart skipped a few beats, and tears were now stinging my eyes.

"No, what? When did that happen? Oh my God," I said in disbelief. *Papa* was who my children called my father-in-law, my husband's father. He had lived with us for six years and had just only recently moved out. My thoughts were now with my husband and how he must be feeling.

"I went to the funeral today, mom. Dad is sad. Where were you, mom?" he asked me I didn't know what to say.

"No one told me, baby. I'm so sorry. Thank you for telling me. Are you okay? I wish I could give you hugs. You know that Papa loved you very much," I said, trying to comfort my son in the best way I knew how. I was shaking and crying, trying not to break down and stay strong. My son had a close relationship with my father-in-law. They were buddies, and I knew that this was very hard for him.

"I didn't think you knew, that's why I called. I'm okay, mom, but I have to go. I will talk to you later, okay?" he said in his strongest big—boy voice.

"Okay, sweetie. Mommy loves you so very much. Never forget that," I said to him as we hung up. Maddy overheard the conversation and insisted on driving because I was so distraught.

"No one called me, Mad. I didn't know he was even sick. My husband must be going through hell. Oh my God, and I can't even be there for him. I can' t comfort my husband in his time of need," I told her as she drove us home. I needed to get a grip here. My heart hurt as I remembered hearing through the grapevine that my father—in-law was upset with me because of the divorce. This man that I took care of for six years, who listened to me and tried to comfort me when my husband and I would fight, insisting that his son was spoiled and that I was the best thing that ever happened to him. I felt as if I had lost my father. I mourned the man who died despising me without ever being able to ask his forgiveness. It was more than I could bear. I needed a Xanax badly and realized that I didn't have any left because I took them all. I asked Maddy if she had anything to calm my nerves I broke down in uncontrollable sobs.

"I thought that your doctor just filled them for you?" she asked.

"Um,no. I need to call her for them, and it's Sunday," I lied through my tears.

"I have something that would work. Let's just get you home. You don't look good," she said to me. I don't know what I would do without her. All of my friends had abandoned me. I really didn' t have anyone but my family and maybe a few friends left. Not counting all the *bulls* who just wanted to get down my pants. I thanked God that moment for her and for Will and the few friends that I *did* have, even though I was sure he didn't hear the thanks given.

It was against the protective order, yet I called my husband. He answered and then hung up on me when he heard my voice. I called his manager, and she assured me that he was surrounded by friends and family and had lots of support. I felt a bit left out and hurt that no one called me to tell me of the death, not to mention call me to see if I was handing it well. Everyone who knew me knew how close I was to my father-in-law, and I felt so abandoned and alone. It was as if I were already divorced and that I didn't matter. That I was no longer a part of the family and that I had no right to know of or mourn his death. I called my children later that night to make sure that they were handling it. My concern was now for my children, not my husband. My ex husband's wife answered.

"Hi, are the kids there?" I asked her.

"No," she answered coldly. I wondered what I had done to her to make her so distant and cold. This was someone that I welcomed into my home and threw baby showers for when she had children with my ex husband. We were close friends, and I was confused to why she was so angry with me. Maybe it was the way I told my ex husband to back off. Regardless, I was still confused with her behavior.

"Okay, I wanted to check on them, to see if they were okay. Hey, if my husband calls you, I know that he has been calling everyone, just please don't discuss me with him, okay?" I asked her.

"Teri, you aren't going to like this, but I am going to say it anyways. You are a liar and a cheater, and you have said horrible things about my husband, and really I am not on your side here, so don't ask me that," she said in a wicked tone.

"What the hell are you talking about?" I snapped back, not in the mood to hear insults thrown my way. I felt beat—up enough, like a punching bag that everyone wanted to take a shot at. I wasn't going to take any more punches without punching back.

"You are a shitty mom, and your kids think you are crazy," she said again in an even more wicked tone. I pictured the wicked witch from the *Wizard of Oz*, since she had just dyed her shoulder-length hair a gothic-like shade of some kind of black that made it look frizzy and fried. I was livid at hearing her bold remarks since my kids told me that they are afraid of her temper and how she went off on them and thought she had more nerve than I gave her credit for.

"Actually, my kids think you're nuts. They are afraid of you most of the time. I know that your father is dying, but you lose your temper with them quite a bit, and you need to get a grip and stop telling me about what kind of a mother I am and concentrate on what kind of mother you need to be!" I snapped back proudly, and I hung up on her after saying this. It was only moments later when the phone rang, and it was from their house. I didn't want to fight with the Wicked Witch of the West anymore, but I answered it anyways. It was my daughter.

"MOM! Why did you tell my stepmom we are afraid of her?" she screamed.

"Um, because you are. I'm sorry, baby, she made me angry, and I shouldn't have said that. But she *does* need to know."

"But it's not true! We aren't afraid of her! We love her! Why do you have to always lie?" she screamed at me. Then I understood. The wicked witch was listening. It hurt me that my daughter would do this. It hurt me that my daughter would consider her feelings over mine, and I was weary as it was.

"Okay, I see. I'm very sorry that I said that to her. My mistake. I apologize, Sis," I said, giving in because I had no fight left within me. All the life had been sucked out of me.

"Well you shouldn't lie! And make us look like we are afraid of her!" she kept going.

"Okay Sis, enough . . . I get it. She is there listening, but I am still your mother, and do not talk to me that way just to appease her. I've had enough, Sis,

I can't do this. So I will say goodbye for now." I hung up the phone feeling as if I meant nothing to anyone anymore, not even to my daughter. My children were frightened of their stepmother's tempter, and everyone knew it, including her. It was my mistake to bring it out knowing that they had to live with her, so that was why I swallowed my words and let her think that she had won. I did it for my children. They were all who mattered to me in the world. They were all I had left.

CHAPTER THIRTY

April '07

I wondered why God wasn't ready for me when I swallowed those pills, and as I hung up the phone with my daughter, I had to wonder if he wanted me to live if only to experience more pain. Was this worse than hell? Was I being punished? Dying would be so much easier, and he wasn't going to let me out this easily, I determined. I called the only person that could possibly understand what I was feeling, and that was Jason. It was also a big mistake that I did turn to him. I would soon learn not to do this anymore.

"What do you expect? You are a shitty mom and a shitty wife and girlfriend," he said when I told him of the conversation. "You are a shitty person in general, T."

"Is this fun for you? I'm at my lowest here. I just lost someone I loved so very much, and I am in great pain here, Jason," I said, hoping for just a hint of sympathy thrown my way. "And now you kick me when I'm down and throw punches just like the rest of them. I don't know why on earth I called you," I said, disgusted that I actually had hoped that he would have given me some comfort in this situation.

"You have to look at yourself in the mirror. Tell me what you see when you do. Because I know what I see when I look at you," he stated.

"I'm working on it. But when I look in the mirror, J, I see broken glass," I said as I knew what was coming next.

"You are the one who shattered the glass, don't forget that," he said coldly. I wondered which scale was heavier, the "Teri Haters" or my "Bull fan club." It didn't seem as if either mattered, really, as I decided that I would stop feeling sorry for myself. I hung up the phone without saying goodbye to him in all of his rudeness.

I drank two bottles of wine as I visited cyber-land that night, pretending to be mentally stable as I chatted with several guys who pushed to meet me. I was hoping to see Will or Adam online, the only two who really could have helped get me though this night, but I knew that Will was out of town, and it had been months since Adam talked to me. His last words to me back in February were "I can't be there for you anymore if you continue to talk to Jason. He's not good for you, Teri, and I can't listen to this anymore. I'm here for you when you realize that you don't need him."

I put in the stereo a CD of songs that I had burned a long time ago, songs that were mine and Jason's. I sang to the one that reminded me of him the most. The one that I played two hundred times that first time we broke up in October.

"So far away, been far away for far too long, so far away . . ." I sang to this song by Nickelback and felt very sorry for myself while doing so. "I keep dreaming you'll be with me and you'll never go, stop breathing if I don't see you anymore . . ." I held my breath for a short moment after I sang the words. I poured the last glass of wine from bottle number two and swigged half of it down in one gulp.

I sat in my husband's chair in the dark. The wine was gone, and I stared into the darkness, lost in a place which felt much like I imagined hell to be like. My biggest fear was being alone. And I sat with my biggest fear, alone in the dark. There was no one that I could call upon this time of night, and I was in no mood to chat online with horny men who didn't care about me. I was lost in this darkness, trying to find my way into the light.

There was a small gun safe next to the chair, and I turned on the lights and opened it. It had some sort of sleeve on it, so I took it out of the harness and put it to my head. I decided this time that I would leave a letter behind for those I loved. I started to write them, and I wrote my good—byes to my husband and to my daughter first. I didn't have any words left to finish what I wanted to say to them, so I figured that I would just get it over with.

I held the gun to my head and pulled the trigger. Nothing. I looked at it and shook it a few times and tried it again, still nothing. I banged it against the table and put it against my head once more, pulling the trigger. Nothing. I was getting frustrated with the gun and figured that it was on some safety lock, and I called my husband.

"Don't hang up! This is important!" I yelled to him when he answered the phone. "I need to ask you something."

"It's midnight. You sound drunk again. Go to bed, Teri," He said in a sleepy voice.

"Okay, but I must tell you something and ask you something," I insisted, and before he could respond, I added, "I want you to know that I love you very much, and I am asking if you will forgive me."

"Teri, it's late, baby, go to bed," he said.

"How does this gun work? I think it's stuck," I said matter-of-factly.

"What gun? What are you doing?" he asked, awake now.

"The gun from the small safe. I don't think it works. How do I get it unstuck?" I asked

"Put the gun down! What are you trying to do?" he asked me with annoyance in his voice.

"Papa died hating me, huh? He hated me, didn't he? I give up. I've had enough. Tell me how this thing works," I said in almost a whisper.

I don't know how long it was that he kept me on the phone, but it was only minutes later when there was a knock on my door. It was the police. I hung up the phone and noticed that one of the officers was the cute one who walked me to my house that night I was kicked out of my husband's bar a month or so ago.

"Hi, is there something wrong, officers?" I managed to ask in my best sober voice.

"Can we come in, Mrs. Brooks? We got a call from your husband saying that you had a gun and that you were going to shoot yourself." The familiar-faced officer said to me.

"No, you can't come in, and I am not going to shoot myself. Goodbye," I said as I attempted to shut the door. His partner held out his hand and stopped the door from shutting.

"We are coming in to check it out. You can make this easy or hard, it's your call," the other officer, who was equally as handsome, said to me.

"Fine, come in already, sheesh," I said, trying to sound annoyed. They walked into the room and saw the empty wine bottle and glass sitting on the coffee table.

"How much have you had to drink tonight?" the familiar-faced officer said to me. I liked his face, and he was kind. I felt as if I could trust him.

"What's your name, your first name?" I asked him.

"Steve. How much have you had to drink? Where is the gun?" Steve asked me.

"Two bottles of wine, and the gun is in here," I said as I walked toward the kitchen.

"Stop! Don't move. I will find it. Is it in the kitchen?" Steve's partner asked.

"Yes. You asked me where it was, and I was going to just go get it. I'm not gonna shoot you, Mr. Cop Man," I said facetiously.

"Have you taken any pills?" Steve asked me as his partner made his way into my kitchen to retrieve the gun.

"Um, no. And I wasn't going to kill myself," I told him.

"What's this, then?" he asked as he picked up one of the letters that I had written.

"Okay, yeah, I was going to shoot myself. Why don't you just shoot me and make it easy here on me?" I asked him.

"I'd like for you to come with me, Teri. You need help," Steve said to me in a gentle voice and then added, "I am going through a divorce myself. It's not worth ending your life over. Be strong, and you will get through this, I promise."

"I'm not going to go anywhere but to bed, and you have no idea what my life is right now, so why don't you just go arrest some bad guys and leave me alone!" I yelled to him.

"You have a choice—go with him or go to jail," Steve's partner said to me. I knew that I needed to be nice and to calm down. Jail would not be good.

"Go where?" I asked Steve, ignoring his partner, who was starting to irritate me.

"Let me take you to the hospital. They will make sure you are okay," he said to me.

"No way. I am not going to a hospital. I'm just drunk! There is nothing wrong with me!"

"Please come with me, Teri? The alternative is not a better choice, I promise," he said.

"Fine! Let me lock up, and I will go if I can sit in the front seat! I'm so not sitting in the backseat of a cop car," I snapped. He didn' t have to agree to this, yet he did. I was silent on the drive to the hospital, angry and cold and very tired.

"I'm not the bad guy here. I want for you to be well," he said, trying to make me feel better.

"It's cold. I'm cold. Please turn on the heat and don't talk to me. I have nothing further to say to you," I told him, feeling a bit betrayed by the cop who once made me feel safe. He turned on the heat and didn't speak to me for the rest of the drive. We pulled up to the emergency room, and I panicked. What were they going to do to me, I wondered.

"Please don't leave me here! What are they going to do?" I asked him.

"I won't leave you. I won't leave," he said to me as he touched my arm. "You are safe, and you need to trust me," he added.

We walked into the emergency room, and they walked me to one of the back rooms. A nurse came in to draw blood, and I was irritated that he couldn't find a vein in my arm and had to put a needle in my hand instead.

"This hurts! Find the fucking vein already! What are you going to do to me?" I asked in frustration.

"We are going to take some blood samples, Mrs. Brooks, and then we are going to give you an IV filled with vitamins. You are very dehydrated." The male nurse said to me. I knew that he was trying to be nice, and I was rude and annoyed with this whole situation, so I calmed myself down so as not to take it out on him, even though he did poke me and miss my veins a few times.

"Where is the cop who brought me in?" I asked the nurse.

"He had to go on a call. He will be back. Try to get some rest until the doctor and crisis worker comes to see you," he said to me as he walked out of the room. It dawned on me that I had to be in court at nine in the morning for my divorce. I panicked and called Maddy, but she didn't answer. I left her a message saying where I was without any explanation and started to have an anxiety attack at the thought of my missing the court hearing.

The doctor came in and asked me several questions and left. He told me that my blood alcohol content was .20 and that a crisis worker needed to speak to me before I could be released. I pleaded with him to let me go home, explaining that I had a court hearing in less than seven hours. It did me no good; he insisted that I be heard by the crisis worker.

I decided to call Jason, knowing that this was probably not the best idea. Before I could dial his number, the social worker came in. He was a chunky man in his midthirties and not very tall.

"Tell me what happened tonight," he asked me as he found a chair to sit in next to the bed I was lying on. I pulled myself up to a sitting position and tried to compose myself.

"Well, my husband set me up! See, we have court in the morning, and so this is his way of making me miss it! It's so a set-up, and you have to believe that," I lied, and these words that came out of my mouth were even convincing to me. I didn't know why I told him that and was amazed that I thought of it so quickly in my intoxicated state of mind.

"So you are telling me that you didn't try to shoot yourself?" he asked me. "And that your husband is making this up? What about the gun and the suicide notes?" he asked me.

"Those notes were written months ago, and I live alone, so the gun is always out at night," I lied some more. He went through a questionnaire that I had to answer.

"Do you have feelings of guilt?" he asked.

"Nope, not at all."

"Are you unable to concentrate, remember things, or make decisions?"

"Nope, not at all," I said again. This pattern of questions continued as I lied my way through them and knew that he knew I was lying.

"Okay, Mrs. Brooks, I think that maybe you should go somewhere for a few days. They can help you," he said to me when the evaluation was over. Obviously, I failed the test.

"No way, never. I have court in the morning. You have to release me now," I insisted.

"You were here a month ago. You took pills and almost overdosed," he said to me as I thought back to when that was. It was true. I had taken pills back in March, and my husband took me in. I had been online with Jason that night and took several prescription pills after I had too many drinks. I didn't take them to kill myself, rather to just sleep for a while, and as I walked downstairs to the bedroom, I fell down the steps, waking my husband up. He knew that I was more than intoxicated, and I finally admitted to taking the pills. He took me to the hospital that night and waited there by my side, never leaving me. I wished he were here with me on this night.

"Oh, that? Well I just wanted to sleep for a while. I didn't want to kill myself," I told him.

"So you have no intentions to harm yourself at all?" he asked me.

I thought back to only a few nights ago, when I *did* take sixty pills, and knew that I did intend to harm myself that time.

"Nope, not at all," I said, using the standard answer which had failed me earlier.

"I will be back, Mrs. Brooks. Try to get some rest," he said to me as I realized he didn't believe me.

"Turn the lights off, please, and I need a warm blanket. It's freezing in this place," I demanded as if I was in a resort hotel rather than a hospital. I looked at the time, and it was almost three in the morning. I called Jason.

"I'm at the hospital. They won't release me," I told him.

"What did you do now?" he asked irritated. It was five in the morning his time, and I knew that I had woken him. I told him the truth, not the lies that I had told the crisis worker.

"You need to get some help, Teri. This is the second time this week. Think about your kids for once!" he yelled in a small voice, trying not to wake his parents or brothers who were down the hall. Steve the officer walked through the door.

"Are you okay, Teri?" Steve asked me.

"NO! I'm so not okay! I want to go home!" I screamed. I asked Jason to tell Steve to persuade the hospital to let me go, handing over my phone to Steve. Steve took the phone and stepped outside, and I couldn't hear what was being said. *Don't fail me now, J. I need for you to help me,* I thought to myself. Several minutes later, Steve came back into the room and handed me the phone, telling me that he would be back soon.

"Did you tell him to help me?" I asked Jason as I was handed back my phone.

"No, T . . . you need to go to the hospital for a few days. He asked me to try to persuade you to go, and I have to agree that you need some help. Go to the hospital and get some help," he said to me, and I felt betrayed by the both of them.

"Never. I won't go. I have court in the morning, and I don't intend to miss it. I needed your help, and you failed me again. Thanks, J, good-bye," I said, and I hung up the phone. I was angry that I was still here and felt sober by now. The chunky crisis worker entered the room and sat down.

"I'm committing you to Mountain High Hospital for seventy-two hours, it's called a blue sheet, and I can do this without your consent, and I think it is in your best interest to go," he said to me.

"No way. I am going to call my lawyer and sue your ass!" I yelled at him, shaking by this time at hearing his words.

"That's fine, but we have a legal right to commit you for at least seventy-two hours," he said again.

"You need to get laid! You are a frigid mean man!" I screamed this insult at him, verifying to myself that I was still intoxicated. I instantly felt regret as I said this to him as it didn't make me feel better.

"The ambulance will transport you there. They will be here shortly," he said, ignoring the insult directed at him.

"I need a cigarette, please," I said in a meek voice, feeling beaten down and defeated by now.

"I can't let you do that. You can't leave the hospital and go outside," he said to me as I fought back the urge to throw another insult. I took a deep breath and cracked a small smile.

"Please? I really need a cigarette badly. I won't flee, I promise," I said, hoping that he would believe this as it was the truth.

"I will think about it," he said as he started to walk out the door.

"I'm sorry, by the way. I didn't mean what I said earlier," I told him, and he turned and nodded and left the room. Moments later, a young security guard in his early twenties came into my room and sat in a chair. He was tall and thin and had acne, making him look more like a teenager.

"Guess you are the jail keeper, eh?" I asked him.

"Yeah, they want me to sit with you until the ambulance gets here," he said as he looked down at his shoes.

"This is a setup, you know. My husband set me up. I will miss court in the morning, and that is what his intentions were. Guess he outwitted me this time. Hey, can I get a smoke? I'm dying here."

"I will see what I can do, and I'm sorry about your court thing," he said to me, looking away once again. I realized why he couldn't look at me—the hospital gown I was wearing was slipping off my left shoulder, almost exposing my breast. I instantly adjusted it and smiled at him. He was sweet, and I didn't want to cause him any trouble.

"Thank you, I would appreciate it. And I have to pee," I said bluntly as I pulled the IV out of my hand. Blood squirted everywhere, and the young security guard jumped up out of his chair to grab me something to wipe up the blood.

"Don't think you are supposed to do that. They won't like that you did that," he said as he handed me over several paper towels.

"Yeah, well, I was never one to follow rules. I have to pee, and will you see about that smoke?" I asked as I wiped up the blood. A nurse came in and scolded me for removing my IV and took me to the bathroom. I figured that my chances for a cigarette now were next to none, but I didn't care anymore. I was done pleading and begging these people. I would rather go nicotineless than give them one more ounce of my pride.

The ambulance came to transport me at seven in the morning. I hadn't slept all night, and I was exhausted. I left several messages for Maddy and my lawyer and knew that he would be angry with my latest stunt. I tried to think of this as a minivacation and then quickly dismissed the "vacation" as a mini "rest." I didn' t want to be reminded of this event on my next vacation. The drive to Mountain High Hospital was only ten minutes, and on the way, I finally got through to Maddy.

"What the hell is going on?" she asked me. "I just woke up and got your messages. What happened?"

"I was going to shoot myself, didn't work. You need to call my lawyer, Mad. Court is like in two hours, and I can't seem to get through to him. I need for you to bring me some clothes, and I need a cigarette in the worst kind of way. I' m not only suicidal but going to be homicidal as well if I don't get some nicotine in me!"

"DO NOT REPEAT THAT!" she yelled.

"I was just kidding, Pop-Tart. I don't want to go, Mad. This won't be good for my divorce."

"Do not admit that you tried to kill yourself. Stick to the story you told the doctors. I will call you later and bring your things. And don't call Jason. He doesn't need to know about this. I don't trust him," she said. I didn't want to tell her that I already did call him, so I thought I would save that fact for later.

"Okay, but please hurry. I will keep my composure so I can get out of here. I know what to tell them. Love you, Mad, and thank you. We are here now, so I have to go." I said goodbye to my friend, and the paramedics lifted the stretcher I was on off the ambulance. I read the sign on the building and felt sick to my stomach. I needed to get out of there, and fast.

Chapter Thirty-One

April '07

The hospital lobby was painted a depressing shade of gray. It looked more like a funeral home waiting room with the outdated tacky floral upholstery on the old—fashioned furniture. I wondered how people could get well in an atmosphere which was so cheerless. What was behind the locked doors was even worse What kind of place was this? They took away my cell phones, and I had to write down the phone numbers of the people I would want to call. I left text messages with the phone number of the hospital for Will and Jason. They took away my jewelry and clothing that was in a bag from the emergency room hospital. I was still wearing the hospital gown given to me from the hospital emergency room, so they gave me another one to use as a robe until Maddy could bring me my clothes.

The first thing they did was take my vitals and ask for a urine sample before they showed me to my room. It was worse than I had imagined. The walls were painted a sterile white, and there was cheap grayish carpet on the floors. The main room, where the television and games were, had beat-up pink linoleum flooring and furniture that looked as if it were from the Salvation Army. It was fairly clean, yet ugly. The rooms were not private, and the mattress on the bed was made of rubber. I was surrounded by ugly rooms and strange people who walked around in circles and some who talked to themselves. What kind of place was this? I didn't belong here, and I was now more than eager to put on my best act and leave as soon as possible.

The next thing they did was ask me to come into a room. I was led there by this thin young girl in her twenties with short brown hair, wearing little makeup. She asked me to undress.

"Excuse me? Why must I undress?" I asked her, a bit confused.

"I have to do a body cavity search. It's just the rules, I'm sorry."

"A what? You *are* kidding me, right?" I asked her in disbelief.

"Tell you what—you aren't in here for substance abuse, you are an attempted suicide, so what I will d o is just have you disrobe and just turn around. I don't think I need to do a body search on you."

"Okay, but this is the most humiliating thing I have ever done," I told her as I complied in what she asked me to do. I stripped off my gowns and turned around quickly and put my gowns back on.

"See, that wasn't too bad, was it?" she asked

"No, I guess it wasn't. Thanks for not doing whatever it was you were going to, though."

"I will show you to your room now. Your friend is bringing some things for you?" she asked.

"Yes. She should be here soon. Do I have to share a room? Is there a possibility that I may have my own room?" I asked her in hopes that it was possible.

"You are supposed to be in room 308, but I think that if I put you in 310 instead, you shouldn't have anyone in there with you while you are here."

"Thank you. I don't do well with roommates. One more thing—can I get some paper and a pen? I have some writing to do, and I know that you don't allow laptops," I asked, then added, "and is there anyone I can get a cigarette from? I'm dying here!"

"Yes, let me show you where you may smoke. You can smoke as much as you want, but only in this designated place," she said to me as she led me out past the ugly television room and out to a patio area. There was a chained fence area that went from floor to the ceiling, and I felt as if I were in a cage. She asked someone for a cigarette for me and showed me where the electric lighter was.

"I'd rather smoke out there with those people," I said, pointing several yards away at a group of people smoking in the sun. "I feel like a caged bird in here," I added.

"Oh, sweetie, you can't go out there. You are in a psych lockdown unit. The main doors are kept locked, and you are confined to only this part of the hospital," she told me.

"What? I can't go out? And I can only stay in this wing? Why?" I asked as this was news to me.

"You are in the psych unit, sweetie. Those people you see out there are able to go outside and roam around the hospital. This unit doesn't allow that."

"Who are these people in here with me? Are they all suicide attempts?" I asked, now curious to know who I would be smoking with.

"No, there are only two of you here for that right now, the rest are addicts in detox. But they are nice, and you are all here to get the special help you each need," she said to me. "I can tell you that if you go to the group therapy meetings and sit in on those as much as you can, you have a better chance of getting out of here sooner. You will meet with a nurse after you finish your cigarette and then see the doctor for your evaluation."

"They said I was in here for seventy-two hours. Does anyone ever get to leave sooner?" I asked, trying to pick her brain for any helpful information that may get me out of this place sooner.

"Sometimes, yes, but not often," she stated as my heart sunk. "Are you ready to see the nurse? After that, I will get you some food. You are shaking, and you probably haven't eaten."

"I am not hungry, thank you, but yes, let' s go meet the nurse. I want out of here," I said impatiently.

The nurse was my age, but she looked older than me. She had long strawberry blond hair, and in the first fifteen minutes, we went over hospital contracts for my insurance. She then asked me the same questions that Mr. Chunky crisis worker guy asked me earlier. This time, my answers were not all the same, and I played it off well. I explained to her that I was supposed to be in court, and this was a ploy by my husband to get me to miss court and to win him some leverage over the divorce. I told her that I had a protective order out on him and told her he was abusive and that I was afraid of him. I almost felt guilt as I told her these lies, knowing that she fully believed my story and felt sympathy for me.

"Tell the doctor what you just told me. Sometimes people are sent here that should not be in here, and you sound as if you are one of these people," she said to me, and I regained some hope that I might get out before the seventy-two hours. "I will bring you something to eat. Just hang in there until the doctor sees you. Try to relax," she said to me as I finished signing the last of the documents.

"I'm not hungry, thank you. I just really need to see the doctor so I can explain this misunderstanding. I have children at home who need me," I said.

"I understand," she said as the phone rang and she answered it and only said a few words before hanging up. "Your friend just dropped off some things for you," she said as she hung up the phone.

"Oh, can I see her?" I asked in excitement.

"Sorry, visiting hours start at six in the evening," she replied, sensing my excitement which turned into disappointment. "She can come back to see you later. If you just want to sign this last document, we are done, and then you can take your things to your room."

I signed what I needed to, and when I returned to my room, the young girl who spared me the body cavity search was there going through the suitcase that was left for me. I watched her sort through it and pull several things out and to the side.

"Hello!" she said as I walked into the room. "I have to go through your bag that your friend brought. Can't have some of the things in here," she said as she sorted through my belongings. Maddy had brought me an abundance of comfortable clothing, making me shudder as to how long she thought I would be here for.

"Okay, but why can't I have my shampoo?" I asked as it was in the discard pile.

"It has alcohol in it. Nor can you have these unless you let me cut off the drawstrings," she answered.

"My sweatpants? Why do you have to cut off the drawstrings?" I asked her.

"You can hurt yourself with the string," she said matter-of—factly. "I will let you keep your brush, even though paddle brushes aren't allowed either."

"Why's that? Who can hurt themselves with a paddle brush?" I asked her.

"Not that—it's that they can hide drugs in it," she answered again as I squinted in disbelief of what she was telling me.

"That's crazy," I said as I watched her put my unacceptable things back into my suitcase.

"You can keep the sneakers if I take the shoelaces off. It's up to you. And you can't have this robe unless I take off the tie."

"I don't need the sneakers unless you have a gym here," I said, trying to be funny in this sad situation. "I want the robe, though, so take the tie if you must. Don't cut off the drawstrings on my sweats. I won't be here that long," I said with confidence and assurance that what I was saying was true.

"No gym. Okay then, let' s see what we have. I need to take an inventory of what you have here that I can leave you. Three pairs of shorts without the drawstrings, a pair of slippers, five pair of panties, baseball cap, five pair of socks, four pair of jeans, a nightgown, six tee shirts, hey this BeBe one is cute," she said as she held it up to admire it.

"Yeah, thanks. Can I take a shower now?" I asked, feeling tired and sticky.

"Sure but don't close the bathroom door. I have left you the hair conditioner, lotion, and toothbrush and toothpaste. No makeup or perfume though, sorry," she said as she zipped up the suitcase

"I'm not too worried about how I look or smell. When can I see the doctor?" I asked her.

"He won't be in until later. I suggest you get some rest and join the group therapy meeting at three o'clock."

"Like when is later?" I asked her, and she walked out the door without responding to my question. I decided to take a shower and do some writing. The shower was refreshing, and I felt a bit better. I sat on the lumpy mattress on the bed and started to write. I was still writing about the month of November in my book, yet I decided that I didn' t want to think about Jason and what went on at that time, so I fast-forwarded to now, what was happening now. After drafting up six pages of freehand scribbling, a young girl who looked to be in her early twenties came to my door. She was heavyset, with mousy brown hair and glasses. Her robe was dirty, and she spoke in a quiet voice.

"Are you Teri?" she asked me.

"Yes, can I help you?" I replied, wondering what it was she wanted.

"There is a phone call for you."

I jumped up from the bed and wondered who it was, almost running from my room down the hall to where the phone was. It was mounted to the wall, and the receiver was dangling. I picked it up, hoping that it was Jason.

"Hello?" I asked.

"Teri? It's Marian. Will called me and gave me this number He told me what happened, and he told me to tell you that after his meeting he will call you."

"Mar! Oh my God, I hate it here. I want to go home," I cried not realizing that I was in tears.

"I know, babe, but you need to get some help. Will and I are worried about you," she said in her beautiful soft voice. It d awned on me then that I had only ever spoken to her on the phone but a few times over these past months. We chatted only when she had issues with her Ben or I with Jason. I missed the sound of her voice, and it was calming to me, reminding me of the first time I heard her voice back in October. It seemed like a lifetime ago.

"I have no strength left within me, no desire to go on living," I said, instantly regretting that I said this to her on this phone, wondering if it were bugged. "My cross is too heavy, Mar," I added, not caring if it were bugged or not. I needed to talk to someone I trusted.

"Yes, I know. You have been through a lot, and you must be strong for the sake of your children," she said. "You must live for them." We talked for several minutes before a woman who looked to be Hispanic and in her middle forties walked up to me, telling me that she needed to use the phone. I said goodbye to Marian and hung up the phone. Tears stung my eyes as I realized in my absence of freedom never to take freedom for granted again. I felt caged and alone in here, even though I was surrounded by people.

I waited by the phone, hoping to use it again before the group meeting, but the Hispanic lady talked for forty minutes. I was getting a bit agitated but decided not to say anything and decided to attend the meeting. I took a seat by the soft—spoken mousy girl who told me I had a phone call earlier.

"My name is Teri, what's yours?" I asked her.

"April. I'm April."

"This looks like its going to be a blast," I said to April as more people entered the room and took a seat.

"They aren't too bad. Just don't ask any questions, and it will end faster," she said in a soft voice.

There were about seven of us there as the young woman who searched my suitcase came in to lead the meeting. I looked around me and glanced at who I was sitting with. There was a heavy older woman in her sixties who seemed drugged out of her mind. She was falling out of her robe and swaying back and forth. She said something to me that I couldn't understand since she slurred her words and rolled her eyes. There were several older gentlemen that were in their late fifties who just stared at me with a frown. I tried not to look at them and noticed that there was also a young man there who appeared to be in his early twenties, wearing a white tee shirt and jeans. He had a tattoo on his muscular right arm, and he reminded me of a young James Dean. Sitting next to the drunken older lady was a bubbly young redhead who appeared to be in her early twenties as well. She was talking and laughing and appeared to be enjoying her visit here.

The meeting was about self—esteem. I tried to stay awake through it but felt sleepy as the bubbly redhead kept interrupting with her opinions and comments. I wanted to smack her for two reasons: because she wouldn't shut up and I was done with this meeting and because she was so happy. The drunk older woman just sat there talking to herself as no one paid much attention to her odd behavior. The young meeting leader held up a black-and-white drawing of flowers that appeared to be daisies drawn by a child. The daisies had smiling faces and stood tall and proud.

"Flowers are beautiful, are they not? Do we all agree?" she asked us as I tried to appear alert.

"They are SO BEAUTIFUL! I never had none sent to me, but one day I will," the bubbly young redhead said.

"What that supposed to be? Them ain't flowers," the drunken older woman said, and this was the first thing that I did understand that came out of her mouth.

"Now look at this one," the meeting leader said, ignoring both remarks. "This is how the flowers see themselves," she said as she held up another childlike black-and-white drawing. The flowers in this drawing were warping and had big noses.

"Oh no! They don't look like that at all! Poor widdo flowies," the bubbly redhead said in a baby voice. I really wanted to smack her now. She annoyed me.

"So we sometimes see ourselves in a negative way, but others may see something else, something beautiful," she said as she held up both drawings now. I heard what sounded like snoring, and the drunken older lady was asleep with her head tilted backward. She looked as if she were going to fall out of her chair.

"Wake up, Wilma!" the bubbly redhead said as she shook her. "WILMA!" she screamed and laughed, shaking the poor woman, who jolted upward, letting out one last loud snort.

"Don't be wakin' her up. Now we have to hear her jibberin again," one of the older gentlemen in his fifties said. He scared me with his rugged, wrinkled face; he looked like the meanest man I had ever seen. I quickly glanced away when he looked at me.

"Hank, I heard that, ya asshole," Wilma said, now wide awake.

"Let's call this meeting over. Thanks for attending, and there will be another one at eight o' clock this evening," the young meeting leader said, and I could tell she had had enough as well. I got up as quickly as I could and headed to the phone. The Hispanic woman was sitting in the metal chair under the wall-mounted phone, now screaming at whoever it was she had been talking to for the past hour. I needed to talk to Maddy, and I felt anxiety building up inside of me. I decided to go outside to the smoking area and have a cigarette. Hank, the meanie, was out there. I started to turn around, deciding that I didn' t need to smoke that badly until he said something to me.

"Come here and smoke with me." I turned around, and he was glaring at me, and then his tanned wrinkled frown turned into a grin.

"Okay," I said reluctantly as I took the farthest seat I could away from him.

"It's here or prison for me. Thought that this would be better than prison again. It ain't all bad in here once you get used to it, little girl," Hank said to me.

"I'm leaving soon. It is a mistake that I'm even here."

He let out a big laugh, and I decided to say as little as possible to this horrible man. Wilma, the drunken older lady, came outside and sat next to me.

"Go away, old lady, you don't smoke," Hank said to her

"Shut up, Hank! I wanna know who this pretty thing is. Is he being mean to you, sweetie?" she asked me as she grabbed a handful of the long hair hanging off my shoulders. She stoked my hair and tugged at it as she did this, not meaning to hurt me.

"No, he's been kind, Wilma, thank you."

"Well, he thinks he owns this place, and he tries to scare the young girls," she said as if he weren't sitting there. I didn't want to glace in his direction, but a laugh came from his way. One of the nurses came out to give Wilma some sort of breathing treatment, but I soon understood that it was not for her breathing. She inhaled something that was inside a long plastic vial pipe.

"I need my fix. I'm a drunk and detoxing. What are you in for, baby girl?" she asked as she inhaled another hit of whatever was in the plastic vial.

"I'm not an addict," I said, not really wanting to answer her.

"Oh, you tried to whack yourself?" she asked.

"No, well it appears that way, but no," I lied. The nurse took Wilma inside, and I was going to get up when Hank got up.

"You coming inside, little girl?" he asked me.

"No, I think that I will stay out here for a bit. It's beautiful outside."

"Suit yourself," he said. *Oh no!* I thought as the bubbly redheaded girl came out as Hank was leaving.

"Hi! What's your name?" she asked as she took a seat right next to me. There were at least a dozen chairs, and I wondered why she chose to sit right next to mine.

"Teri," I answered.

"Hi, Teri! My name is Barbara Jean, but you can just call me Babs," she said, and I thought her nickname suited her since it rhymed with *gabs*.

"Hello, Babs."

"Oh, you look sad. It's okay! How long are you in here for?" she asked.

"Seventy-two hours, supposedly."

"I have to leave today. I have been here for a week, and my time is up," she said sadly.

"Are you ready to go? Did you get the help that you needed?" I asked her.

"No, but what can you do? I'm a *meth* addict. You an addict too?" she asked.

"No. So what are you going to do?" I asked her, genuinely concerned. She told me that she was headed for Florida, if she could raise the money for a one—way ticket. She was twenty-four and had two children who lived with their father. She left her kids when her boyfriend introduced her to the wrong crowd and she became an addict.

"I have family in Florida. I need to get away from my boyfriend or I won't stay straight."

"Then go, and be strong. Are you leaving for Florida tonight?" I asked.

"No, I only have eighty bucks, and the ticket is more. I'm crashing with some sober friends until I get the rest of the cash."

"Can your family help? It would be tempting for you to use again if you are here for too long."

"My family ain't got no money. Think I will clean some houses or do whatever."

I dared not ask what "do whatever" meant.

"How much do you need?" I asked.

"'Bout a hundred and fifty."

"I don't know how long I will be here. Hopefully I get out tonight or tomorrow, but I will give you the rest of the money. Well, I won't give you the money, but if you want me to book you a flight, I will." I said this without thinking of what I was offering. I was not getting any money from my husband, nor was I working much.

"You would do that for me? Why?" she asked.

"Because I want for you to be well." I gave her my phone number and told her to call me so that I could help her with her ticket. Someone came out and told me that I had a phone call. My heart jumped as I thought it may be Jason.

"Hello?"

"Hi, Teri. I have been calling you. This phone's had a busy signal all day." It was Will. I was glad to hear his voice. I talked to him for several minutes, and then I called my father and Maddy.

Dinner was something that looked like ham but tasted more like rubber. I barley ate a few bites when I started to feel ill. I went to the front desk to ask if the doctor was ready to see me.

"Oh, he went home for the night. He will see you in the morning," a male nurse said to me without even looking up.

"What? I have to stay here tonight?"

"Honey, they never let anyone leave the first night anyways. Do you need something to help you sleep tonight? I do believe that the doctor gave orders for a sleep aid if you need it." I was upset but decided that I would not show it. I didn' t want to appear to be angry or hostile.

"Sure, can I have it now?" I asked. If I had to stay the night, then I would rather sleep through the rest of my visit.

"No, but you may have it at nine o' clock. I have some antianxiety meds here for you as well if you would like that."

"I'd love that. Give me two of them please," I joked. He handed over a Xanax to take for my anxiety. I wanted to make a phone call, but the Hispanic lady was on it again. I was done being nice and made a gesture to her that I needed to use it. She held up a finger and looked down to the floor as she began yet another argument with whoever the lucky person on the other end of the receiver was. April, the mousy young girl, approached the front desk with some of her belongings.

"There is a time limit of fifteen minutes when you use the phone, but she ignores that rule," she said to me in a frail voice, looking over at the Hispanic lady, who seemed calmer by now. "You are the other suicidal attempt? I heard that there are two of us in here for that. The rest are addicts," she added.

"Oh, word travels fast around here. So are you excited to go home?" I said without answering her question.

"No, I am afraid to go. I don't want to go."

"Is there someone you can talk to if you need to?"

"Yes," came out of her mouth, but I read her lips because she didn't actually say it.

"Don't hurt yourself anymore. Be good to yourself," I said to her as I gave her a hug. These words should have burned coming out of my mouth. I was not one to be preaching anything to anyone. I didn't let go of her until she pulled away, and when she did she had tears in her eyes.

"I have nothing to live for," she said to me through her tears. This meek, mousey, almost childlike young woman was opening up to a stranger who was probably in worse shape than herself.

"Do you have children?" I asked.

"No."

"Then live for your future children," I told her.

That night, as I went to bed, I said a prayer for my children and for the people who I had met in this hospital. I prayed that God give them hope and strength. I prayed that I would get out of this place, and for the first time in months, God must have heard my prayer because the following morning, when I did see the doctor, I was released within an hour. *God is great, God is good,* went though my head as I walked into my home that day. *God will save me as he should.*

CHAPTER THIRTY-TWO

July '07

I was sitting in my closet, carefully cutting squares out of cardboard and taping the pieces together as to form furniture for my Barbie dolls. Sifting through the box of Crayola Crayons, I selected my favorite colors and drew fat daisies on the furniture pieces. I was careful not to color out of the lines. I positioned the colorful furniture around my closet, creating "rooms" for my dolls. I heard someone walking into the closet.

"Dara! Look! It's beautimous!" I squealed in delight as I turned around to find Mr. Buck standing there.

"It is beautimous! But its time to play our game now," he said unzipping his pants."

"I don't want to play it. I don't want to."

He didn't respond to my comment, not that I expected him to. He never did. He slid his fat fingers down the front of my stretch pants and I closed my eyes, knowing that it would be over in a few minutes anyways. I closed my eyes and thought of happy dancing flowers and pink and yellow skies.

"DON'T TOUCH HER! LEAVE HER ALONE! LEAVE HER ALONE!" I screamed.

"Ter, wake up. Wake up honey. You're having a bad dream," Maddy said, shaking me. She was staying with me for a few days. I found it hard to be alone lately because my children were taken from me for a few months. I missed them terribly and my life was emptier than ever before. I was paying the "piper" for the suicide attempt.

"Oh, I'm sorry Mad. I'm okay, go back to sleep"

"Do you need some water?"

"No, I'm okay. Just a nightmare. Go back to sleep now. Thank you though."

I rolled over to my side, clutching a pillow to my chest and holding it as if it was a six year old little girl with long dark hair. *Its okay now, you're safe.* I thought, squeezing the pillow with a tighter grip. *He can't hurt you anymore. I won't let him. I won' t let anyone ever hurt you again.*

How could I end up back in the hospital emergency room once again within three months? It was surreal that this could happen when I woke up happy one morning and found myself twelve hours later in the same place I was at only three short months ago. I had lost control of my life once more. It was a Sunday, July 1, and the phone rang at about four o'clock in the afternoon. I was mopping my floors, and Maddy was online, helping me with client billing and chores. My younger sister, Dara, was coming into town for the Fourth of July holiday.

"Hello," I answered, out of breath.

"Hi, why are you breathing so hard?" my older sister, Kirstin, asked.

"'Cause I'm cleaning. It's not like I have cleaning ladies anymore, you know! My life of luxury is over! Oh well, I need the exercise. What's up?" I asked as I sat down to take a much—needed cigarette break.

"Have you heard from Jason lately?" she asked.

"Yes, why? He texted me yesterday, I believe. What's this about? What's up?" I asked, feeling a knot tightening in my stomach.

"You know that he has been texting me. I have told you that," she said.

"Yes, because he's been concerned about me and what's been going on. You told me that."

"No, it's been more than just that, Teri." I wanted to vomit by now. I sat down and lit up a cigarette preparing to hear what I already knew she was going to tell me. "I wanted to tell you this when you were stronger, but I can tell that you are still holding on, and he's not worth it, sweetie."

"What are you trying to tell me, Kirstin? Just spit it out!" Maddy was folding clothes and overheard the conversation. She knew I hated laundry, and I would joke that if I ever went to prison and had laundry duty, I'd hang myself with the dirty laundry.

"Who are you yelling at, Ter?" Maddy asked. I held up a finger to her, not answering her.

"What are you trying to tell me, Kirstin?" I repeated to my sister.

"Oh, is Maddy there? I can just call you back later then," she said.

"NO! Please just tell me what is going on! For God's sakes spit it out!"

"Teri, I wanted to tell you this a long time ago, but you were so vulnerable and raw. At first I thought that Jason was calling me because he was concerned about your well-being. Then his calls became more personal. He started to ask me to meet him when I would be flying to New York. Then he started to send me e-mails with pictures of him. Inappropriate pictures of him."

"What kind of pictures? And how did he get your e-mail?" I asked.

"I wanted to see how far he would go. I led him on at first, to see how far he would take it. I wanted to prove to you what kind of man he was. I never intended to meet him. He sent me pictures of him in his uniform, one of him lying on his bed—I suppose that's the one you took of him that you had told me about, and . . . one of his penis."

I walked over to the sink and vomited.

"Teri? Teri?" Moments past.

"I'm here," I said, shaking. Then the tears came. They were silent tears. No loud sobs. I don't even know if she realized I was crying. "What else, Kirstin?"

"A week ago, I was in New York, and he called me, asking me what I was doing. I told him that I was out partying with my crew. He wanted me to call him when I got back to my room, so I did."

"And?"

"And when I did, he proceeded to have phone sex with me. I told him that I could not do this, that you are my sister and that you still loved him. He said that no one needed to know. I hung up on him, Teri."

"That was big of you," I said.

"Don't be angry with me. I didn't even want to tell you until you were stronger."

"YOU LET THIS GET OUT OF HAND! And why would you even do this? Why would you not tell me this was going on?"

"I wanted to see what kind of guy he was, if he really loved you. I never intended to meet him, ever."

"Why you? Why you? I love him, Kirst. I won't love anyone else again," I told her.

"He doesn't love you, Teri, he never did. He just wants a sugar mama. Someone to take care of him, anyone who will take care of him." I knew that she didn' t mean to hurt me, but her words were as sharp as a knife, cutting through my heart, and she didn't stop there.

"He asked if there was a chance for us, if we could see each other." I don't know if she realized that her words were becoming borderline cruel now. "I told him that I was in a relationship that I didn' t want to risk losing and that you meant the world to me, that I could never go there with him. He said that he saw my pictures that you took of me on the MySpace that you created for me, and that is the reason, Teri, that I really deleted my account. It was because of him. I felt funny about him checking my page."

My head was spinning, and I wanted to throw up again. I knew that Jason was still checking my MySpace page, and I had created a page for my sister, who was on my page, but he was now checking her page as well?

"You didn't have to PROVE anything, Kirstin. I already know what he has been doing. I think I was the one who told you that he was on that one site where he was webcamming for strangers when I set up that fake profile weeks ago. I just don't know who he is anymore. I don't understand him," I said. Moments which seemed like minutes passed.

"Are you there? Teri?" she asked. "Teri?" I was stupefied, and although my mouth was moving, no words escaped my lips. "Please talk to me." She was clearly upset now. I could tell this hurt my sister, but I was now numb and in shock. I had no tears left within me. I could hear her saying something, but my thoughts took me to the previous night's prayer. I went to bed and started to pray. Before I said my second sentence, I did something that I hadn't done in years. I got out of my bed and dropped to my knees.

"Dear Father in heaven, please give him back to me. Bring him back to me because this pain is too much to bear. I know that he's not good for me, but I love him with all that I am."

I never did name who "him" was, but it was not my husband I was referring to, and God knew this. I started to cry uncontrollably as I prayed and begged the Lord to grant me something that I knew was so very wrong for me. It wasn't until this minute that I realized that he did answer my prayer.

"Teri! Please talk to me!" My sister was upset. I was too angry to feel sorry for her. I felt betrayed by the two people I trusted the most this past year, the two people I loved so dearly even though deep down inside I knew my sister could never betray me and this was not her fault.

"I don't know what to say Kirst. But I have to go do something, something that I should have done long ago."

"You told me that you have been seeing that Grizzly hockey player and dating, Teri, I thought that you could handle hearing this right now."

It was true. I was still online and on several sites and had more dates than there were days of the week, and I was seeing a Grizzly hockey player occasionally, but I was waiting for Jason. After all these months, I still loved him with all my heart, and I finally realized that what I was looking for the entire time was always right in front of me.

"Just because I am dating doesn't mean I don't still love him Kirstin. I'm such a fool. Know what? I have been waiting for him. Yep. I figured that I would let him get through the summer and do what he needs to. It doesn't matter anymore. I can't talk to you about this. I have to go."

"Can I speak to Maddy then?" she asked. I handed the phone to Maddy and walked over to the computer. I deleted all of Jason's photos from both my laptop and desktop. I tore up all of his photos and blocked and deleted him from my Yahoo and MSN. He was dead to me. I calmly finished mopping my floors and folding my laundry. I cleaned my toilets like nothing had happened.

"You are scaring me, Teri," Maddy said to me.

"Why?"

"I don't know if I should leave you. I know that you are upset, and you are acting so normal here. What's going on in your little head?"

"I have no idea what you are talking about, Mad. Go, I will be fine, really. I have writing to do," I said convincingly.

"Sure?"

"Yes! Now go! Thanks for your help. Really, I am fine. He's a pig, and I'm so over him!" I lied. She must have believed me because she left. I don't think she even made it out of the driveway before I poured the first shot of tequila, but all I remember was that by nine o'clock that night, I was wasted. I picked up the bottle of Seroquel, and it had about thirty pills left in it. The bottle of Clonazepam (similar to Xanax) had about thirty as well. I put the bottles down and poured myself another shot.

Don't do this again, Teri, the little voice in my head said to me.

Fucking do it . . . What do you have to live for? You are miserable and your own kids think you are nuts, the other voice said.

I waited to hear from the "good" voice, but I heard nothing. I picked up the bottles and swallowed all of the pills left in both of them. I lay on the sofa, and I don't know how much time went by when the phone rang. I don't know why I even answered it really.

"Hewo?"

"Teri?" my father asked.

"Who this?" I asked, and that was the last thing I remembered.

My father would later tell me that he came over and called the police, who then called an ambulance, and I ended up in the emergency room. I had overdosed, and it took them twelve hours to wake me up. The first face that I would see would be the one of the chunky crisis worker who committed me the last time.

"Welcome back, Mrs. Brooks. Looks like you will be staying at Lakeshore this time. Enjoy your stay," he said as he wobbled out of the room. If I had a bowling ball, I would have rolled it in his direction to knock him over, and that would have made this all somewhat worth it.

CHAPTER THIRTY-THREE

July '07

I'm looking out of the window of my hospital room on the fourth floor on this Fourth of July night. I have been sitting here at this window for several hours, watching the sun sinking, in the blood red and orange dusk sky behind the miles of the dark silhouette of the mountains. When I see the first firework of the night, I close my eyes and pretend it is a birthday candle and make a wish. I just don't know what to wish for anymore. My sister Dara is in town, and I know that I am for sure going to lose my children again for a few more months as I did the last time. My ex husband will see to this. Punishment for standing up to him is how I would view it, however. I'm angry, and I have no one to blame but myself.

This hospital is worse than the last one. The staff is mean, and there are not many privileges. There is "cruelness" about this place. Most of the time, the nurses forget to give you your meds, and you need to ask for them. They sit in the nurse's station, telling racist jokes, and deliberately ignore you or make you wait if you ask a question. The only time the staff is on good behavior would be when the doctors are here, which is not very often. Coffee is not allowed, and only two cigarette breaks are allotted a day if you attend all group therapy meetings.

I was told that I would have to stay an entire week, so when Maddy brought me my things, she only brought me two pair of shorts and three tee shirts this time, thinking that I would be out sooner. I am too numb to be upset about how much time I am to be staying here or how I will be missing the time with Dara and my children. My emotions have left me. My parents, Maddy, and Will call me every day. Surprisingly, I did get a call from both my husband and ex husband, but I never did return their calls, and I only spoke with Kirstin once. The phone is only available for two hours a day in this hospital, making it hard to make or receive calls. The only good thing is that there are three of them.

The food is awful. What they called beef stew reminded me of dog food, so I decided to skip lunch one day and wait to use the phone. The phone is by a room to where the doctor visits with patients. Nurse Sally, a hefty older Swedish lady with long red hair she wears in a bun had been a bit "snappy" with me from the moment I arrived.

"There is no need for you to stand by the door and listen to the doctor and his patient. He will see you when he is ready," she said, not even looking at me as she walked by, writing something on a chart. I had had it with her attitude.

"I already saw the doctor, and if you bother to look up and clean those one-inch-thick glasses you are wearing, you would see that I am waiting to use the phone here," I said rather calmly.

"Just for that, you have lost your phone privileges for the rest of the day. Messages will be given to you."

"Yes, Nurse Snooty," I said, not letting her intimidate me. "I mean, Nurse Sally."

"Group is in twenty minutes. I suggest you go," she said and walked away. I wondered what made her so mean. Why where people like her? Was she always like this, or did it change someone over time who worked in an environment of this sort?

On my way to group, I realized that I needed fresh towels. Gary was the only nice nurse, and I was glad to see he was on duty.

"Hi, Gary, I need fresh linens, please." He pointed to the closet. "Right, I forget that I'm not at the Marriott," I laughed. We were responsible for changing our own bedding and changing out our towels.

"Couldn't help hearing your conversation with Sally," he said.

"Yeah, she loves me, I think."

"She's a crazy old bat. Don't take it personal—she hates everyone, Teri."

"Really, Gary, she is the last concern I have. But thanks for being kind, that's a novelty in this place. Know what? Fuck going to group, I'm going to go write. Who needs to use the phone or smoke or eat? Thanks for the towels." I went back to my room and started to write.

I had no desire to make "friends" or connect with any other patients as I had at Mountain High Hospital. I wanted to get better, but I knew that this wasn't the place that I was going to be able to do this at. Minutes later, Nurse Sally walked into my room.

"Teri, I need to speak to you for a moment."

"I'm not going to group. You can starve me, take away my phone privileges, not let me smoke, I don't care. You people are mean. Go away please."

"There is a young girl here. Her name is Heather. She is a heroin addict. She will not talk to anyone. She asked me about you. Please try to get her to go to group. For some reason, I think that you may be able to get through to her."

"Why me?"

"I don't know, and maybe I am wrong, but she hasn't said more than twenty words since she has been here, yet she asked about you. Will you help? You may use the phone if you do."

"I will try. Not because I want to use the phone. By the way, that crazy old lady two rooms down just used my bathroom and did the "big icky" in my toilet . . . can you please have someone clean it. I know that we have to clean our own things, but God . . ."

"Go talk to Heather. I will take care of it."

"Deal."

Heather was twenty-seven, with long auburn hair and hazel eyes. Her hair reached down to her waist, and her features were chiseled, with a small pointed nose, high cheekbones, and a full bottom lip.

I walked into Heather's room, and she was lying on her bed in a fetal position. I picked up a pillow on the next bed and hit her in the butt with it.

"Hi, I'm Teri, and I'm a shoe-a-holic." She laughed and sat up.

"Hi, I'm Heather."

"Okay, girlfriend, pillow fight or group therapy? Personally I would rather have a pillow fight, but I really do want to smoke later, so wanna go with me?" I asked.

"But I only have this hospital gown until my husband brings my clothes later," she said.

"Hold on, I will be right back." I went to my room and put on my ugly hospital gown and grabbed two ponytail holders. I went back to her room and put both of our hair up in ponytails.

"Teri, you are crazy!"

"Shh, that's a bad word in this place." She laughed again.

Sally was teaching therapy, and I could tell she was pleased to see that we showed up.

"Today we do *clay* therapy," she said as she handed the group rubber gloves and a ball of hard gray clay the size of an orange.

"The clay will warm up in your hands as it is oil based. Once you have softened it, I would like for you to create what you are *feeling*. In other words, sculpt something about your life as you know it now," she said to the group.

The people in the group appeared confused, and I could sense that Heather was adamant about doing this. I didn't know her, yet I knew that she didn't share her feelings well. As I was fixing her hair, she did share some things with me. She was also married to a heroin addict, and she supported their habit by being an escort, and they didn't even own a stick of furniture. They had sold everything. I never asked her anything. This was what she chose to tell me. I only listened.

"I can't do this, Teri," Heather whispered to me.

"Yes, you can. Not everything in your life is bad, babes. Think . . . of just the simplest of things, even," I told her.

I formed two six-inch tubes and rolled them out flat with a small rolling pin and cut the ends off making it approximately 6"x1"x 0.5" wide. I repeated the same thing with the other tube, but this time making it only 3"x1"x 0.5" wide.

I laid the smaller piece over the longer one, forming a cross. I pinched it down gently, securing the two pieces together so they were fixed firmly.

Next I rolled a small ball into my hands, taking careful effort to proportion it smoothly until it became a perfectly symmetrical ball. I took the end of a pencil eraser and dug a hole into the ball. I rolled the ball around my palm as well as rotating the pencil in the opposite direction, forming a "bowl."

I pinched the sides of the bowl, stretching it up to form a thin "neck," and curved the edges over slightly. I stuck my gloved index finger in my diet Coke and smoothed the edges of my vase until it was not lacking the quality I was seeking. I then took a sharpened pencil and started from the top of the vase, digging a deep crooked groove in it until it reached the bottom of the vase. I repeated this, going over the lines again until the groove was clearly a dominant crack. Once again, I dipped my finger into my diet Coke and smoothed out the rough edges.

I turned my cross upside down and created a "shelf" to secure it on to the center of the cross, and then I set the cracked vase on the shelf on this upside-down cross.

When I was done, all eyes were on me. Had I taken that long? Why was everyone staring at me?

"Wow, Teri," Heather said. "That is beautiful. Is it the Holy Grail?"

"Ha-ha! Hell no! Nothing holy pertains to my life, these days!"

"Let's share then, shall we?" Nurse Sally said. "Kim, what is your sculpture?"

Kim's sculpture was a girl holding a baby.

"This is me and my son," she said, then burst out into tears. I had noticed the bandages on both of her arms and wrists. No one asked about why she was there. No one needed to. It was obvious. What wasn't obvious was what she said next.

"He just turned twenty-two last week you know. We found out a few days ago that he has AIDS. My baby has AIDS. I will not survive my baby. It isn't right to survive your kids," she cried.

A tear dropped onto my clay cross, and suddenly my cross seemed lighter to bear.

"I'm sorry," I mouthed, with no words actually escaping my lips. I could not have found my voice if I had even wanted to. She nodded back to me, acknowledging my gesture.

"Heather, what is it that you sculpted?" Sally asked. I looked over to what it was. I saw just a ball. A very large ball.

"A world," she said meekly.

"What was that?" Sally asked.

"It's a world. A world of possibilities, a world of hope, freedom," she murmured.

I suddenly saw the beauty in this ball. Here sits this girl, who has never left the state of Utah, who sold her body for drugs. So young and beautiful. She told me that she would go to Home Depot parking lots and find receipts and then go into the store to steal whatever merchandise was on the receipts to return it for cash for drug money. She was so lost, yet her sculpture was the most simple, and all she wanted was the world

I took her hand in mine and found the words to say, "The world is yours, so take it."

"Mick, what is your sculpture?" Sally asked. It looked like a house with a woman preparing to jump from the roof, arms spread, head first.

"It's my ex-wife taking the plunge."

"Oh, that's not nice," I said.

"Yeah, well you don't know the bitch. If you did, you'd probably be sculpting a big hand behind her to give her a push!"

"I rather doubt that, but it's your clay therapy, so whatever pleases you, I suppose," I said to him.

"You're a dolly, Teri, in your little hospital gown and ponytail. Maybe we can hook up in the snack room later," Mick said.

"Okay, Teri, tell us what your sculpture is," Sally asked, throwing Mick the look I wanted to.

"Let me guess?" Mick asked. "It's some kinda Roman vessel filled with poison that will kill your sorry-ass no-good wife, but she dies too quickly, denying for you to witness her agonizing death," he said.

"Um, no. And by the way, I would never meet you in the snack room, Mick, you scare me," I said and he laughed.

"So, what is it, Teri?" Sally asked again.

"Well, when I was a young girl, my mother told me a story of an emperor of China who could afford all of the most precious of vases that money could buy. He never married but had many concubines. One day, a beautiful peasant girl came to the village, and he fell madly in love with her, but she refused to be one of his mistresses. She agreed to marry him under the one condition. That he give up all of his concubines and be only faithful to her forever. She told him that if he were ever unfaithful, she would know this because of a precious Ming vase handed down to her family for many generations. Legend had it that if infidelity occurred, then the vase would crack. Marriage was as precious as this Ming vase and as fragile. You must handle it with much care and respect. If it cracks or breaks, it can always be mended, but it will never be whole again."

"Wow, Teri, is this a true story?" someone asked.

"Hold on, I'm not done. So one day the empress saw a crack in the vase."

"'What is this crack, my husband?' she asks. The emperor did not answer."

"'Are my words too faint to hear?' Again the emperor still did not answer."

"'Was my bed not warm enough or my skin not soft?' The emperor did not answer."

"'Were my words not gentle and my touch not pleasing?' The emperor did not answer."

"The empress traced her finger down the crack of the vase, knowing that the emperor had been unfaithful. She broke of a piece of the vase and ran the sharp edge down the back side of her arm. Her blood ran into the vase, and the thick red liquid escaped through the cracks of the vase. Before the emperor realized what she had done, the empress was dead."

"Blaming his mistress for the empress's death, he mixed poison into the vase of his wife's blood and had his mistress drink from the vase which would kill her," I said, finishing my story as everyone sat in silence. Seconds later, Mick broke this silence.

"See! I knew it was a vessel for poison!" Mick said.

"Shush, Mick. Why don't you make Gumby for me? I love that guy. Go play with your clay," I said.

"Okay, I will make you Gumby. But tell me why you would put the vase on an upside-down cross?

"I cracked the vase, Mick. And the cross, well, it's for me to bear. I'm not worthy of it standing upright."

This time everyone was in tears, including Mick. Funny thing, though, I was the only one who didn't have tears in my eyes. I could not cry for myself.

CHAPTER THIRTY-FOUR

August '07

It began sixteen months ago with a glimpse of a fuchsia screen on the news. It may take a lifetime for things to come to a full circle, but you can bet that it will. I have lived and lost much in sixteen months, yet through this I have learned much about myself and about a scary world called *cyber land*. As I log online and fight the urge to chat, Albert Einstein's definition of insanity comes to mind: *doing the same thing over and over again and expecting different results*.

I've walked through the darkest parts of hell and I have found my way back to the surface. A surface which seems solid and stable as I cross my fingers that I won't slip into a crack and find myself back in the VIP section of the coolest part of hell again. As I have lost both my husband and Jason, it is my hope that maybe I will find Teri. The cracks in the mirror are starting to fade as I become stronger, in my search of a soul, however wan it may be. A soul I handed over to the devil fifteen months ago, the day Designgirl was born. I do believe I see one less crack each time I look at my reflection, and the monster who stared back at me each time is now either asleep, hiding, or if I am very lucky, dead. I look back, but the cracks aren't as deep as before, which gives me hope that one day I will look into a clear mirror and see Teri smiling back at me.

Ryan has since moved away, and I've lost the one that I would always run to, the one I thought I could always depend on. I have no one to run to now, yet Will is still my rock these days. And Tony, my Italian guy, calls often to make sure that I'm sane. I still chat with most of the characters in my book and dozens that I didn't get the opportunity to mention. I am dating now, which is different from my "meetings" because I am now single and don't have to hide. Yet I still find myself looking over my shoulder anyways. My trust in men has faded, like the colors of fall when winter nears. I am cautious now. I am not quick to meet anyone new. Sexual obsession has been replaced for my search for "love," something that that I was probably always seeking to begin with. Dating does terrify me these days. I find myself sitting at home most of the time because my alter ego has left me for now. She was the brave one, the bold one. Someone who now scares me—someone who I once was.

The desire for binge drinking has left me. The night my husband moved out was the night I didn't feel compelled to drown myself in a bottle of tequila every night.

Over a thousand chats and one hundred "secret" meetings later, I had lost my way. I hope that I may be able to love again because I still do believe in fairy tales and know that one day my prince will come. But for now, my best guy is still this computer. Some things just don't change overnight.

EPILOGUE

Some things just don' t change overnight. I recently joined a singles site and have been exchanging messages with a few—what I now refer to as "men" instead of "bulls." One in particular caught my eye because he is not only handsome and my age but seems to be a genuinely nice guy, something that I actually care about now. I'm done with the bad boys, the "bulls." After weeks of sending messages back and forth through this site, we finally exchanged Yahoo addresses. His name is Jeff, and he is a pilot.

Yahoo IM:

Jeff:	Hi Teri
Teri:	Hello Jeff
Jeff:	It's finally nice to chat with you, messaging emails can become monotonous
Teri:	Yes it can be
Jeff:	So tell me, what is it that you are looking for?
Teri:	Something I haven't found yet . . . Real. I'm looking for something real.

www.ingramcontent.com/pod-product-compliance
Lightning Source LLC
Chambersburg PA
CBHW051225050326
40689CB00007B/812